DAILY DEVOTIONAL

365 NAMES OF GOD

UNLEASHING THE POWER AND THE BLESSINGS OF GOD'S NAMES

JOYCE A. BOOHENE

365 Names of God Daily Devotional: Unleashing the Power and the Blessings of God's Names

Trilogy Christian Publishers A Wholly Owned Subsidiary of Trinity Broadcasting Network

2442 Michelle Drive Tustin, CA 92780

Cover design by: Peter Boateng

For information about special discounts for bulk purchases, please contact Trilogy Christian Publishing.

Manufactured in the United States of America

10 9 8 7 6 5 4 3 2 1

Library of Congress Cataloging-in-Publication Data is available.

ISBN: 978-1-63769-466-4

E-ISBN: 978-1-63769-467-1

Dedication

To give all Glory, Praise and Honor to El Elyon, The Most High God
This book is dedicated to
God The Father, The Son and The Holy Spirit

'And those who know Your name [who have experienced Your precious mercy] will put their confident trust in You, For You, O Lord , have not abandoned those who seek You.' Psalms 9:10 AMP

'For from the rising of the sun, even to its setting, My name shall be great among the nations. In every place incense is going to be offered to My name, and a grain offering that is pure; for My name shall be great among the nations," says the Lord of hosts.'
Malachi 1:11 AMP

'For I proclaim the name [and presence] of the Lord ; Ascribe greatness and honor to our God!' Deuteronomy 32:3 AMP

Acknowledgements

I gratefully acknowledge......

I am eternally grateful to my husband, Dr Leeford, for your love and support, your understanding and encouragement is astounding, I am really blessed to have you by my side through the years.

To Kezy, Jeshurun and Nili, the precious gifts from the Heavenly Father, for your endearment and encouragement, may you manifest the Glory of God in your life and in your generation.

I am very grateful to these great men of God for their valuable support and direction through the years, Dr. Joseph K. K. Baisie of Fountain of Glory Church, and Apostle Bismark Akomeah of Jesus Power Church.

Of course, to the loving members of Christ Center of Hope Church in Chicago, for your great support, I say the Lord bless you and favor you endlessly.

Presented To:

From:

Date:

Introduction

The Name of a person represents the being of the person, it portrays the features that distinguishes the individual, such as qualities, ethics and lifestyle. God displays His power through the revelation of His name and His acts of wonders. He revealed His name to Moses and the people of Israel. "....... I know you by name" (Exodus 33:17 NKJV). He knew Moses personally to reveal Himself to Him. The wonderful deeds of His name cannot be denied, calling Him brings deliverance in situations. 'There is salvation in no one else! God has given no other name under heaven by which we must be saved."' (Acts 4:12 NLT) We have been given The name of the Lord to experience His power!

365 Names of God daily devotional are designed to draw you into a deeper revelation of His character and reality. Knowing Him as your Portion of inheritance, Shield and Strength, means He will not allow the enemy to exact upon you any longer, you are filled with His might, love and mercy, He remains unchanged and manifests Himself as you walk with Him. "I have manifested Your name [and revealed Your very self, Your real self] to the people whom You have given Me out of the world; they were Yours and You gave them to Me, and they have kept and obeyed Your word. John 17:6 AMP. Jesus is the manifestation of the Father, He humbled and offered Himself as a sin offering, God exalted him with the name that is above every other name. When we call Jesus the Christ, tongues confess that He is Lord of all. Maybe you do not know Jesus yet as your Lord and personal Savior, I pray you ask Him to forgive your sins, receive His gift of everlasting life, let Him perfect your ways, and be blessed eternally.

Studying the names of God daily confers His power and His divine nature into your life everyday, you get to know His plans, His will and purposes. We can practically experience him as the only Faithful God who keeps His covenant of peace and blessings with us, "So they shall put My name on the children of Israel, and I will bless them."' Numbers 6:27 NKJV Discover and release the power and goodness of His names into your life.

Joyce A. Boohene

January

May the Lord answer you in the day of trouble;
May the name of the God of Jacob defend you;'
Psalms 20:1 NKJV

January 1

ELOHIM

אלוהים

The Creator

"In the beginning, God (Elohim) created [by forming from nothing] the heavens and the earth" (Genesis 1:1, AMP).

The Elohim who formed the heavens, and the earth makes you His residence, you are His temple, and You are His habitation. When He lives in you, He is in you with all His sovereignty and His Awesomeness, "Bara" the Hebrew term to "create," is solely used for a divine action which illustrates that man cannot form anything like Elohim creates. It means no other god can hold the stand of the Creator. "Bara" likewise expresses the form of setting things in place and function. Elohim's creative activity brings order to the cosmos and all creation.

He's setting events in order in your life to make you fruitful and to have dominion over what He created. He is mindful of you to set you above and not beneath, the first and not the last. You can move mountains of challenges at your command. You have the authority to command actions to be. As the year begins, He is visiting you to bless the moment, make Him first in all your endeavors, turn to Him and His Word first for strength and directions, and let blessings and happiness be your portion.

Prayer: *I pray the Creator be with you today, the former concerns be wiped out, I pray He makes a unique thing in your life, and cause it to shoot forth and spring up for you in all areas of your life.*

Launching Deeper: Psalm 8:3-9, Acts 17:24, Proverbs 8:22-24, Hebrews 1:9.

Hebrew Word Study: "Bara"—to shape, to bring about, to create (Strong's Hebrew: 1254).

January 2

El Elyon

אל עליון

God, Most High.

"And blessed, praised, and glorified be God Most High, Who has given your foes into your hand! And [Abram] gave him a tenth of all [he had taken]" (Genesis 14:20, AMPC).

When the Lord provides solutions and answers to our prayers, we give Him the honor. When we celebrate and glorify The Most High, we acknowledge Him as the Mighty Man in Battle; He shows up and takes control of the challenge; He takes ownership of the warfare and every storm. So, long as you keep praising and blessing Him, fear fades away, and you can experience the tabernacle presence of the Lord where miracles happen, and His glory is revealed. The Hebrew word Elyon comes from the root word "olah," which means "to ascend." The name of God Elyon gives us the certainty the LORD has ascended on high, above everything on our behalf. He is the Ascended One. If there is wickedness in high places working against you, know He is the Most High. There is nothing higher than Him. He will show up and bring you deliverance; the right Hand of the Lord is magnificent to fight for you and shine the light of His presence upon you. As you pray to God for the promise, praise Him for promises fulfilled.

Prayer: *I pray to El Elyon, the Most High for you, as you dwell in His secret place, may He cover and protect you in His mighty shade. May He inhabit in your praises and be loaded daily with His Divine benefits.*

Launching Deeper: Genesis 14:18-24, 2 Chronicles 20:14-16, Psalm 72:17-19.

Hebrew Word Study: "olah"—to go up, to ascend, to climb, to rise (Strong's Hebrew: 5930).

January 3

El Shaddai

אל שדאי

Almighty God

"When Abram was ninety-nine years old, the Lord appeared to Abram and said to him, "I am Almighty God; walk before Me and be blameless" (Genesis 17:1, NKJV).

The song "El Shaddai" was written by Michael Card and John Thompson in 1981. It was made famous by Amy Grant in 1982, honoring the name of the Lord God Almighty. She sang, "Age to age you are still the same, by the power of your name El Shaddai," "We will praise and lift you high El Shaddai." The well-known meaning of El Shaddai is "Mighty" and "All-Sufficient." He gives you all the authority and all strength you will ever need. More than sufficient, taking away every insufficiency and replacing them with His provisions. When we think of the great inventions of man and how fascinating they may be, we understand the awesomeness of the God who created man. He is the Almighty and All-powerful God. When you have Him in you, He takes away your weaknesses and frailty and fills you with His power, presence, and provisions. He has empowered you with His might and the ability to win. Praise and bless the Lord for His Divine visitations this day.

Prayer: *May The El Shaddai, All-Powerful, Who is over all powers there be, overall forces there be and over all principalities there be, take away your inadequacy and give you sufficient resources to fulfill His plans and purposes for your life.*

Launching Deeper: Exodus 6:2, Genesis 28:3,4, Romans 15:13, Job 42.

Hebrew Word Study: "amar"—to utter, to say (Strong's Hebrew: 559).

January 4

Ben Elohim

בן אלוהים

The Son of God

But these are written (recorded) in order that you may believe that Jesus is the Christ (the Anointed One), the Son of God, and that through believing and cleaving to and trusting and relying upon Him you may have life through in) His name, through Who He is.

John 20:31 (AMPC)

"Tell us if you are the Christ, the Son of God," the Pharisees asked, and Jesus answered, "Yes, it is as you say." The Jewish leaders accused Jesus of blasphemy when He responded to their question. His answer as the "Son of God" meant He had the same nature of God, The likeness of God, and the One that is of God, which was an offense worthy of a death sentence in the Levitical laws. They crucified Him as a sacrifice for the atonement of your sins, and through His death and resurrection, you have eternal existence and will not come under judgment. He is the power that destroys the stronghold of sin and works of the devil; at the mention of His name, every knee bows and proclaims Jesus is Lord to the glory of the Father. In Jesus, the Son of God, you have redemption through His blood. He gave His Son because He loved you so you can be connected to Him eternally. You will not be condemned; you are forgiven and have life more abundantly.

Prayer: *I pray the Son of God gives you abundance of life, as you give Him praise for the forgiveness of sin. as you believe may He use you to do great works in Him.*

Launching Deeper: 1 John 5:20, Luke 1:35, John 3:16, John 5:18.

Hebrew Word Study: "ben"—son (Strong's Hebrew: 1123).

January 5

Elohei Avraham

אלוהי אברהם

The God of Your Father Abraham

"And the LORD appeared to him the same night and said, "I am the God of your father Abraham; do not fear, for I am with you. I will bless you and multiply your descendants for My servant Abraham's sake."

Genesis 26:24 (NKJV)

The bond of genuine friendship never dies; friends dedicate themselves to support and care for each other, there is confidence and consistency. When there is a situation, friends reach out at the earliest time to support or call for aid. Anytime we reached out to help a friend, we proved ourselves to be loyal and trustworthy. The friendship of God the Father and Abraham was on a powerful bond as a covenant. God found Abraham to be dependable and trustworthy of a covenant. God knew him as the one who would order his offspring and children's offspring to follow the statutes of the Lord and bear the promise to fulfillment (Genesis 18:19). The fulfillment of the blessing depended on Abraham trusting God, walking with God in faith and in obedience to His Word. Your faith and confidence in God will bring Him to fulfilling His promises in your life. The God of Abraham will direct you and your children to walk in His Word as well. You are descendants of Abraham as you believe, both Jews and gentiles are all one in the covenant. Believe in what The God of Abraham has said in His written Word, there will surely be a performance of what He says in your life today.

Prayer: *The God of Abraham is your Shield and reward, His covenant of blessing is established in you, He will multiply and increase His blessings upon you and your children's children. All curses are broken by the blood of Jesus.*

Launching Deep: Acts 7:32, Genesis 12:2, 15:1, 17:7,8, 26:2-4, Exodus 3:6.

Hebrew Word Study: "rabah"—to be or become much, many or great (Strong's Hebrew: 7235).

January 6

HaGafen HaAmittit

המגן המעתי

The True Vine

"I am the vine; you are the branches. He who abides in Me, and I in him, bears much fruit; for without Me you can do nothing" (John 15:5, NKJV).

The branches of the vine cannot bear fruit by themselves unless it is attached to the vine. Christ is the origin of our spiritual growth and fruitfulness; maintaining our spiritual unity and keeping our relationship with Him is very significant. In Him, we live, move, and have our being. Remember, the branch flourishes as long as it is joined to the stock of the vine; it partakes the nutrients being transmitted through the stem to the leaves. It also cannot support their weight; it needs physical structure to rest on. The Lord moves you to a deeper relation with Him when you stay connected to Him as the provider of your strength and life. Through the divine cleansing of the Word, the vinedresser prunes His branches for more production. This exercise might not be pleasant, but, at the end, it produces the perfect fruits expected and the fullest of your blessings and joy as He promised. As branches spread out and mount up with the help of a structure, so are you being transformed by the Help of the Spirit, growing from grace to grace, strength to strength, fruitful to fruitfulness, and from glory to glory by the power of the Holy Spirit as you depend on Him.

Prayer: *I pray your life be productive and fruitful as you abide in the True Vine, and through His strength and power, you will continue to flourish and prosper.*

Launching Deeper: John 15:1-8, John 17:23, 1 Corinthians 3:18.

Hebrew Word Study: "shakan"—to abide, to settle down, to dwell (Strong's Hebrew: 7931).

January 7

ELOHIM HASHAMAYIM

אלוחים השם

The God of Heaven

"So that they would desire and request mercy of the God of heaven concerning this secret, that Daniel and his companions should not perish with the rest of the wise men of Babylon" (Daniel 2:18, AMPC).

Daniel fasted for weeks and prayed to the God of heaven to deliver the Jews from the hands of Belteshazzar. While bringing the answer to his prayers a principality delayed the angel in the heavenly realm, it took reinforcement for the angel to be released as Daniel continued to pray. God rules in the heavens and rules in the affairs of men. Even though the rulers of the nations might not acknowledge that He is the Creator of the earth, the dwelling place of men, He reigns and gives kingdoms to whomsoever He will. The heavens and the highest heavens belong to the God of heaven and all that is on the earth, He is more than able to accomplish what concerns your life and establish you with His gifts in the land of the living. Keep trusting in Him, He hears your prayers, and He's sending you help without obstructions in the heavens, as Christ intercedes for you before the Father.

***Prayer**: I pray, the God of heaven, open the heavens' doors and pour His favor and kindnesses upon your course, His hand of prosperity be upon you and His kingdom manifest in your life today and cause you to eat the good of the land in Jesus' name.*

Launching Deeper: Deuteronomy 10:14, Genesis 14:19,22, 2 Kings 19:15, Nehemiah 2:20.

Hebrew Word Study: "shamayin" —heaven, sky, space. (Strong's Hebrew: 8065).

January 8

The Elohei Kol HaAret

אלוהי קול הארת

The God of the Earth

"For your Maker is your Husband–the Lord of hosts is His name–and the Holy One of Israel is your Redeemer; the God of the whole earth He is called" (Isaiah 54:5, AMPC).

The deeds of the Lord are beyond description. Creation displays the magnificent works and power of the God of the earth. When the earth is without form and void, the immediate service of the Spirit comes to effect, He broods over the waters, the Word is declared, and there is fulfillment upon the earth. There is formability, order, and functionality in God's creation. Darkness means unfulfilled condition. He did not create without a purpose. He has ordained a plan for all He made, so does He have a purpose calling you His child and placing you on this earth. His presence in your life makes the difference. As a child of God, recounting the great things, He has accomplished in your life and proclaiming His righteousness is a source of faith that brings into existence the work of His mighty hand. There is no god in the earth, and beneath the earth like our God, He gives existence to creation and throws discretion and understanding to kings to rule and to establish His plans. He downloads His blessings, mercies, goodness, and favor upon you and commands you to manifest His glory this day.

***Prayer**: I pray, let the Spirit brood over the earth and bring revival in the nations, and let the earth be full of the knowledge of the Lord as the water covers the sea. Let Him walk with you and talk with me. You are His child, and He is your God.*

Launching Deeper: Isaiah 45:18, 1 Peter 3:12, Genesis 24:3.

Hebrew Word Study: "rachap" means to brood, to relax, to flutter. (Strong's Hebrew: 7363a)

January 9

AVINU SHEBASHAMAYIM

רם שבסמאים

Heavenly Father

"Look at the birds of the air, for they neither sow nor reap nor gather into barns; yet your heavenly Father feeds them. Are you not of more value than they?" (Matthew 6:26, NKJV)

The perfect rule of God is instituted in heaven. He dwells and rules in the highest above the galaxies. His majesty is above the heavens, and the heavens declare His glory. He commands the supernatural and controls the natural. The beauty and the enormity of the cosmos are inconceivable; as vast as it may be, He still cares about the minute element of the earth, the tiniest details of your life matters to Him. If He can sustain the birds of the air who do not sow to harvest and makes sure they do not perish in hunger, without hassle these creatures get what they need, how much more your life that is so dear to Him, Your Heavenly Father has bought you with the blood of His precious Son, and you are His forever. When you cry upon Him, He answers your request and reveals every secret to you. Bless His name and let your incense of prayer: ascend to Him in heaven, for His mercy endures upon your life. He who alone is sovereign over all the kingdoms of the world is your Helper this day.

Prayer: *I pray Heavenly Father, who knows every need upon your heart, sustains you. Marvelous are His works. As you believe in His Word, let Him be pleased to provide your needs and give you good things and shine His countenance on you.*

Launching Deep: Genesis 26:3,4, Luke 21:18, Matthew 10:29-31, Psalm 145:15,16.

Hebrew Word Study: "samak"—to sustain, to lean, rest, support (Strong's Hebrew: 5564).

January 10

ELOHEI AVRAHAM ELOHEI YITSCHAK VELOHEI YA'AKOV

אלוהי אברהם אלוהי יצחק ולוהי יעקב

The God of Abraham, Isaac and Jacob

God said also to Moses, This shall you say to the Israelites: The Lord, the God of your fathers, of Abraham, of Isaac, and of Jacob, has sent me to you! This is My name forever, and by this name I am to be remembered to all generations.

Exodus 3:15 (AMPC)

The name God of Abraham emphasized the covenant God made with Abraham and his seed, the promise of a great nation to his descendants. At this point, the Lord is commanding Moses to correlate the Lord God by this Name when he goes to Egypt to speak the message of deliverance to the Israelites. By this name, He will be distinguished from the gods of Egypt, and they will remember the Word given to their predecessors, the patriarchs. This name is known through generations as the God of Abraham, Isaac, and Jacob. His name is remembered from generation to generation. He never failed them and kept them in His covenant of blessings for His name's sake. The Lord will add to you a thousand times as He did to the fathers and bless you as He promised, as He divided the Red Sea for them, so is He removing every obstacle out of your way. The God of Abraham, Isaac, and Jacob grant you success and show you kindness this day.

***Prayer**: I pray the blessings of Abraham into your life, may all who bless you be blessed and be a great nation, declare it established in Jesus.*

Launching Deep: Genesis 17:7,8, 24:12, Deuteronomy 1:11,35, Psalm 102:12.

Hebrew Word Study: "zakar"—to remember, to be mindful (Strong's Hebrew: 2142).

January 11

ELOHEI HARUCHOT I'CHOL-BASAR

אלוהי הרושות אחול בזאר

The God of the Spirits of All Flesh

"Let the Lord, the God of the spirits of all flesh, set a man over the congregation" (Numbers 27:16, AMPC).

The glassblower creates designs of glasses by puffing air through the blowpipe to expand the glass into a bubble of the desired size and shape. Just like the glassblower, your spirit is the breath of the Father. He exhales into you the breath of life, and His breath functions as a spirit to fill your soul. In Exodus 3:14, His name is present. He is present whenever you need Him, He is as close as your next breath, and without His breath, there is no life. The promise of the Father is to pour the Holy Spirit upon all flesh so we can walk in His strength and authority. No matter the challenge, He can provide a ready individual to fulfill the most formidable roles. He qualified Noah to build the ark for a new world. He qualified Abraham to raise His chosen nation, He qualified and raised Moses to lead His people out of Egypt's oppression, He lifted and qualified Joshua to bring them to the promised land, He's qualified you for something great, His divine purpose, He has filled you with His breath, His Spirit of power and might. Therefore, you mighty person of valor arise and shine and let His glory be seen in you.

***Prayer**: I pray the Spirit of the Lord rests upon you and use you mightily to bring transformation and revival to many and cause you to replenish your resources with the seed of prosperity in you this day in Jesus' Name.*

Launching Deep: Numbers 16:22, Jeremiah 32:27, Zachariah 12:1.

Hebrew Word Study: "Ruach"—breath, wind, spirit (Strong's Hebrew: 7307).

January 12

Elohim Chayim

אלוהים חים

The Living God

"For who is there of all flesh who has heard the voice of the living God speaking out of the midst of fire, as we have, and lived?" (Deuteronomy 5:26, AMPC)

The Hebrew word "chai" is living, it's also connected to the root word "exist," to breathe and to live. Our God is the Self Existing God and lives forever, A direct encounter with God is a life-threatening experience, Yet He is the all-merciful God. In Judges 6, when elders of Israel demanded that Gideon be killed for tearing down the altar of Baal, the father defended him, saying, "If Baal is god let him defend himself when someone breaks down his altar" Baal was a worthless and lifeless idol that could not defend himself nor protect the people, just like the idols people worship in our days, these images need to be carried from place to place. They can't talk with their mouths, they have ears but cannot hear, they have eyes but cannot see, they cannot use their hands nor walk with their feet, those who worship them become like them. But our Living God speaks with the voice of thunder. He hears the prayers of His people, delivers with His mighty hand, and walks in the midst of His people. Believe and trust in the God Who lives eternally. The Living God is your impenetrable fortress and your Shield Who defends and protects you and lives to take care of you today, tomorrow, and all your days.

Prayer: *I pray, the Living God, Who does mighty acts and displays His power, delivers you from adversaries as you call upon Him today.*

Launching Deeper: Psalms 29, 115:3-9, Judges 6, Exodus 32:20, Genesis 32:30.

Hebrew Word Study: "chai"—alive, living (Strong's Hebrew: 2416).

January 13

Elohei HaChayim

אלוהים השאים

The God of the Living

"He is not the God of [the] dead, but of [the] living! You are very wrong" (Mark 12:27, AMPC).

One of the prominent groups in the time of Jesus was the Sadducees, a group that denied the supernatural and the resurrection. They believed the soul ceases to exist at death with no resurrection. Their rejection of the resurrection was emphatic even to the teachings about Jesus as the origin of resurrection. They devised a question of marriage after death to Jesus, and He answered that God is more concerned about those who are alive than the dead. Jesus rose from the dead as the first fruit and lived for us to know that there is eternal life when we believe in Him. He is the God who is mindful of the living. The God of the Living quickens the dead and gives life to the mortal, and all creation lives unto Him. Be aware He is very concerned about your well-being, and His help is always available to you; not only will He give you life but will sustain your life and maintain His covenant relation with you. He will provide your needs and protect your existence from any form of evil and grant you His grace for sustenance.

***Prayer:** I pray that the God of the living will bring into existence His Word concerning your life and cause you to enjoy the increase in the fields in Jesus' name.*

Launching Deeper: Acts 23:8, 17:31, John 11:25,26.

Hebrew Word Study: "chay" means "alive, living" (Strong's Hebrew: 2416a).

January 14

ELOHIM HAAV

אלוהים האב

God the Father

"And every tongue [frankly and openly] confess and acknowledge that Jesus Christ is Lord, to the glory of God the Father" (Philippians 2:11, AMPC).

Jesus mentioned that whoever acknowledges Him will be acknowledged before God the Father (Matthew 10:32), without reservations or any fear of men, we confess the name of the Lord Jesus and give honor to Him as we give honor to the Father, for He has given all authority and power unto Jesus and reveals everything unto Him. Yet Jesus did nothing of Himself except what God the Father will tell Him to do. Obedient to the will of the Father brings fulfillment in life and rule over the works of darkness. Call upon Him now and see His Mighty Hand of deliverance. The promises of God the Father concerning your life are true. He cannot lie or turn away from what He said in His Word. You are His child by the Spirit's adoption, and you can cry Abba Father and ask anything in the name of Jesus, and He will answer, remember your expectations will not be cut off. At the mention of the name Jesus, every tongue will declare He is Lord, and every challenge in your life will bow to Him, honoring and glorifying the Father and the Son.

Prayer: *I pray God the Father removes every reproach and distress, let there be the distinction that brings honor and favor upon your life. Let Him hear your petition and extend defense to deliver you in Jesus' name!*

Launching Deeper: John 5:23, 13:31, 1 John 2:23, Romans 10:9, Isaiah 45:23.

Hebrew Word Study: "shebuah"—an oath (Strong's Hebrew: 7621).

January 15.

Elohim Emet

אלהים אמת

The God of Truth

So that he who blesses himself in the earth Shall bless himself in the God of truth; And he who swears in the earth Shall swear by the God of truth; Because the former troubles are forgotten, And because they are hidden from My eyes.

Isaiah 65:16 (NKJV)

Truth centers on the realm of obligatory tasks that arise from one's position. God is the God of truth, ever faithful and constant to His words; in Him, there is no mismatch between who He is and what He says. He is worthy of confidence and reliability, His words and actions are united and dependable, no one can accuse Him of any unfaithfulness, for His words are flawless and trustworthy and impossible for Him to lie, He abounds in truth and perfection and to abide in His tent requires speaking the truth in the heart. He preserves His children by His truthfulness and sends forth His truth to all. It reaches even to the clouds and endures through all generations. Knowing Him reveals who He is and His true words, that when you obey His word of truth, you also receive His revelation and set loose from bondage. His truth enlightens and releases you from every prison gate bringing every rich spiritual blessing from Him.

***Prayer:** I pray the God of truth grants unto you illumination into His Word and receives the authority to invoke blessings in His Mighty name.*

Launching Deeper: Numbers 23:19, Psalm 12:6, Hebrews 7:21, John 17:17, Jeremiah 10:10.

Hebrew Word Study "Emet"—truth, firmness, stability, reliability (Strong's Hebrew: 571).

January 16

ELOHEI AVOTENU

אלוהיי אבוטנו

The God of Our Fathers

"And when we cried to the Lord, the God of our fathers, the Lord heard our voice and looked on our affliction and our labor and our [cruel] oppression" (Deuteronomy 26:7, AMPC).

Father as a title is sometimes applied to any male ancestor of a person. The patriarchs, Abraham to Isaac to Jacob and to the twelve tribes, walked with God, and He made a covenant with Abraham that transcends through all generations. At any time, any descendant who walks right in Him can call and make a claim of the benefit of the covenant in an hour of need, and He will hear their cry. In the days of the Israelites' residence in Egypt, when their bondage became very severe, they cried to the Lord, and He recognized the covenant He performed with the fathers and acted on their behalf. The word "remember" here in Hebrew is "zakhar," which appears in connection with some activity, a memory that prompts a specific action. When the Lord remembers He takes prompt action, the Lord will not only remember every aspect of your life but will assign you help swiftly. He will assign the wind, the breath to hover over every storm and bring peace to every tempest, like Sarah, Rachel, and Hannah He remembered and opened their wombs. The same God of our fathers is opening doors for you and turning situations around on your behalf in Jesus' name.

Prayer: *I pray the God of our Fathers will look upon you and offer you kindness and show you His signs and wonders this day.*

Launching Deeper: Exodus 2:23,24, 3:9, Isaiah 40:8.

Hebrew Word Study: "zakar"—remember (Strong's Hebrew: 2142).

January 17

ELOHEYNU

אֱלֹהֵינוּ

Our God

"There is none holy like the Lord, there is none besides You; there is no Rock like our God" (1 Samuel 2:2, AMPC).

I remember a schoolmate who had an illness with a periodic crisis. There will be days she is happy, and another time she's experiencing pain. Certain situations can make life very miserable and sap any joy of life in a person, but when we cry unto Our God, He intervenes. This was the situation of Hannah. She had a remarkable and loving husband but was barren. Barrenness was ridicule and reproach in her time. The intensity of this anxiety and shame occurs every year the family goes worship at the tabernacle in Shiloh. Her Rival mocked her and will cause her to lose her appetite for the prepared meal of the sacrifice. One day, she cries unto the Lord in prayer and goes boldly to the throne room of grace to pour her heart to the Lord Our God. There her prayers were answered. Our God wants us to come to Him with no reservation. He is your God who reigns on High but looks down to love and care for His children, He will take away every anxiety and shame out of your soul, you are in His mind, and He knows the wonderful thoughts He has concerning you, all will come to pass in your time, and You will see them all happening in Jesus' name.

Prayer: *I pray, let His Word regarding your life manifest and cause you to rejoice in the salvation of Our God.*

Launching Deeper: Matthew 6:9-13, 1 Samuel 2:1-11, Psalm 55:22.

Hebrew Word Study: "shalak"—to throw, fling, to cast burden (Strong's Hebrew: 7993).

January 18

Elohei Tehillati

אֱלֹהֵי תְהִלָּתִי

God of My Praise

"O GOD of my praise! Keep not silence" (Psalm 109:1, AMPC).

The song keeps ringing in my spirit as I woke up this morning "Higher higher higher, when the praises go up His glory comes down" He is the God of my praise. When we lift praise to the Lord, His blessings come down, like water vapor ascending to the skies and turning back to liquid water, rain drops of His miracles and power. Praises empower us over the powers of darkness. It is part of the arsenals we used to pull down strongholds of evil. It confuses and unstable adversaries in their camps. When we celebrate the Lord as our praise, we proclaim our belief in God's sovereignty and presence and establish our victory over every foe. The Hebrew word "tehilla" is derived from "halah," which means to shout your praise or sing songs or honor. Our purpose of being is to praise God, to be awed by whom the Lord is, and to declare His awesomeness. Doing this will change your way of life. He is the God of your praise. Praising God is a powerful transformer. Keep the atmosphere of praise despite every challenge, and the Lord's zeal will fulfill His promise for Your life.

Prayer: *I pray, let your lips be full of His praises, and see the God of your praise display His mighty power in your soul. Proclaim His blessing upon your life today.*

Launching Deeper: Deuteronomy 11:21, 2 Chronicles 20:22, Habakkuk 3:17,18

Hebrew Word Study: "tehillah"—praise, song of praise (Strong's Hebrew: 8416).

January 19

ELOHEI TZUR

אלהי צור

God of My Rock

"The God of my rock; in him will I trust: he is my shield, and the horn of my salvation, my high tower, and my refuge, my saviour; thou savest me from violence" (2 Samuel 22:3, KJV).

The battle was at rage, David had fought to the edge of his strength and had become weary at this point as the Philistines pursued. Ishbi-Benob, a son of a giant with a heavy sword, attempted to kill David, thank God for Abishai, who saw from afar and ran to the aid of David and killed the giant. David and his warriors brought an ultimate defeat of the Philistines by the power of God (2 Samuel 21). He turns and praises the God of His Rock for His deliverance and His faithfulness in His covenant. David realizes that he was gullible to defeat; if it had not been for the Lord, He wouldn't have made it. The Lord is His Rock (2 Samuel 22:32). Rely on and count on the Lord God. He is The unmovable, unshakable, unchangeable, and dependable One who never fails when you put your faith in Him. The Lord is pulling you out of every trap and pit and setting you upon the Rock. He is the never-failing God. Your Rock, which has become your Security and your Stability. He will also give you power and be your Shield of protection.

Prayer: *I pray, as you trust in the Lord, may He continue to defend you and lift you up above those who rise against you and cause them to stumble before you in Jesus' name, declare!*

Launching Deeper: 2 Samuel 21, 2 Samuel 22:31,32, Psalm 31:3,4.

Hebrew Word Study: "batach"—to trust. (Strong's Hebrew: 982).

January 20

ELOHEI TSEVA'OT

אלהי צבאות

The God of Host

"David became greater and greater, for the Lord God of hosts was with him" (2 Samuel 5:10, AMPC).

A presenter invited a child of about eight years old and gifted in singing to a show thousands of people see. After he had finished singing his song, the host asked him why he was not intimidated at all by the enormous crowd. His response was intriguing, "When I say the Lord's prayer, I am an extraordinary person". That was profound. Saying the Lord's prayer makes him a unique person. Praying and calling upon the Lord brings a transformation. The God of Host caused David to proceed in His kingdom and in His battles to be very great. When He leads your way of life, the difference is obvious. When the Lord is with you, your success is inevitable, and life becomes relevant in His sight. Even if it looks bad with delays and uncertainties, know that as you have called upon Him, He has a plan for every move, do not be moved, the God of Host is in control. He transforms the ordinary to be extraordinary, the poor to be prosperous, the weakest to be the warrior, and the powerless to be powerful, the God of Host will distinguish you and bring honor to your life this day.

Prayer: *I pray, the God of Host be the difference in your lifestyle and let nothing intimidate you, be transformed to be the champion and extraordinary in Jesus' name.*

Launching Deeper: Genesis 39:23, 21:22, 2 Samuel 3:1, Psalm 24:10, Haggai 2:4.

Hebrew Word Study: "YHWH ELOHE tseva'oth" stands for "Yahweh, God of Hosts," Commander of Armies—those of Israel and the heavens' angel warriors. (Strong's Hebrew: 6635).

January 21

ELOHAI

אֱלֹהָי

My God

"Heed the sound of my cry for help, my King and my God, For to You I pray" (Psalm 5:2, AMPN).

Nehemiah was a man who loved to pray consistently. We see the Mighty Hand of God upon his life in every step of his assignment. From the time he heard the Babylonian captivity were in extreme distress, the Lord put it upon his heart to reconstruct the broken walls, there were many dangers surrounding his assignment, but he prayed through every one of them. Nehemiah prayed; "according to the perfect hand of the Lord My God, the king granted me favor to fulfill my assignment, by the perfect hand of the Lord My God we will arise and build despite the mockery" He also prayed, "Remember me for my good deeds according to your great mercy My God, recognize what my enemies are doing against me and pay them back My God," In all that He went through, His supplication was "My God, My God" and His God helped Him and saw Him through to complete the monumental task. When challenges and distress come, call upon the Lord your God. and He will take care of that trouble. His perfect hand be with you every step of the way, remember you, grant you favor before kings, and grant you every resource you will need to complete your divine assignment, therefore arise and build.

Prayer: *I pray for you; you receive favor before men for every need. He commands you to invoke His blessings upon your life, let the good hand of the Lord be with you in Jesus' name.*

Launching Deeper: Nehemiah 9, Exodus 15:2, Psalm 3:7.

Hebrew Word Study: "qashab"—to incline (ears), attend (Strong's Hebrew: 7181).

January 22

ELOHIM AVINU

אֱלֹהִים אָבִינוּ

God Our Father

"Grace (favor and spiritual blessing) be to you and [heart] peace from God our Father and the Lord Jesus Christ" (1 Corinthians 1:3, AMPC).

See what grace is like a person who persecuted the church but finds himself in the hands of God as a tool used to spread the gospel throughout the nations. Paul was the Lord's great tool: His greetings in the epistles to the ancient churches sums up his message of salvation through the grace of our God found in Christ. When Paul says, "God our Father," he shows that the Jews and non-Jews are the same before God the Father; in Christ Jesus, we all have become his children. Through His wonderful work of grace, there is deliverance from the bondage of sin to a peaceful relationship with Him, with the provision of eternal life to those who believe. To many believers, grace is "unmerited or undeserved favor" that unmerited favor is being extended to you and your descendants, receive the free, good gift that comes from God our Father, no matter the situation you are in now or where you come from, your tribe or nationality or language if you believe in Christ as your Lord, receive His perfect peace and His grace. The favor and spiritual blessings of God our Father be unto you in Jesus' name.

Prayer: *I pray, as you put your trust in Him every moment of your time of living on the earth, the power of His grace rescue you from every evil, may you excel in His grace mightily to fulfill your purpose.*

Launching Deeper: Romans 1:7, 1 Corinthians 1:4, Titus 2:11,12, John 1:12.

Hebrew Word Study: "Av" or "Ab"—a leader or strength of the family (Strong's Hebrew: 2. ab).

January 23

ELOHEI MISHPAT

אֱלֹהֵי מִשְׁפָּט

God of Justice

Therefore, the Lord will wait, that He may be gracious to you; And therefore He will be exalted, that He may have mercy on you. For the Lord is a God of justice; Blessed are all those who wait for Him.

Isaiah 30:18 (NKJV)

King David was so enraged when the rich man took the poor man's lamb for his guests, he reacted to the injustice carried out on this poor man. You could imagine how furious he was as Nathan continued telling the story. David's response also evokes a sense of unfairness in us as the story unfolds his own injustice in taking Uriah's wife. His repentance displays the recognition of his sin against the God of justice. The Lord waits for us to repent and surrender for His blessings and requires that we do justly, love mercy, and walk in righteousness and humbly before Him. God's justice requires that we avoid sin since it entails everything contrary to His holiness. He also brings justice to His children when the enemy takes from them their blessings; He will not allow you to be treated unjustly by the enemy for His name sake, He will defend you and uplift you out of any distress, He will bring justice to you, heal and deliver you by the power of the blood of Jesus.

Prayer: *I pray the God of justice will have mercy on you and bring you justice against the works of your enemies.*

Launching Deeper: Malachi 2:17, Micah 6:8, 2 Samuel 12:1-14.

Hebrew Word Study: "Mishpat" meaning "justice," is which also stands for "judgment," it's an act of deciding a case. (Strong's Hebrew: 4941).

January 24

ELOHEI MIKKAROV

אֱלֹהֵי מִקָּרֹב

The God Who is Near

"For what great nation is there that has God so near to it, as the Lord our God is to us, for whatever reason we may call upon Him?" (Deuteronomy 4:7, NKJV)

The Lord is near and close as your breath, you can call Him anytime for anything and for any reason. There are more deep oracles to receive, instructions to your next dimension, not only for you but for your assignment. He is the progressive God who wants to see you grow in your calling. The more we experience Him as One near, the more empowered we become as His church to release this promise into any environment we touch. What hinders us is the willingness to obey, as living gates of heaven, we need to prepare ourselves to have encounters with Him; we walk in obedience and the willingness to go through the process and willingness to leave certain things behind. The Lord wants to get closer to you more than you want to. He is near to all who call upon Him in truth. When you are close to Him, you can hear clear revelations and instructions from Him and walk in His perfect ways, and He will raise high your horn of strength and cause you to prevail.

Prayer: *I pray as you get closer to the Lord: May His glory rob on you, may He show you great things in your life.*

Launching Deeper: Psalm 46:1, 145:18, Isaiah 55:6, James 4:8.

Hebrew Word Study: "qarob"—near (Strong's Hebrew: 7138).

January 25

HaTamim kol Derekim

התמים עד דרקים

The Perfecter of Ways

"It is God who arms me with strength, And makes my way perfect" (Psalm 18:32, NKJV).

Despite the flaws of men, the Perfecter of Ways can make us perfect through the blood of Jesus. The atoning sacrifice makes us perfect and blameless in his sight: He is the maker of intellectual gifts and moral grace provided for men. He raises men from low estate, enthrone and makes them perfect to fulfill His purpose. He raised and perfected Deborah to judge the Israelites and to conquer the Midianites; He raised and perfected Esther to stand in the gap to save the Jews from the hand of wicked Haman. The perfecter of your ways crowns you and condemns the wicked. He instructs us to be above reproach and be perfect because he wants us perfect in the knowledge of Him: we can know what is right and be pure and blameless, being filled with the fruit of righteousness through the Lord Jesus Christ. Not conforming to the patterns of the world, trying in our daily lives to be found blameless, He cannot bless men contrary to what he has said in His Word, but He will bless them to every letter of the word when they walk in His ways, continue to excel in the work of God as He perfects your ways.

Prayer: *I pray, May He raise and make you perfect to do what is in His mind and heart in Jesus' name.*

Launching Deeper: 2 Peter 3:14, 1 Corinthians 15:58, Philippians 2:15, 1 Thessalonians 5:23.

Hebrew Word Study: "tamim"—to complete, unscathed, blameless, and without fault (Strong's Hebrew: 8549).

January 26

ELOHEI MA'UZZI

אֵל סַלְעִי

The God of Strength

"The LORD God is my strength; He will make my feet like deer's feet, And He will make me walk on my high hills. To the Chief Musician. With my stringed instruments" (Habakkuk 3:19, NKJV).

When someone asks, "What is your strength?" It might be difficult to answer such a question because there are different kinds of strengths, some can look at their achievements and what they can do well to answer the question. It can be some skills they have gained; being it knowledge-based strength or personal strength, they are manmade strength that does not last much. The indwelling presence of the Lord in the believer's life empowers them and vanquishes every form of weakness and fear. His power and strength are enough for the believer in time of any form of trouble. His power takes away your weaknesses, and Paul talks to the Corinthians about that (2 Corinthians 12:9). God strengthens those who put their trust in Him and have faith in Him. He gives you confidence and equips you for any battle. When Habakkuk talks about hinds feet, it represents the swiftness that God gives to enables you to escape any trap of the enemy and outrun those who have gone ahead of you.

Prayer: *I pray, receive that swiftness to overtake and overcome every challenge, and know the joy of the Lord is your strength.*

Launching Deeper: Psalms 18:1, 27:1; 46:1, Isaiah 12:2, 2 Corinthians 12:9.

Hebrew Word Study: "chayil"—strength, efficiency, wealth (Strong's Hebrew: 2428).

January 27

Elohei Haelohim

אֱלֹהֵי הָאֱלֹהִים

The God of gods

"For the Lord your God is God of gods and Lord of lords, the great, the mighty, the terrible God, Who is not partial and takes no bribe" (Deuteronomy 10:17, AMPC).

The God of gods is superior over all other deities and feared among the gods of the nations. David praised the name of the Lord when the Lord revealed His secrets to him, it was proven to the king that any means of worshiping evil spirits does not bring excellent results, The God of gods reveals secrets and maxims of men. His divine judgment comes when leaders of nations rely on enchantments, witchcraft activities, dealings with evil spirits, mystic insights, and consulting lesser gods for powers and for solutions. The heathen gods handcrafted by humans, backing corrupted imaginations and workings of evil forces, are subdued by the God of gods as He defeated all the nations that came against His covenant nation Israel. In His justice, the God of gods brings His judgment upon them and triumph over them, He is the one who owns and controls the universe. The people of the nations are to fear Him above all gods and greatly praise His name. He is the terrible God, and His mercies endure forever: do not be afraid of their craftiness. He thwarts and frustrates their intentions and delivers you out of their snares.

Prayer: *I pray the Lord be your judge, let Him hear your cry and you to overcome traps and snares of the enemy and terribly destroy them*

Launching Deeper: Deuteronomy 7:21, Nehemiah 1:5, Revelation 17:14, 19:16.

Hebrew Word Study: "gadol"—great (Strong's Hebrew: 1419).

January 28

ELOHEI CHASDI

אֱלֹהֵי חַסְדִּי

The God of Mercy

"Unto thee, O my strength, will I sing: for God is my defence, and the God of my mercy" (Psalm 59:17, KJV).

(Psalm 59:17, KJV).The Ark of the covenant is a representation of the presence of the Lord God amidst His people, the sacred cover or the atonement cover of the Ark is called "Kapporet" in Hebrew (Exodus 25:17), as the throne room of grace, which is the place of the Seat of Mercy, in the Holy of Holies. In judgment the Lord does not keep His anger for long. His mercy triumphs over judgment, and it's upon whoever He wishes. The Lord God of mercy shows His mercy through the atoning sacrifice of Christ, and by that, we see His loving kindness to thousands of generations of those who love Him and keep His word. When He chooses you, He sets you aside and establishes you in His plan with loving kindness on your life from His Seat of Mercy. He saves you not by your works of righteousness but by His mercy through the Holy Spirit and transforms you to be a vessel of mercy, accepted and beloved. Receive more of Him as you share His lovingkindness in your world.

Prayer: *I pray the God of Mercy be good to you and open His hand and satisfy your desires and help you from His Mercy Seat.*

Launching Deeper: Psalms 145:8,9,16 101:1, 52:8, Exodus 33:15,16, Romans 9.

Hebrew Word Study "Kaporeth" means "propitiatory" (Strong's Hebrew: 3727).

January 29

Netzach Yisroel

נצח ישראל

Strength of Israel

"And also the Strength of Israel will not lie or repent; for He is not a man, that He should repent" (1 Samuel 15:29, AMPC).

The joy of the Lord is our strength. It is interesting how joy is connected to strength. Science has proved that just a smile can cause mood elevation, and being joyful increases a healthy lifestyle; it boosts the immune system, battles stress and pain, and also supports longevity. The Strength of Israel helped Nehemiah be a cupbearer to the king in a foreign land, The Strength of Israel helped him to gain the position as a governor in Israel. The Lord listened to his prayers of intercession for the nation. With a willing heart, the people came to help in building the wall. Nehemiah triumphed over many adversaries, for The Strength of Israel is faithful to keep His promise. He is the great one with His Mighty hand to drive out every enemy and save His children. He is not a man to change His mind any time that you change. The Strength of Israel empowers you to accomplish what He has put upon your heart and be your strength.

Prayer: *I pray the Lord arm you with strength from on high and exalt your horn and let His word give you comfort.*

Launching Deeper: Deuteronomy 33:27, Psalms 18:1, 29:11, 68:35, Nehemiah 9.

Hebrew Word Study: "netsach"—eminence, enduring, everlastingness, perpetuity (Strong's Hebrew: 5331).

January 30

El Kanno

אֵל־קַנּוֹא

The Jealous God

"For you shall worship no other god; for the Lord, Whose name is Jealous, is a jealous (impassioned) God" (Exodus 34:14, AMPC).

In the sixth Month, in Ezekiel 8, the hand of the Lord fell upon Ezekiel In a vision, he saw the Lord in the appearance of fire and amber. Yahweh took him to the temple where the image of jealousy was at the gate, provoking His jealousy which calls for His wrath against them. God is a jealous God who will not give His honor to another. The promise of the Lord for you is to do you good and not to harm you, an awesome thing the Lord will do, He will not fail and will not lie, He will drive every enemy away from you, and His countenance will not leave you alone, but you do not worship any other god beside Him, you put nothing before Him that will take your worship more than Him; He does not accept rivalry; do not provoke Him to jealousy. Anything that takes His place in your life provokes His jealousy, He desires all of your heart upon the altar, unreservedly, honoring Him with all your strength, your mind, and your soul. Set the Lord always before you and let His zeal be upon you, by that, you will find His perfect peace within. He will reveal Himself to you as you worship Him in spirit and in truth.

Prayer: *I pray let your zeal for the Lord increase and your love and faith in Him increase, may you put nothing before Him as He blesses you in Jesus' name.*

Launching Deeper: Exodus 20:3,5, Deuteronomy 4:24, Joshua 24:19, 1 Kings 14:15,19:10.

Hebrew Word Study: "qanna"—jealous (Strong's Hebrew: 7067).

January 31

El Echad

אֵל אֶחָד

The One God

"There is only One God and One mediator to God and Father, and He is Jesus Christ the Son" (1 Timothy 2:5).

The keynote of the Jewish faith "We worship One God in Trinity, and Trinity in Unity." The Unified God, God the Father, God the Son, and God the Holy Spirit. One God Who created all and fashioned all humans in the womb, He created and formed you for His glory. "Hear, O Israel: The Lord Your God is One" (Deuteronomy 6:4). We are people and sheep of His pasture, and He is willing all men to be saved and come to the knowledge of the truth in Jesus. He redeemed you and called you by your name; you are His, He is over all and in all. All things derive their existence from the Only God, so-called images of gods, being it the sun, moon, and stars, any image of worship upon the face of the earth are worthless and lifeless. He is the Savior of all people. We serve Him with one mind and one heart and with a united and perfect heart. Obey and yield to His commands and His word. He is the absolute One, whom alone we worship and adore.

Prayer: *I pray, Our Lord and mediator makes intercession for us before the only God. Let your will and purpose for our lives be in Jesus' name.*

Launching Deeper: Deuteronomy 6:4, Isaiah 44:6, 1 Corinthians 8:4-6, Galatians 3:20, Malachi 2:10.

Hebrew Word Study: "Echad," meaning one or to be united in one (Strong's Hebrew: 259).

February

So they shall put My name on the children of Israel,
and I will bless them."'
Numbers 6:27 NKJV

February 1

El Hanne'eman

אֵל הַנֶּאֱמָן

The Faithful God

Know, recognize, and understand therefore that the Lord your God, He is God, the faithful God, Who keeps covenant and steadfast love and mercy with those who love Him and keep His commandments, to a thousand generations.

Deuteronomy 7:9 (AMPC).

El Hanne'eman is the Faithful God who gives promise and seems to accomplish what He says. He performed His promise by leading Israel out of Egypt to a prosperous land. As He delivered them, He vowed Himself to take care of them, to supply their needs and protect them. God displayed His faithfulness in the lives of the children of Israel, how He's kept His covenant with them, how He worked all things together for their good. His faithfulness is unconditional to His covenant children. You can trust Him to work all for your good. Before He begins, He has already finished. Faith in Hebrew is "Emunah," meaning that which comes from faithfulness, recognition of the faithful. You put your faith in what has been faithful to you. The Lord has been good to you, trust, and He will never forsake His promise to you. Because the Lord your God loves you and cares for you, He's chosen to perfect what He had said concerning your life. The one who has begun the outstanding work is always faithful to bring it to completion.

***Prayer:** I pray His will is done in your life. Let Him watch over you and keep you to do what He has promised.*

Launching Deeper: 2 Timothy 2:13, 1 Thessalonians 5:24, 1 Corinthians 1:9, Genesis 25:15.

Hebrew Word Study: The word "emunah" itself comes from "aman," which means to securely trust or rely upon, and from which we get the word "Amen." (Strong's Hebrew: 530).

February 2

El Tsaddik

אֵל־צַדִּיק

The Righteous God

Consult together, argue your case. Get together and decide what to say. Who made these things known so long ago? What idol ever told you they would happen? Was it not I, the Lord? For there is no other God but me, a righteous God and Savior. There is none but me.

Isaiah 45:21 (NLT)

God chose Cyrus, Koresh, who was a foreign king, anointed him as an agent of restoration to give orders to the rebuilding of the temple and to restore the nation of Israel. He has the power over all, including foreign kingdoms, to equip them with power and prosperity to do His bidding of righteousness. Because He is God and doing right is Who He is, His Word cannot fail. He is the just God; He raises men to bring righteous justice to His people and to enforce His judgment against their enemies. His righteousness justifies you the believer and gives His promise of the Spirit Whom He poured upon you to bring transformation and to obtain His righteousness through Christ. You have the right standing and peace with God, and the righteousness of Christ is making your life spring forth salvation, peace, rest, prosperity, and fruitfulness.

Prayer: *I pray as He chose Cyrus, may He appoint and anoint you to bring a transformation of righteousness through the power of the Holy Spirit in you.*

Launching Deeper: Deuteronomy 32:4, Psalm 71:19, Isaiah 45:5, 43:11, 44:7, 46:9.

Hebrew Word Study: "Tsadaqah," which is "righteousness" or "just," pertains to doing right or being just (Strong's Hebrew: 6664).

February 3

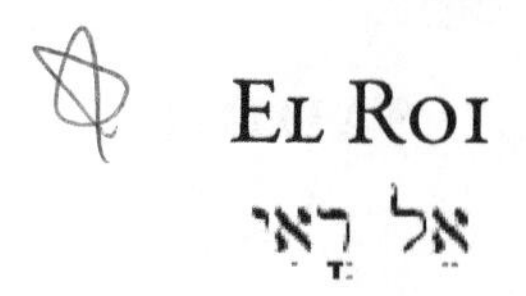

El Roi

אֵל רֳאִי

The God Who Sees Me

"Then she called the name of the Lord who spoke to her, You-Are-the-God-Who-Sees; for she said, 'Have I also here seen Him who sees me?'" (Genesis 16:13)

In the time of Hagar's distress in fleeing from His mistress, the Lord revealed Himself to her in the form of an angel; the Lord came and comforted Hagar and gave her a promise. He is the God Whom no one sees and lives, but reveals Himself to His people in different ways and still preserves them by His mercy. At Beer-laha-roi, "the well of living after seeing." El Roi manifested His providence to Hagar, and She remembered the mercies and goodness of "the God who sees." He sees all things, including your needs. He knows you from His throne room. His eye of love, mercy, and grace watches over you. He is keeping you as the apple of His eye and will never take His eye off you. The Lord who sees you hear your prayers and knows your desires. He will strengthen your heart and open the book of remembrance for you to do you good and cause His face to shine upon you.

Prayer: *I pray May the Lord continue to be pleased to take notice and care of you in Jesus' name.*

Launching Deeper: Genesis 32:30, Exodus 24:11, Psalm 139, Psalm 10:17, Malachi 3:16.

Hebrew Word Study: "raah"—to see (Strong's Hebrew: 7200).

February 4

El Yeshurun

אֵל יְשֻׁרוּן

The God of Jeshurun

"There is none like the God of Jeshurun (Israel), Who rides the heavens to your help, And through the skies in His majestic glory" (Deuteronomy 33:26, AMP)

In life, people have the desire to know the future and how things will turn for their good, but our hope and courage are in the God of Jeshurun, the Keeper of hope. No matter the present matter, He has a record of absolute devotion to His word, to keep His children in safety and to make His providence available to them. The God of Jeshurun honored the declarations of blessings Moses made to the tribes of Israel to show how faithful He is (Deuteronomy 33:1-26) and to remind them of the love, His goodness, and protection in which Israel is to celebrate in all their days. Have the confidence that the everlasting arms of the God of Jeshurun prevail on your behalf in any challenge. He will ride through the heavens to help you and destroy every enemy. He makes sure no trouble overwhelms you. Your security and establishment in the promised land are decreed. God Himself is your help and defense. He is the One Who empowers you to take your possession and your divine supplies.

Prayer: *I pray the Lord come quickly to your aid and cause you to rejoice in His salvation and deal with you bountifully.*

Launching Deeper: Deuteronomy 32:15; 33:5,26; Isaiah 44:2.

Hebrew Word Study: "Yeshurun"—the upright ones (Strong's Hebrew: 3484).

February 5

El Gibbor

הגיבור

The Mighty God

For to us a Child is born, to us a Son is given; and the government shall be upon His shoulder, and His name shall be called Wonderful Counselor, Mighty God, Everlasting Father [of Eternity], Prince of Peace.

Isaiah 9:6 (AMPC).

The Lord is the omnipotent God and maker of all things. Creation rehearses the greatness of God, for their Creator is the eternal One, infinitely wise, mighty, and good. Even counter-changing of day and night is substantial proof of the authority of God, and this calls us to reenact, "And let them sacrifice the sacrifices of thanksgiving and work out His deeds with shouts of joy and singing! (Psalm 107:22) The Psalmist describes his intensity and commitment in giving praise and celebrates Elohim's power and acts. We see a glad remembrance of God's actions and operations. Adonai is not simply powerful, He is also compassionate toward His people and faithful to His commitment to them, "as His divine power has given to us all things that pertain to life and godliness, through the knowledge of Him who called us by glory and virtue." (2 Peter 1:3 NKJV) We should acknowledge God's authority and goodness in what he does for us and, in much greater work, our redemption by Christ.

Prayer: *I pray the Mighty God give you the wisdom mouth that your adversaries cannot resist and grant you success this day in Jesus' Name.*

Launching Deeper: Isaiah 25:1; 40:9-11; Matthew 28:18; Luke 2:11, Romans 9:5, Titus 2:13.

Hebrew Word Study: "misrah"—dominion, rule (Strong's Hebrew: 4951).

February 6

El De'owt

הדאווט

The God of Knowledge

"Talk no more so very proudly; let not arrogance go forth from your mouth, for the Lord is a God of knowledge, and by Him actions are weighed" (1 Samuel 2:3, AMPC).

When it seems like God does not see what you are going through, He's not listening to your prayers, you are alone and neglected, know that the God of knowledge knows you by your name. He has perfect intelligence of all things. His knowledge originates within Him. He recognizes the past, present, and future and what's in your heart, what you need and desire, your frame, the way He formed you, and how to respond to your call. What man cannot see is visible and uncovered in the sight of God. He will give you rest from days of trouble, for His understanding has no limit. He knows his works and words, all creatures and men, everything they think about, and the things they do, whether good or bad, are before His eyes. The God of knowledge is aware of what He has put upon your spirit, the plan and purpose for your existence, an excellent one to bring you to an expected end, remember no eye has seen, ears heard, or heart received what He has prepared for you tomorrow. Through the Holy Spirit, He has made known to you His wonderful agenda for your life, walk and live in His abundance and grace to fulfill them!

Prayer: *The Lord who knows what you need before you ask, send you help from Zion, stretch forth His hands and rescue you from any trouble, and supply you with His benefits, and may you bless the name of the Lord. Declare these blessings!*

Launching Deeper: Psalm 139, Psalm 33:18, Revelation 2:23.

Hebrew Word Study: Da'at" comes from "yode'a"—to know, have knowledge (Strong's Hebrew: 3046).

February 7

El Haggadol

אל הַגָּדֹל

The Great God

"And I said: 'I pray, LORD God of heaven, O great and awesome God, You who keep Your covenant and mercy with those who love You and observe Your commandments'" (Nehemiah 1:5, NKJV).

He is a great God and greatly to be praised, to Him, all the gods of the earth bow in the splendor of holiness, they tremble before Him, the great God who is the giver of strength, power, and wealth. He will do everything for His excellent name. When it pleases the Lord to call and choose you as His own, He will not forsake you. His name and reputation are feared among the nations, with tremendous power and an outstretched arm and terror. He delivers His people from Egypt, the King of those who rule as kings and Lord of those who rule as lords of the earth and in the greatness of His majesty. He overthrows those who rise against Him. By His absolute authority at work in you, He can do immeasurably more than you imagine or ask. He demonstrated by the working of His great strength in the resurrection of the Lord Jesus, whom you are also raised with and made alive so you can be a partaker of His great grace and live in hope of the Great God.

Prayer: *May the El Gaddol who does great things work in you greatly and show you His great mercy, love, favor, and grant unto you His mighty gifts.*

Launching Deep: Deuteronomy 10:17, Nehemiah 1:1-8, 1 Chronicles 29:11-14.

Hebrew Word Study: "gadol" means great, grand, awesome (Strong's Hebrew: 1419).

February 8

El Hakkavod

אֵל־הַכָּבוֹד

The God of Glory

"The voice of the Lord is upon the waters; the God of glory thunders; the Lord is upon many (great) waters" (Psalm 29:3, AMPC).

Mount Sinai was all wrapped in smoke when the God of Glory descended upon it. There was thick cloud, thunder, and lightning, loud sounds of trumpets as the mountain kept on quaking violently with the smoke going up like a burning furnace, chills of reverential fear and trembling will engulf you. If you were around the mountain and hearing the thunderous voice of God. Even though we know God is everywhere, such an act makes us appreciate His merciful grace. When Moses spoke to God, His glory appeared in the fiery cloud, and they could hear His voice in the mountain's midst. He answered in the secret place of thunder and declared His covenant to them. His words are an extension of Him and reflect His nature. The cloud by day and flaming fire by night, the Shekinah that appeared on the mountain is moving with you every step of the way; it will never leave until you arrive in your promised land as evidence of His covenant. His commanding presence helps you to stay connected to Him and helps you keep focus on Him. He abides with you.

Prayer: *Be impacted with the reflection of El Kabod, as you have a continuous communion with Him, become a possessor of His special benefits of constant presence and protection and rich grace*

Launching Deeper: Psalm 81:7, Exodus 19:16-20, Exodus 33:9-10.

Hebrew Word Study: Kabod means glory, weight, and honor (Strong's Hebrew 3519b).

February 9

ADONAI HA'ELOHIM HAKKADOSH

'אדוני ה'אלוים הקדוש

The Holy Lord God

"And the men of Beth Shemesh said, 'Who is able to stand before this holy Lord God? And to whom shall it go up from us?'" (1 Samuel 6:20, NKJV)

Flashes of lightning and rumbling sounds of thunder could be heard from the great throne, seven fire-blazing lamps were in front of the Mercy Seat, around the throne were the four living creatures with their wings full of eyes, they kept on crying, never taking a break "Holy, holy, holy is the Lord, God Almighty, Holy, holy, holy is the Lord, God Almighty" as the twenty-four elders join casting their crowns before the throne, and bowing down to ascribe glory and honor to the Holy God, for the whole earth is full of His glory (Revelation 4). Join them to lift up worship and honor His Holy name today. Holiness is God's nature and His name. His Holiness is glorious and outstanding; the perfection of His ways, His mercy, His justice in governing all things, and His righteous acts are attributes of His Holiness. The Holy Spirit conforms believers to walk in holiness. He calls us into a holy life by His purpose and grace and names us a kingdom of priests and a holy nation. So we set ourselves apart from that which is unholy and strive to live lives pleasing unto Him as we celebrate and bless His Holy Name.

Prayer: *I bless the Holy Lord who has the key of David, let Him open doors of favor for you.*

Launching Deeper: Revelation 4:8, 1 Timothy 1:9, Exodus 19:6, Isaiah 5:16. Joshua 24:199.

Hebrew Word Study: "Kaddosh" means sacred, holy, set apart, utterly unique, and one of a kind (Strong's Hebrew: 6918).

February 10

El Chaiyai

אֵל חַיָּי

The God of My Life

"Yet the Lord will command His loving-kindness in the daytime, and in the night His song shall be with me, a prayer to the God of my life" (Psalm 42:8, AMPC).

The God of my life gives me life, sustains my life, and preserves my life. I call upon Him day and night, and He opens the heaven on my behalf by His mercy. My God ordains and commands victory for me and causes me to have sufficient harvest in the work of my hands. He blesses everything I put in my hand and endows me with His strength and favor. He is faithful to keep His Word and will decree a blessing for me. He commands a word of promise and fulfills it, just like the centurion told Jesus; "I don't need you to come to my house. All I need is just say a word." (Matthew 8:8) Jesus heard his prayers and gave a word that the sick be healed, and it happened. The centurion believed in Jesus; he knew Jesus has all the power; he trusted Him that whatever He says would be fulfilled. His Word will come to pass in your life, keep believing it. In the dark times, the God of your life would protect you and surround you with victory songs. When you call upon him in the night, He will hear and cause you to shout for joy in the morning.

Prayer: *I pray the Lord commands His blessing, deliverance send forth His loving devotion and His truth unto your life.*

Launching Deeper: Psalms 27:1, 44:4, 57:3, 63:6, 71:3. 77:6, 119:55, Colossians 3:3.

Hebrew Word Study: "chayyim"—life (Strong's Hebrew: 2425).

February 11

El Yisrael

אֵל יִשְׂרָאֵל

The Lord God of Israel

"May the LORD repay your work, and may you receive a rich reward from the LORD, the God of Israel, under whose wings you have taken refuge" (Ruth 2:12, BSB).

In a time where a nation had become faithless, Ruth, the epitome of loyalty, remained faithful to the God of Israel and declared to Naomi, "your God will be my God, I will serve and worship the God whom you worship." The Lord God of Israel honored and exalted Ruth. He honors and rewards those who honor Him. The object of worship of the people of Israel is the God of Israel. This title gives us the idea and the nature of the God who delivered his people from the gods of Egypt. He is above every other god, the Supreme Being, who declares and it comes into existence. He descends into the midst of His people and walks among them and reveals Himself to them. He does not condone sin and unrighteousness, and His Word is true. His tabernacle presence abides with you, as He did for the Jews and for Ruth. He is making a way in the wilderness and rivers in the desert as He did for Israel, and He is of the power to establish you in the season of harvest, keep watch over you and take every pain away from you.

Prayer: *Let the Lord God of Israel reward you and fulfill what His mouth has spoken concerning your life and work miracles for you today.*

Launching Deeper: Jeremiah 28:2, 2 Chronicles 6:4, 2:12, 1 Chronicles 4:10.

Hebrew Word Study: "sekar"—reward, wages, payment (Strong's Hebrew: 7939).

February 12

EL EREKH APAYIM AVI HA-TANCHUMIM

ל אֶרֶךְ אַפַּיִם אֲבִי הַתַּנְחוּמִי

The God of Patience and All Consolation

Now may the God Who gives the power of patient endurance (steadfastness) and Who supplies encouragement, grant you to live in such mutual harmony and such full sympathy with one another, in accord with Christ Jesus.

Romans 15:5, AMPC).

God's time is not the time of men. He lives in the heavens and in eternity, and a thousand years is just like a watch in the night in the sight of the Lord. Every day is a day of Grace for a soul to get saved. He is patient for all, the reason the Father has delayed the coming of Christ. The Lord wishes that all would come to believe in Him and be redeemed. The God of Patience was patient with Noah to take him over hundred years to build the ark, commanded all the animals to come in, and saved eight souls. His nature is compassionate and patient to all who call on him. Sometimes we wonder why His promises and his word have not yet been, He takes His time to work the best, or the coming of the Lord has not yet come. He doesn't want anyone to perish. He as well requires us to be like-minded as Christ, that we would also be patient with one another, live in peace, be in the interest of others, love one another, and be united in spirit and in purpose walking in love as Christ loved us.

***Prayer**: I pray the Lord fills your heart with joy and bound in hope through His power.*

Launching Deeper: 2 Peter 3:9, Jeremiah 32:39, Philippians 2:4, 1 Peter 3:8.

Hebrew Word Sturdy: "channun"—gracious (Strong's Hebrew: 2587).

February 13

El Yeshuati.

אֵל יְשׁוּעָתִי

The God of My Salvation

"Behold, God, my salvation! I will trust and not be afraid, for the Lord God is my strength and song; yes, He has become my salvation" (Isaiah 12:2, AMPC).

Our adoption by the Father into his kingdom changes our status as sinner into the righteousness of Christ. From the Hebrew word "yeshuah," meaning salvation, deliverance, and victory, our Yeshua has delivered us from the shackles of the slavery of sins and given us victory over the bondage of sins. Anyone who calls upon the name of Yeshuah and believes in His heart is saved. In Him, the God of our salvation, we are safe and have redemption. We have peace with God and are brought near to Him through the blood of Jesus and united with Him, and at His throne, we find mercy and grace in time of need. As you have received and believe in Him, you have salvation. He has given you the power to become a child of God. You have forgiveness of sins and citizenship with God's holy people. You are justified by faith and have become a new creation. As a believer, you have the new birth, and the Holy Spirit dwells in you and grants you the ability to do God's will. You have the power and the grace to manifest His glory and to do His purpose.

***Prayer:** I pray let your meditations and supplications be pleasing to the God of your salvation as you rejoice in Him.*

Launching Deeper: Romans 8:22, Ephesians 1:7, 2:19, Romans 1:17, 6:4.

Hebrew Word Study: "yeshar"—salvation (Strong's Hebrew 3468).

February 14

El malei Rachamim

רחמים מאלי

All-Merciful God

"For the Lord your God is a merciful God; He will not fail you or destroy you or forget the covenant of your fathers, which He swore to them" (Deuteronomy 4:31, AMPC).

Moses reminded the people of Israel to be obedient to the commands and judgments of the Lord and be careful to observe them. By doing that, they would have power and victory over their enemies and possess their promised land. He continued to caution them to take notice of how the Lord has kept them and delivered them from the nations. Israel should remember to do his will, and he will not forget them. He has sworn to keep his covenant of mercies unto you, for his compassion never fails. They are new every morning. He keeps His mercies to the generations, living to a thousand generations. He is gracious, and for those who return to Him, He will not turn His face away from them. Even in judgment, the Lord remembers mercy. He is rich in mercy and delays in sending disaster. Mercy is the nature of God. He recalls his covenant and does not break it.

Prayer: *I pray the mercies of God be upon you and to everyone around you. God full of mercy, remember you and show you favor.*

Launching Deeper: 2 Chronicles 30:9, Nehemiah 9:31, Psalm 116:5.

Hebrew Word Study: rachum—compassionate (Strong's Hebrew 7349).

February 15

HaTiferet Kocham

אתיפרט אני אוהב

The Glory of Their Strength

"For You are the glory of their strength, And in Your favor our horn is exalted" (Psalm 89:17, NKJV).

Everyone wonders about the survival of the people of Israel. Nations marveled at how they've been able to stand, how they are sustained and even how they become a state now. Israel's strength is amazing. Their authority and might are wonderful. The Lord Himself has been their power to sustain them all these years. He is the strength and the splendor on their might. Their horn is exalted. As you keep on trusting in Him, He will not dismay you. His goodwill for you is everlasting and will cause you to be high above every society; that is His pledge to you. The strength of Israel is extraordinary, and He has imparted this virtue unto their lives. Everything that made who they are today is of the Lord, the grace upon the people, the glory of their outstanding achievements belongs to the Lord. By the Lord who gave you strength, you conquer nations, you destroy cities and capture kings in the power of His potency, and also live a victorious life.

Prayer: *I pray your weaknesses be overshadowed with His strength in Jesus' Name.*

Launching Deeper: Psalm 28:7, 1 Corinthians 1:30,31, 2 Corinthians 12:9,10, Psalm 89:24.

Hebrew Word Study: "koach"—ability (Strong's Hebrew: 3581).

February 16

HaSabbal

הסבא ״ל

The Burden Bearer

"Blessed be the Lord, Who bears our burdens and carries us day by day, even the God Who is our salvation! Selah [pause, and calmly think of that]!" (Psalm 68:19, AMPC).

Think of a man traveling from afar carrying a load, getting close home he sees somebody running to him to help, he takes the load off his shoulder and hand over the burden to the helper and gives a sigh of relief. I want you to see GOD'S open arm relieving you from every burden. His word says commit every burden, your ways and your decisions, your worries and anxieties, your challenges, your trials unto Him, and He will provide you rest. As you keep trusting Him, He will work out every trial for your good, pour out your heart to your Burden Bearer as His right hand lifts you up. He would support and uphold you with His righteous right hand. Jesus said, "Do not worry about your life what you would eat and wear." He will take care of that. He's calling, everyone carrying yokes, those that are bearing a heavy load, those that are suppressed with the challenges. He has no way to turn them down but has promised to grant His perfect rest.

Prayer: *I pray as you cast your burdens, anxieties, and challenges receive His rest in all areas of your life and may He give you something fresh and powerful, a light at the end of the tunnel.*

Launching Deeper: Matthew 11:28, Psalm 55:22, Psalm 37:5, Isaiah 46:4.

Hebrew Word Study: "sebel"—burden, a load (Strong's Hebrew: 5447).

February 17

Immanuel

עמנואל

God With Us

Therefore the Lord Himself shall give you a sign: Behold, the young woman who is unmarried and a virgin shall conceive and bear a son, and shall call his name Immanuel [God with us].

Isaiah 7:14 (AMPC).

When King Ahaz expected the Assyrians to come to invade Israel, he lost hope and was frightened. He forgot the covenants the Lord had made with His people that He will be with them and protect them. So, the Lord sent the prophet Isaiah to tell him He himself will give him a sign, knowing that His promises are with them. The Almighty God took up residence among His people in the word's form, becoming flesh and full of grace and truth, walked and lived in the midst of His people. The Assyrians' plan would not stand and will not come to pass. The declarations of evil will not manifest. It's because God with us would not allow that, His blessings nullify every pronunciation of curses. When God says He is with you, count on His Word, trust in Him that His presence is with you, His power is with you, His revelation is with you, His glory is with you, His favor is with you, His strength is with you, His dominion is with you, His protection is with you, all of His goodness and mercy is with you, continue to keep your faith in Him.

Prayer: *Let Immanuel give you a sign and do what every plan of evil against you be thwarted and bring you victory over the adversaries.*

Launching Deeper: Isaiah 8:8, 9:6, John 1:1,2,14, Revelation 21:3, Psalm 46:7.

Hebrew Word Study: "yalad"—to bear, bring forth, beget (Strong's Hebrew: 3205).

February 18

El Hannora

האנורההאנורה

Awesome God

And now, our God, the great and mighty and awesome God, who keeps his covenant of unfailing love, do not let all the hardships we have suffered seem insignificant to you. Great trouble has come upon us and upon our kings and leaders and priests and prophets and ancestors—all of your people—from the days when the kings of Assyria first triumphed over us until now.

Nehemiah 9:32 (NLT)

Full of awe and none like Him is our God. Fearful in praise and marvelous in deeds and wonders. By His mighty hand and His outstretched arm, He works salvation to those who believe. And by His great terrors, He's able to deliver His people out of every terror. He is not a respecter of persons or takes reward for His name. He does outstanding things for His people, His Majesty is awesome, and His right hand displays awesome deeds. The Awesome God is the hope of all the earth. By the greatness of His authority, His enemies submit themselves to Him, and He is the One who gives strength and capability to you. He is also in the council of holiness and feared above all. Every mountain before you quake at His presence and shatters the gods of the land. He blesses those who seek Him and calls upon His name in worship. From all places as far as the ends of the earth, El Hanora is great among the nations. The Awesome God will make all things possible for you. His strength will consume every mountain before you and break every barrier for you to run through in victory.

***Prayer**: The Awesome God remembers His covenant with you and bring you to His place of abundance and rest.*

Launching Deeper: Deuteronomy 7:20-25, Nehemiah 1:5, Zechariah 2:11, Joel 2:11.

Hebrew Word Study: "shamar"—to keep, watch, preserve (Strong's Hebrew: 8104).

February 19

HaShem

הַשֵּׁם

The Name

"May the Lord answer you in the day of trouble; May the name of the God of Jacob defend you" (Psalm 20:1, NKJV).

The name of the Lord is the tower, the refuge, the stronghold, the dwelling place, and shelter for the righteous to run into. At the mention of the name Jesus, every knee bows. His name is the revelation of His personality, His power, His glory, and brilliance. When the righteous call upon the name of the Lord, there are manifestations. His name displays His sovereignty, lifted above all, synonymous with His presence and always honored by the righteous. You are called by His name, and for His name's sake, He will deliver and preserve you. Whatever you ask the Father in His name, He will hear and answer your prayer. There is salvation, miracle, and healing in the name of Jesus. Receive the demonstration of His power and strength as you call upon Him, receive grace and great manifestation of His good things for your life.

Prayer: *I pray the name of the Lord protect you. The Lord grant you your heart's desires, breakthroughs, and His glory come upon your life this day.*

Launching Deeper: Isaiah 30:27, 28, Psalm 20:5, 111:9, Proverbs 18:10, Deuteronomy 28:58, John 20:31.

Hebrew Word Study: "anah"—to answer, to respond (Strong's Hebrew: 6030).

February 20

Ehyeh asher Ehyeh

אֶהְיֶה אֲשֶׁר אֶהְיֶה

I AM THAT I AM

"And God said to Moses, I AM WHO I AM and WHAT I AM, and I WILL BE WHAT I WILL BE; and He said, You shall say this to the Israelites: I AM has sent me to you!" (Exodus 3:14, AMPC).

The human body goes through changes and undergoes stages of growth. Change is inevitable in human life. We always aim at becoming something better, something greater, and something stronger, but our God remains the same. The Lord spoke to Moses and told him when "they ask you who has sent you to deliver the Israelites, tell them I AM sent you." This title was to give Moses the confidence to stand before Pharaoh and proclaim the One who set him on the mission of deliverance of His children. The self-existing "I AM GOD" is the one who gives you the audacity and the authority to stand before kings and to accomplish your mission. The God of Israel is the God of immortality and eternity. The full nature of Him is that He is incomprehensible. His absolute power is unfolded in His name. He is all we will need in life. Jesus presented Himself "I Am" as I Am the Bread of Life, I Am the Good Shepherd, I Am the Way, Truth and the Life, I Am the Resurrection and the Life, and I Am the True Vine. Whatever good you can think of or ever will need, He is the "I AM," He is your everything.

Prayer: *Let the I Am who exists like nothing else, none beside Him, the immutable, and the self-existing be praised and be exalted in your life and let Him be all you desire in Jesus' name.*

Launching Deeper: Exodus 6:2,3, Isaiah 52:6, John 8:28, 58, Hebrews 13:8, Revelation 1:8, 4:8.

Hebrew Word Study: "hayah"—come to pass, become, be (Strong's Hebrew: 1961).

February 21

ADONAI-ELOHIM

יְהוָה אֱלֹהִים

The LORD God

"This is the history of the heavens and of the earth when they were created. In the day that the Lord God made the earth and the heavens" (Genesis 2:4, AMPC).

By the words of Adonai Elohim, all being and all things were made. He laid the foundations of them all and gave life to every creature. All the heavens' army worship Him. Elohim' is mostly refers to Yahweh in scriptures, "The Strong One, of His creative power, the very existence of the universe rests." Considering the enormity of the milky way galaxy, with its countless clusters of stars, the overwhelming power of Elohim becomes obvious. His beautiful masterpiece is done in an unimaginable size. Elohim is in the form called the plural of majesty and intensity. "Lift up your eyes on high, And see who has created these things, Who brings out their host by number; He calls them all by name, By the greatness of His might And the strength of His power; Not one is missing (Isaiah 40:26, NKJV). He knows the number of the stars and calls them each by name. Before everything, He was the First. He is Infinite God. He knows your name, it is written in the palm of His arm, and remember He is very mindful of you. The riches of His Divine grace are made available to you. Elohim has cleared you blameless before Him by the blood of Jesus and seated you with Him in the heavenly places, rule and have dominion.

***Prayer:** I pray let Adonai Elohim, who laid the foundations of the earth, make way through the impossible and give you rest in Jesus' name.*

Launching Deeper: Exodus 15:3, 1 Kings 18:39, 2 Chronicles 20:6, Genesis 5:1

Hebrew Word Study: "asah""—make, manufacture, do, construct (Strong's Hebrew: 6213a).

February 22

HAHAD SHAUFEKD AL HACHAROVIM

חה"ד שאופק אל-חרובים

The One Enthroned Upon the Cherubim

"Give ear, O Shepherd of Israel, You who lead Joseph like a flock; You who dwell between the cherubim, shine forth!" (Psalm 80:1, NKJV)

The covering of the ark made of pure gold is the mercy seat. Upon the ends of it are two cherubim with wings spread out above to cover the ark. The Mercy seat between the cherubims is where the high priest sprinkles the blood of lambs in the Most Holy place. Moses literally hears the voice of the Lord between the cherubim. This position of the cherubim of the ark is where the Lord manifests His presence to the Israelites. He sits enthroned and reigns as a shepherd to protect His flocks, care for them, carry them in His bosom, and gently lead them. The ark as a symbol of His presence always shows that He is with us continually every step of the way. Your King and your tender Shepherd, who guards and guides you to greener pasture, provide you with His manna for your soul and spirit, as a king rule over your life against any kingdom of darkness that will rise to contend with you. He will continue to strengthen, empower and watch over your day and night.

***Prayer**: I pray let the One Enthroned shine forth upon your life, and His presence continues to be with you.*

Launching Deeper: Exodus 25:18-25, 2 Kings 5:15, 19:19, 1 Chronicles 13:6, Nehemiah 9:6.

Hebrew Word Study: "nachah"—lead, to guide, to drive (Strong's Hebrew: 5148).

February 23

ELOAH. YA'AKOV

אֱלוֹהַּ יַעֲקֹב

The God of Jacob

"Tremble, O earth, at the presence of the Lord, at the presence of the God of Jacob"(Psalm 114:7, AMPC).

This title tells us how God was faithful to Jacob and his descendants. Through Jacob, the nation of Israel was raised. Their relationship encourages us to put our trust in the God who keeps His covenant and promises that He will make his people great and fulfill it. The God of Jacob is the God who blesses His people, increases and multiplies them a thousand times. His name is a weapon and powerful to deliver, restore, and protect them. He is gracious, remembering his mercies even onto the children's children. The God of Jacob is faithful and absolutely trustworthy and performs His promises to you as a believer in Christ Jesus. He never changes. Keep trusting in him with perseverance and obedience. His Spirit abides with you and with His word in your mouth, commands every challenge and situation to tremble at His presence, and declares His power, favor, blessings, wisdom, understanding, and strength upon your life.

Prayer: *I pray let the God of Jacob give you revelation and show secrets of the past, the now, and what is about to happen.*

Launching Deeper: Genesis 32:27,28, Psalms 14:7, 46:7, 75:9, 76:6, 114:7.

Hebrew Word Study: "peneh"—face, front, presence (Strong's Hebrew: 6440).

February 24

ELOAH SELICHOT

אֱלוֹהַ סְלִיחוֹת

The God of Forgiveness

They refused to obey and did not remember the miracles you had done for them. Instead, they became stubborn and appointed a leader to take them back to their slavery in Egypt. But you are a God of forgiveness, gracious and merciful, slow to become angry, and rich in unfailing love. You did not abandon them.

Nehemiah 9:17 (NLT)

Think of a debt record with your name on it before the judge, with your prosecutor and lender present, and the judge declares he cancels the debt. You don't have to pay them any longer; you are free, a decree of indebtedness ascribed against your life erased. The nature of our God is forgiving and shows lovingkindness. Through the blood of Jesus, He exercises love and great compassion for all who believe in Christ the Son, according to the riches of His grace. He forgives your sins and remembers them no more. His mercy is extended to those that humble themselves, cry unto Him for pardon, turns away from their sin, and recognizes His holiness. He forgives our iniquity and keeps his compassion even to a thousand generations. You are his own as His inheritance in Christ. He hears your plea and prayers from his dwelling place. The God of Forgiveness is just and cleanses us from all unrighteousness; He does not turn his face away from you, for His namesake He will not cast you away from His presence; He rejoices in doing you good and will faithfully establish you in His blessings.

***Prayer**: I pray according to His loving devotion may He blot out every fault and remove stumbling blocks out of your way in Jesus' name.*

Launching Deeper: Exodus 34:7-12, Numbers 14:18, Nehemiah 9:31, Psalms 86:5, 103:8, 130:4.

Hebrew Word Study: "verachum"—compassionate (Strong's Hebrew: 7349).

February 25

Esh Okhlah

אש אוקלה

Consuming Fire

"For the LORD your God is a consuming fire; He is a jealous (impassioned) God [demanding what is rightfully and uniquely His]" (Deuteronomy 4:24, AMP).

When the Lord asked Moses to come to the summit of the mountain where He was in the cloud's mist, the appearance of the glory of God was like a fire in the eyes of the people looking from afar and the mountain like a blazing furnace. Moses gives them the command that the presence of the Lord will go before them as a consuming fire to protect them and to destroy the enemies before their eyes. But if they provoked him to jealousy with the worshipping of idols, then His anger will kindle like fire. He is the gracious and great God, full of goodness and glory given unto you as His child. He urges you to keep being faithful in serving Him and not to worship any other god or set your heart to love anything more than Him or bow down to conform to what is not righteous, but keep seeking Him and fear His name to stay in His presence. The name of the Lord is like dens of smoke and his tongue life-consuming fire to destroy any form of evil (Isaiah 30:27). The nations tremble because none can stand before the everlasting flames; He impels you to seek Him and live for He is good and gracious.

Prayer: *I pray the Lord be jealous over you, and His love continues to shine upon you as your affection in Him grows.*

Launching Deeper: Ezekiel 1:26,27, Psalm 50:3, Hebrews 12:29, Exodus 15:7, Isaiah 30:27, 33:14.

Hebrew Word Study: "esh"—fire (Strong's Hebrew: 784).

February 26

BOREI YISRAEL

בּוֹרֵא יִשְׂרָאֵל

The Creator of Israel

I am the LORD, your Holy One, The Creator of Israel, your King" (Isaiah 43:15, NKJV).

The One who made Israel to be who it is, He created the nation into existence by His promises to their fathers, for His glory, and for His purpose. The God of Israel declared to Pharaoh to let His firstborn, His people go so they will worship Him; He chose them to be special people unto Him. He is their God and has entrusted them with His oracles, the giving of the law, the covenants, the worship, the promises, and the promise of the Savior, Jesus Christ, born to Israel to bring salvation to all people. He provides for them and does not abandon Israel only when they continue their relationship with Him; for in them, all nations are blessed; Keep your faith in the God of Israel. You are an heir of the covenant. He remembers you and will restore you. As He created Israel and made them to be what the nation is today, so has He made you. The God of Israel is taking the responsibility to make you what He has determined you to be and to bring you to an expected end, maintain your relationship with Him, and nothing will thwart His purpose for your life.

Prayer: *I pray the Lord reveals His glory unto you, give you a title of honor to you and your generations, and strengthen you.*

Launching Deeper: Psalm 149:2, Romans 3:1-3, 9:4,5, Isaiah 43:1; 44:6, 45:11.

Hebrew Word Study: "beriah"—a creation, thing created (Strong's Hebrew: 1278).

February 27

Elohei Marom

אֱלֹהֵי מָרוֹם

The God on High

"With what shall I come before the LORD [to honor Him] And bow myself before God on high? Shall I come before Him with burnt offerings, With yearling calves?" (Micah 6:6, AMP)

God on High is sovereign over national authorities and powers. He gives kingdoms to whomever He desires and also administers kingdom affairs. Our God is the God who is gloriously enthroned and dwells on high above the heavens and the earth as His footstool. He is High above all evil powers, high above principalities, high above divination, enchantments and spells to turned the enchantment and curses of Balak into blessings, high above the witchcrafts of Jezebel and brings her kingdom down, High above any satanic conspiracies against His people and overturns them. Yes, He is the undisputed ruler, the High King, and the High God. Heavens and the heavens of heavens cannot contain him as he rides on the clouds above all nations. His countenance fills the temple and the universe, exalted above all gods, none holy and none besides Him. Though He is high and above, He sees the lowly and takes care of the lonely. His presence is seen among the humble. He lifts you up and raises you to sit with princes and to inherit the throne of glory; you are lifted up and seated with Christ in the high places, walk in power, and in live dominion with the grace of the Spirit.

***Prayer:** I pray let all the heavens and the earth give honor to the God on High and bless His Holy name. And let Him overturn every enchantment against your life in Jesus' name.*

Launching Deeper: Isaiah 57:15-17, Daniel 4:17 Psalm 138:6, Psalm 97:9, Isaiah 6:1.

Hebrew Word Study: "rum"—to be high or exalted, rise (Strong's Hebrew: 7311).

February 28

El-Channun
אֵל־חַנּוּן
The Gracious God

So he prayed to the LORD, and said, "Ah, LORD, was not this what I said when I was still in my country? Therefore, I fled previously to Tarshish; for I know that You are a gracious and merciful God, slow to anger and abundant in lovingkindness, One who relents from doing harm.

Jonah 4:2 (NKJV)

Jonah, concerned that the Lord will relent on His judgment against Nineveh, diverted his journey from Nineveh to Tarshish in disobedience to the Lord's commission. He knew how forgiving and merciful the Lord is; the lord is so gracious that when he goes to give the message of God's judgment to Nineveh, the nation will repent and turn from their wicked ways, escaping God's wrath. Truly, The God of Grace forgave them and withdrew His punishment. Like Jonah, we can be unforgiving but still attain the mercies and grace of the Lord. We are to extend the grace unto others who deal with us wrongly. The God of Grace releases grace to all who willingly repent and believe in His Son Jesus, receiving His salvation. His grace gives you the ability to turn away from ungodliness to do His will and purpose through the Holy Spirit, exercising discipline (Titus 2:10,11). By His grace, His covenant is to provide every help when you call upon Him, and from His fullness, you receive grace upon grace to fulfill your calling.

Prayer: *I pray the grace of God be with you, may He plant you and take root deeply in Him, and let Him build you to bear great fruits in Him.*

Launching Deeper: Exodus 34:6, Numbers 14:18, Deuteronomy 4:31, Psalms 86:5,15. 103:8. Jeremiah 20:7, 26:13.

Hebrew Word Study: "nacham"—regret, to be sorry (Strong's Hebrew: 5162).

March

'That they may know that You alone, whose name is the Lord ,
Are the Most High over all the earth.'
Psalms 83:18 AMP

March 1

Adonai

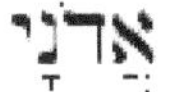

The Lord

"In the year that King Uzziah died, I saw [in a vision] the Lord sitting on a throne, high and exalted, with the train of His royal robe filling the [most holy part of the] temple" (Isaiah 6:1, AMP)

Isaiah goes to the temple for the usual worship routine. On one of the days, something different happened, the day the king died, He had an encounter and saw the Lord seated upon His throne in His glory, clothed with surpassing light saturating the expanse of the temple, the true king and Lord over Israel revealed Himself to Him that day. When the physical throne was empty, he saw the glorious throne of Adonai. When we let go of the weight which occupies the place of Adonai in our lives, we see His fullness, the cares of the world, and dependence on earthly things steal our focus on Him, and we turn to be self-sufficient. When we desire and seek him first, all other things fall in place. Isaiah's encounter with the Lord took him to a deeper revelation of the Lord's assignment for his life. We receive more of Him when we let go. As a ruler over your life, He is mindful of you to answer your prayers, displaying He's kindness and forgiveness, rich in mercy. In His Lordship, He grants onto you His daily benefits renewed each day, keep your reliance on Adonai, and get deeper in the waters of His revelations for His love and faithfulness unto you will never cease.

***Prayer:** I pray as you cast your cares upon the Lord, let him sustain you, fight for you and preserve you from troubles.*

Launching Deeper: John 12:41, Revelation 4:2-10, 20:11, 1 Kings 22:19, Ezekiel 1:1.

Hebrew Word Study: "kisse"—seat of honor, throne, chair (Strong's Hebrew: 3678).

March 2

ADONEI HA'ADONIM.

אֲדֹנֵי הָאֲדֹנִים

The LORD of Lords

"These will make war with the Lamb, and the Lamb will overcome them, for He is Lord of lords and King of kings; and those who are with Him are called, chosen, and faithful"

(Revelation 17:14, NKJV).

The miraculous events in the June 1967 Israeli Six-Day War marvel the world. The war displayed God's mighty hand at work amid His people. Though a small nation, Israel could crush its surrounding nations who waged war against them, they conquered their adversaries to the north, east, and south and enlarged their territories three times. This presents a picture of the beast with ten horns representing ten kings in Revelation 17, rising to do battle with the lamb when they wage war thinking the lamb is weak. He prevails and triumphs as the Ruler and master overall and executes justice. His enemies are defeated on the cross. He is Lord of Lords and warlords with supreme authority in heaven and the earth given to Him. All power belongs to Him, know that challenges and situations have no place in His presence, it does not matter how gigantic they might be, Greater is the one in you and reigns in you over all that will come against you, they are crushed at His command by the blood, and you win. The Lord of the kings of the earth, the ruler of the earth's governments and systems, governs over all and grants you victory.

Prayer: *Let the Lord of Lords reveal secrets unto to you, and to Him, be honor and glory and power forevermore.*

Launching Deeper: Deuteronomy 10:17, Daniel 7:26, Revelation 16:14, 19:16, 1 Timothy 1:17, Psalm 136:3.

Hebrew Word Study: "sholtan"—dominion, power, empire. (Strong's Hebrew: 7985).

March 3

Adonai Adonai

אֲדֹנָי יְהוִה

Lord YHVH. Lord GOD.

O Lord God, You have begun to show Your servant Your greatness and Your mighty hand, for what god is there in heaven or on earth who can do anything like Your works and Your mighty deeds?

Deuteronomy 3:24 (NKJV)

I have known many twin siblings, both identical and nonidentical. Some are very difficult to identify the two, but looking closely, you will find something unique about each of them. With over seven billion individuals on the earth, each one is unique; you will never encounter anyone the same as another, no matter how similar they might look. This is the awesomeness of the God we serve, the uniqueness of His creation, none the same. The Lord YWHW, the unique personal name of God showing He is unequal to any other god and active and always presents. This name also represents Yahweh's unique role as the covenant God, who does not share His glory with another. The name He is to be remembered, honored and feared throughout generations forever, that there is no other god that can save like Him, that will not abandon His people for the sake of His glorious name. His greatness extends to the ends of the earth. He uniquely abounds in mercy and grace. He is unmovable and never changes. He made you and established a covenant with you through His Son Jesus, brought judgment against your enemies on the cross, and restored you to Himself with favor and never-ending richness of His glory.

Prayer: *I pray, receive the fullness of Him, and let your life never be the same.*

Launching Deeper: Micah 5:4, Psalms 110:4, 83:18, Joshua 22:22, Joel 2:27.

Hebrew Word Study: "asah"—accomplish, make, manufacture (Strong's Hebrew: 6213).

March 4

Haol Paratz

האול פרץ

The Yoke Breaker

Then the trees of the field shall yield their fruit, and the earth shall yield her increase. They shall be safe in their land; and they shall know that I am the LORD, when I have broken the bands of their yoke and delivered them from the hand of those who enslaved them.

Ezekiel 34:27 (NKJV).

The woman had been in this posture for eighteen years, contoured and bent walking like she carries a yoke or a burden; when Jesus took notice of her, He had mercy and declared the woman to be loose; the yoke was taken off her neck immediately and was delivered and walked. A yoke, a curved piece of wood that fits on the neck of oxen to draw the plow. Being restless to shake off the yoke as Isaac told Esau when Jacob took His blessing is striving and travailing, calling upon the Yoke Breaker, and He will shatter the bars of yokes, save from any spiritual enslavement, destroy the rod of the oppressor and set you loose form infirmities, With His bands of love, He lifts every yoke. Declare you will not allow any yoke in your life, do not accept the burden, strive to see a change in that situation, I declare you set free no more burdens. Prayer and fasting lose the bands of wickedness, knowledge of His Word, the truth, liberates you from the yoke of ignorance; He reveals Himself to you and shows you what He has made you, walk in power and dominion lift your head up and be filled with His glory.

Prayer: *I pray the Lord deliver you from every yoke and discomfit them and their host, and crush their horses and burn their chariots with fire*

Launching Deeper: Luke 13:11, Ezekiel 30:18, Hosea 11:4, Leviticus 26:13.

Hebrew Word Study: "ol"—yoke (Strong's Hebrew: 5923).

March 5

YESHU'AT ELOHEINU OLAMIM

ישות אלוהינו עולם

The Author of Eternal Salvation

"And having been perfected, He became the author of eternal salvation to all who obey Him" (Hebrews 5:9, NKJV).

In the kingdom of the Lord, an act of obedience can ripple to make a great impact on the lives of others. For example, an usher at a wedding event greets guests, escorts them to their seats, ensures guests' questions are answered, and their needs met. Just to mention a few, if no usher is present to perform this duty, we can see the level of confusion that might erupt in that event. Salvation originates from Jesus. Through His obedience, He left His place in the heavenlies, submitted himself to the Father's directions, and taking upon Himself to atone for the sins of many, brought a ripple effect of many souls saved and being saved every day. He authored eternal salvation. From the obedience of the apostles to taking the gospel to the ends of the earth to the converted believer today, responding to Christ as He obeyed the Father will lead to a successful life and eternal salvation. Adhere to your assignment given to you in the kingdom and make a lot of impact in the lives of other people, it will enrich your life with His goodness and turn many to eternal salvation, author a step toward someone's eternal salvation through Jesus Christ our Lord.

***Prayer**: I pray Lord let me heed to your Word and be obedient to do your will.*

Launching Deeper: Hebrew 9:12,15,2:3, Psalms 45:17, 68:10-20, Isaiah 45:22, 50:10.

Hebrew Word Study: "pallet"—deliverance (Strong's Hebrew: 6405).

March 6

Hakkadosh

הַקָּדוֹשׁ

The Holy One

"To whom then will you liken Me, that I should be equal to him? says the Holy One" (Isaiah 40:25, AMPC).

Joshua's life, he had come to a close end of leading the Israelites to the promised land and allotting the land to the various tribes as their inheritance; he called them and reminded them of the great things the Lord had done for the nation; He is a God Who keeps His promises, right from the beginning to the end, He will make sure He brings all to a beautiful completion what He has promised you, none of His words concerning you will be void, He is the Holy One who calls you and distinguish you as a child of God. He requires that His people separate themselves from sin and any form of unholiness. His Holiness and perfection cannot stand ungodliness. The Lord cautioned them to be faithful to Him and obey His Word. They cannot serve Him and strange gods. If they willfully turn to disobey these commands, He will turn away from them. Then comes the call to weigh the benefits and the inconveniences in serving the Holy God. If you turn away from Him, you forfeit all His great benefits, and if you serve Him, you have bestowed His providence in all areas of your life, stay connected to the Holy One, your source of blessings in life.

Prayer: *I pray the Lord set you apart for Himself and distinguish you for greatness and for favor.*

Launching Deeper: Joshua 23, 24:19, Isaiah 5:16, 1 Samuel 6:20.

Hebrew Word Study: "tiklah" completeness, perfection (Strong's Hebrew: 8502).

March 7

Kedosh Yisrael

קְדוֹשׁ יִשְׂרָאֵל

The Holy One of Israel

"Whom have you mocked and reviled and insulted and blasphemed? Against Whom have you raised your voice and haughtily lifted your eyes? Against the Holy One of Israel!" (2 Kings 19:22, AMPC)

Rabshakeh stood by the highways near Jerusalem to speak to the Jews on behalf of the Assyrian king, saying that putting their trust in their God and king will not be of any help to them. Hezekiah, the king, saw this as a blasphemy and a threat, and went to the temple, spread the letter before the altar, and lifted up his voice, and prayed to the Holy One of Israel. He heard his prayers and declared to the Assyrians that it is He that they lifted up themselves against, The Holy One of Israel. He will fight for His people and deliver them. They will be rooted in their land and bear root upon it and will prosper in all their ways. The Holy One of Israel will establish you in His presence, where you will receive His grace and mercy to bear abundant fruit in your life. His holiness stands for justice for His people. Gods of the nations cannot be compared to Him in redeeming His people. He will arise on your behalf when the enemy comes against you like a flood; the Holy One of Israel will lift up a standard for you and rescue you. Depend and have confidence in Him as you rejoice in His holiness.

Prayer: *I pray the Lord lifts up His standard against the foes and makes them fear the name of the Lord*

Launching Deeper: 2 Kings 19, Isaiah 59:19, Psalm 71:22.

Hebrew Word Study: "rum"—to be high above, exalted, rise high (Strong's Hebrew: 7311).

March 8

CHOKER KOL LEV

קול לב קול

The Searcher of Hearts

"Now He who searches the hearts knows what the mind of the Spirit is, because He makes intercession for the saints according to the will of God" (Romans 8:27, NKJV).

When Samuel got to Bethlehem and saw Eliab, he thought Eliab was the one God had chosen to be king instead of Saul, but the Lord told Samuel, "You will look at the outward part of man to determine his perfection, but I look at the inward part of man I search the hearts of men," the spirit of man is the candle in which He looks through the inward parts. He searches the heart and tests the mind, and rewards us according to our deeds (Jeremiah 17:10). He searches for a heart of remembrance that remembers His faithfulness and is grateful to bless His holy name, a heart that honors Him and glorifies Him, a concerned and zealous heart for service unto the Lord, and a heart that is applied unto the teachings of the word to obtain wisdom of God. He understands the imaginations of our hearts. We should serve Him with a willing heart, and He will be found by us. Christ is our advocate; through Him, we have access to the Father by the Spirit who knows our reins and prays according to the will of God for our lives, and our Father will harken unto us, and His name is glorified.

Prayer: *I pray the searcher of Hearts searches me and fixes all that is needed to be fix and fulfills His Word for my life in Jesus' name.*

Launching Deeper: Proverbs 20:27, Romans 8:34, Jeremiah 17:10, 1 Thessalonians 2:4, 1 Chronicles 28:9, 29:17.

Hebrew Word Study: "bochan"—to test, to examine (Strong's Hebrew: 976).

March 9

Ha'Osekha

נחל האושקה

The Maker

"For your Maker is your husband, The Lord of hosts is His name; And your Redeemer is the Holy One of Israel; He is called the God of the whole earth" (Isaiah 54:5, NKJV).

There can be makers of various things all over the world, but the Chief Maker of all is the Lord, the Maker of the heavens and earth, the Maker of all things is the heritage of the believer, the Lord is making you what He said about you; He is fashioning and shaping you into the form He desires. Like the potter working the clay on the potter's wheel, he first has in mind the purpose of the finished object before he starts. It can be a pot to carry water, a bowl for food, or a vase to carry some flowers. He has the picture of the object in his mind and then begins to fashion the clay to that object. God, the Maker, has the plan and intentions of what He is making you. According to the volume of books written about you, He has made you. He is settling you in His grace and positioning you in all abilities, providing all that you will need to fulfill every purpose of your life. You may not know or understand how He is forming things around you, but keep believing and trusting. He will accomplish and perform what concerns you, the Maker will make the way and make you great. Receive it in Jesus' name!

Prayer: *The Lord is faithful who has started making things to happen for you, to the image of Him, He will bring it to completion.*

Launching Deeper: Isaiah 45:11, Psalms 138:8, 57:2, Philippians 1:6.

Hebrew Word Study: "yetzer"—formed, framing, purpose (Strong's Hebrew: 3336).

March 10

Moshia

מוֹשִׁיעַ

Deliverer

"And he said: 'The Lord is my rock and my fortress and my deliverer'" (2 Samuel 22:2, NKJV).

In our world today, you can mostly find people enslaved in addictions, sicknesses, family issues, deception, and diverse situations. Some yearn for true freedom from these afflictions. The only true origin of deliverance is the Lord Jesus Christ and nothing else and no one else. The knowledge of truth in Him is what makes a person free (John 8:31-36). For His love for humanity, He gives true deliverance. He gave His only begotten Son that whoever believes in Him is saved, there can be all forms of deliverers, false religion, false prophets and false redemption from addiction and sickness, The Deliverer, Jesus came that we might have life and have more abundantly with its fullness and joy. He delivers and opens blind eyes and brings out prisoners from prison and sets the spiritually bound and enslaved free. He is anointed to give you relief from spiritual oppressions, bind up wounds of your heart, and break any form of guilt and power of sin out of your life. You are delivered to enjoy His blessings and fruitfulness in full.

Prayer: *I pray the Lord will not delay delivering you out of Zion. Let Him send forth His help quickly to you in Jesus' name.*

Launching Deeper: Judges 3:9, Genesis 45:5-7, Exodus 3:10, Psalms 40:17, 144:2.

Hebrew Word Study: "palat"—to escape, be free, to bring out, save (Strong's Hebrew: 6403).

March 11

HAMOSHIA

הַמּוֹשִׁיעַ

The Savior

And it will be for a sign and for a witness to the Lord of hosts in the land of Egypt; for they will cry to the Lord because of the oppressors, and He will send them a Savior and a Mighty One, and He will deliver them.

Isaiah 19:20 (NKJV)

The promises of freedom in people's life come in so many ways, it can be a drug that ensures happiness but turns to be enslavement, a relationship to give fulfillment but turns to a wrongful trap, or even a second job for financial security but becomes a master. These promises become an entrapment and never give the freedom expected and a deception when we call on the Lord, the Savior, He saves. He is a very present help in times of challenges and confusion. For all of us once lived a life of deception and false promises of happiness, as slaves in all sort of evil desire, living in bondage but through his grace, the kindness and love of our God. He gives salvation not of anything that we did but by his mercy and grace; he washed us in his blood and gave us new birth, renewed us by the Holy Spirit, and defeated the devil on our behalf. The Savior, through His mighty acts, through His miracles, through His resurrection, saved us from the power of sin, redeemed us from the law, and gave us citizenship of heaven with all spiritual blessings to partake.

***Prayer**: I pray the Lord contends with any force of evil that contend with you and save you to His abundant grace and blessings in Jesus' name.*

Launching Deeper: Isaiah 45:21,22, Luke 2:11, Isaiah 43:11, 63:8, 49:25, 26.

Hebrew Word Study: "mishloach"—sending stretch out, dispatch (Strong's Hebrew: 4916b).

March 12

ZERO'A HASHEM

זירו-ה'

Arm of the Lord

"Who has believed our report? And to whom has the arm of the LORD been revealed?" (Isaiah 53:1, NKJV)

Isaiah issued a prophecy about the Messiah's coming. He made a report of the wondrous works of the Almighty and what he is about to reveal. The Arm of Jehovah Himself was revealed in the life and ministry of Jesus. A symbol of the Lord's sovereignty and His mighty acts amid His people. The Lord comes with authority, and His mighty arm rules for Him. His arm manifests His mighty deeds, working in miracles and redeeming men, the saving force of the Lord is demonstrated to help His people in every captivity, for His arm is not too short to reach out and save them, He brought his nations out of Egypt with His righteous right arm, helped them and upheld them, with His outstretched arm He crushed the enemies of His people and led them through to divide the waters before them, there He gain for Himself an eternal glory, by His powerful arm He made the earth and everything within it and gives to whomsoever that He pleases. His everlasting arms are your dwelling place where you find refuge and security and representation of His holiness and love for all His children.

***Prayer**: I pray the Arm of the Lord preserves your life, and may He grant your request, even length of days forever.*

Launching Deeper: Psalms 77:15, 89:10, Isaiah 63:12, Exodus 6:6, Deuteronomy 9:29, 33:27, Psalm 98:1.

Hebrew Word Study: "asah"—make (Strong's Hebrew: 6213).

March 13

Hannoten Teshuah

הַנוֹתֵן תְּשׁוּעָה

The Giver of Salvation

"The One who gives salvation to kings, Who delivers David His servant From the deadly sword" (Psalm 144:10, NKJV).

Salvation is only in the name of Jesus. He is the source of eternal salvation to those who obey his word. God anoints Christ to offer salvation to all men according to the will of God. Everyone who believes the Son would have eternal life and, by faith, have access to God and become His child. The Father has granted us forgiveness of sins, wiped our transgressions, we are no more outside His kingdom but have become citizens of God's family and partakers of heavenly riches, prepared for those who believe in Him, and also to share the inheritance of the saints of the kingdom of His beloved Son. He has overcome the world for us, and in Him we have peace. Even in this world, we have righteousness in the sight of God and have become a new creation. The old has passed, and all things made new. The Giver of Salvation also gives you power over the works of darkness and freedom from bondage of sin by the Holy Spirit.

Prayer: *I pray the Lord covers your head in the day of battle and gives you strength and power.*

Launching Deeper: Acts 4:12, Hebrews 5:9, 2 Samuel 22:51, Psalms 18:50, 33:16-18, 140:7.

Hebrew Word Study: "yasha"—to deliver (Strong's Hebrew: 3467).

March 14

OZER HAYATOM

עוזר הייאטום

Helper of the Fatherless

"You have seen it, for You have noted mischief and vexation (irritation) to take it into Your hand. The unfortunate commits himself to You; You are the helper of the fatherless" (Psalm 10:14, AMP).

The beggar Lazarus sat at the rich man's gate, and it became his dwelling, quests come in and out, dogs licking his wounds and no food to eat until food are thrown out in trash if the day is good, he will get something if not nothing for days, and this can lead to his death. "Lazarus," meaning "whom God helps" in Hebrew, is a representation of poverty and helplessness, something that the fatherless can experience, but the Lord is his Helper and his Father, He gives him justice; He pleads his course; He protects him; he finds mercy in Him, when the fatherless cry, the Lord hears, He sees the affliction and his anguish, His eye is upon him to relief and preserves him, He is quick to defend and destroys those who oppress Him. Jesus assured the fatherless that he would not leave them; He would not abandon them. He redeems them by his blood and adopts them as His very own children. Through faith in Christ Jesus, He now adopts the spiritually fatherless into the family of the kingdom of God, and by the Spirit, all can cry Abba Father. He extends His blessings and favor to all, His strength and faithfulness to all, and He is the great loving Father to all.

***Prayer**: I pray the grace and blessings of the Lord come upon your house as you call on Abba Father.*

Launching Deeper: Psalm 31:7, Job 29:12, Deuteronomy 10:18, Psalms 68:5, 146:9, Jeremiah 49:11.

Hebrew Word Study: "nathan"—to give, put, set (Strong's Hebrew: 5414).

March 15

Go'el

גֹּאֵל

Kinsman Redeemer

Remain tonight, and in the morning, if he will redeem you, good; let him do it. But if he is not willing to redeem you, then, as the LORD lives, I will redeem you. Lie down until the morning.

Ruth 3:13 (AMP)

The story of Ruth in the scriptures shows God's redemptive love. The kinsman-redeemer is responsible for preserving the life, the family name, integrity, and property of a close relative. Boaz, "in Him is strength," became the go'el to redeem the land for impoverished Naomi and marry Ruth to keep the line of Elimelech and produce an heir for Naomi. Boaz, the near kinsman to Ruth, gives a picture of the Messiah Who redeems the church for Himself. Remember, in Deuteronomy 23:3, a Moabite shall not enter into the congregation of Israel, but grace and favor found Ruth to be redeemed. Naomi's lineage was preserved. The same grace has found us among the nations to pay the ransom for us. He will plead your cause for you, redeem you, and your life be preserved according to His Word in Psalm 119:154. He will make peace for you and silence the voice of the accuser.

Prayer: *I pray the Lord shows you loving devotion and in famine and redeem you, let Him give you might in time of weakness.*

Launching Deeper: Leviticus 25:26; Numbers 5:8; 35:19, 21, 24f, 27; Deuteronomy 19:6.

Hebrew Word Study: "gaal"—to redeem, reclaim as one's own (Strong's Hebrew: 1350).

March 16

Go'el Yisrael

גֹּאֵל יִשְׂרָאֵל

The Redeemer of Israel

> *Thus says the LORD, The Redeemer of Israel, their Holy One, To Him whom man despises, To Him whom the nation abhors, To the Servant of rulers: "Kings shall see and arise, Princes also shall worship, Because of the LORD who is faithful, The Holy One of Israel; And He has chosen You."*
>
> *Isaiah 49:7 (NKJV)*

Imagine the day of the Exodus of Israel from Egypt to the promised land. They gathered at the city gates of Egypt to start the journey. You could imagine the children leaping from one place to the other, waiting for the command from Moses, the leader, to set off. Adults sing songs of praise to the Lord, HaGo'el, the Redeemer, and give Him thanks. He is strong and powerful to redeem His people from the enemy's grip of oppression and slavery. When He heard their cries, He remembered His covenant with them and said, "I will rescue you from their bondage and redeem you with an outstretched arm, and with great judgments" (Exodus 6:6). With great judgment, He paid the Egyptians for what they did to Israel and brought them out of that land. He paid the price for your ransom to restore you to himself, took the place to avenge you, deliver you, and paid off the cost of sins. The blood of Jesus is the price. When He was lifted up on the cross, we received our redemption and are bold to stand and declare we are free from slavery of sin.

Prayer: *I pray in His time of favor, the Lord helps you and appoints you to be a covenant and bring restoration to you.*

Launching Deeper: Isaiah 48:17, 49:26, 63:16, Deuteronomy 7:8, Exodus 15:13, Jeremiah 15:21, 31:11, 50:34.

Hebrew Word Study: "amar"—say, mention, command (Strong's Hebrew: 560).

March 17

Go'el Haddam

גֹּאֵל הַדָּם

The Avenger of Blood

You shall strike the house of Ahab your master, so that I may avenge the blood of My servants the prophets, and the blood of all the servants of the Lord , [who have died] at the hands of Jezebel.

2 Kings 9:7 (AMP)

The son of the prophet got to Ramoth Gilead to anoint Jehu. He called Jehu to a room and gave him Elisha's message, anointed him as king of Israel, and fled as instructed by Elisha. Jehu will be king to avenge the blood of the prophets whom the house of Ahab and Jezebel had killed. After being anointed, he rode his chariot to Jezreel and destroyed Jezebel as commanded. God used him to avenge His prophets. The Avenger is the family member who restores justice to the family in time of any loss, be it losing an individual or property. Anyone who curses his people is cursed, and anyone who blesses them is blessed. Those that rise up against them, the Lord does not spare. His hand will take hold on judgment against their adversaries. He is merciful and does not ignore the cry of the afflicted. He will lift you up from any danger and from any gates of death. The Lord will deliver and redeem you. He will avenge your enemies and anything that afflicts you, anything that suppresses you and any challenge that puts you in bondage. The Lord will avenge on your behalf and remember you with His blessings.

Prayer: *I pray the Lord hears you when you call, draws close to you, and pleads your cause in Jesus' name.*

Launching Deeper: Numbers 35:12,25, Leviticus 4:2, Psalms 10:12, 72:14, 136:23, Revelations 6:10, 19:2.

Hebrew Word Study: "nebi"—prophet (Strong's Hebrew: 5029).

March 18

ADONAI TSURI V'GO'ALI.

יְהוָה צוּרִי וְגֹאֲלִי

Rock and Redeemer

"Let the words of my mouth and the meditation of my heart be acceptable in your sight, O Lord, my rock and my redeemer" (Psalm 19:14, ESV).

Job desired vindication of his ailment, someone to plead his cause. He showed confidence that his redeemer lives. His redeemer will surely come to his aid. He had been through a lot with no fault of his; he lost everything, friends came to him, and they could not comprehend what had happened to him, but he kept hoping in the Lord to see him through. The Lord commands you to put away fear even when it looks hopeless; He is your Helper from the beginning to the end. The latter days of Job were more blessed than the beginning. His Rock and Redeemer granted him the double portion and restored all that he lost. For your sake, He will bring nations down and give you the victory, by His divine restoration receive double for every trouble, He can hide His face for some time, but with everlasting lovingkindness, He will have mercy (Isaiah 54:8) and redeem you from lack and bring you into abundance. He will teach you to profit and lead you to the way of prosperity, heal you from sicknesses and diseases to the place of perfect health and perfect rest.

Prayer: *Your Redeemer lives, and He is mighty. Let the words of our prayer and our heart meditations be pleasing to Him.*

Launching Deeper: Job 19:25, 42:12, Isaiah 48:17, Jeremiah 50:34, 30:31.

Hebrew Word Study: "Go'el" meaning "to redeem" or "to buy back" (Strong's Hebrew: 1350).

March 19

Metzavveh

מצווה (ארץ)

Commander

"Indeed I have given him as a witness to the people, A leader and commander for the people" (Isaiah 55:4, NKJV).

The President exercises supreme control and commands over the armed forces as the head of government over the nation; he gives commands when necessary, in certain situations. The Messiah is the commander to His people and possesses supreme control over creation, a ruler over all whose origin is of eternity. He is the commander-in-chief, and His throne is established forever. All nations will serve Him and adhere to His commands. He issues decrees to restore and rebuild His people, a supreme command that they possess their inheritance, and enjoy all blessings and favor that He covenanted with them. His people follow His ordinances and observe His precepts. His command is that we keep seeking God the Father. Those in captivity will go forth. Those in darkness will see the light. The righteousness of the Commander will be imparted unto you, and His glory revealed in your life by His grace and mercy. The Commander leads you in triumph over the works of darkness and destroys them under His feet.

Prayer: *I pray the Commander rules over every challenge in your life and brings every force of wickedness down in Jesus' name.*

Launching Deeper: Isaiah 49:8-10, Psalm 18:43, Isaiah 16:5, Jeremiah 30:9, Ezekiel 34:24, 37:24,25, Hosea 3:5.

Hebrew Word Study: "nagid"—a leader, an officer (Strong's Hebrew: 5057).

March 20

Haderek Oseh

הדרק אוסה

The Way-Maker

Behold, I am doing a new thing! Now it springs forth; do you not perceive and know it and will you not give heed to it? I will even make a way in the wilderness and rivers in the desert.

Isaiah 43:19 (AMPC).

There might be no sign of fulfillment on the new thing he has promised, but it surely springs forth even though you may not recognize it. He commands that you see he's working miracles is inevitable. He does new things and wonderful things. He made a way through the wilderness from Egypt to Canaan, the promised land; it was a deserted path, a dry place, but he made it fruitful for them and caused the springs to run from the rock in the midst of dryness. He went before them by the fire by night and cloud by day to seek a place for them and to show them the way, for he makes the way of the righteous smooth and leveled and makes the way through the sea, a path through the waters. The Lord is making way for you, and what seems impossible, the Lord will create the possibility, He would smooth your path, every cooked place will be straightened. In your family, He will make a way. In your marriage, He would make a way. In your finances, He would make a way, and in your health, He would make a way. In all areas of your life, the Lord is more than able to bring you to your land of expectation and fulfillment.

Prayer: *I pray the Way-Maker removes every stumbling block out of your way and make a new thing spring forth for you.*

Launching Deeper: Isaiah 42:16, 43:16, 45:13, Joshua 1:8, Psalm 37:7.

Hebrew Word Study: "lach"—a new thing, fresh (Strong's Hebrew: 3892).

March 21

M'SHIACH ADONAI.

מְשִׁיחַ יְהוָה

The LORD'S Anointed

"The kings of the earth set themselves, And the rulers take counsel together, Against the Lord and against His Anointed" (Psalm 2:2, NKJV).

Paul received the message from his nephew that some Jews had vowed not to eat or drink till they kill him. A plot to set an ambush against him when he is sent to the high priest, but the Lord delivered him through the governor Felix. The Lord said to him, "You are to bear witness of me in Rome after testifying in Jerusalem, be of good cheer" (Acts 23:11-30). Paul was anointed to fulfill a mission, to testify about the Lord's death and resurrection to bring salvation to many. Whatever his enemies did to cut him off before his time failed, Christ, the Anointed One, is the chosen One, is set apart for a divine purpose by the Father's plan and foreknowledge. As the Anointed One, the spirit of the Lord rested upon Him with power to heal the sick, to restore true freedom, to carry our weaknesses, and to preach good news to the poor; all about Him came to fulfillment. The Anointed King is righteous, victorious, and humble; His light shines upon us, and we are citizens of his kingdom, by believing in the LORD'S Anointed, you are born of God, baptized into Christ, clothed with Him, and raised to sit with Him through the glory of the Father.

Prayer: *I pray the Lord hear your cry and have mercy, be gracious and answer you.*

Launching Deeper: Acts 10:38, 23:11-35, 2:22-36, Matthew 21:8,9, Acts 5:42.

Hebrew Word Study: "suph"—to be fulfilled (Strong's Hebrew: 5487).

March 22

HaNagid

מָשִׁיחַ נָגִיד

The Prince

Know therefore and understand, That from the going forth of the command To restore and build Jerusalem Until Messiah the Prince, There shall be seven weeks and sixty-two weeks; The street shall be built again, and the wall, Even in troublesome times.

Daniel 9:25 (NKJV)

A touch on Daniel's shoulder and a word of comfort by Gabriel brought great relief to him that morning. After twenty-one days of fasting for God's intervention on their distress, Gabriel assured him that the Messiah the Prince would come at an appointed time, and their distress has ended. Messiah the Prince is of the highest pedigree and holds the highest office, authority and power, and wealth. The Father gives Him His authority to give eternal life to all souls handed to Him, for in Him and through Him, all things exist. As the Preeminent Prince, God gives Him the right and privilege to be the First and above all creation and as an heir to all things, for the Father loves the Son and has placed creation in His hands. He has made Him a leader and a commander to disarm forces of wickedness; He subdued and defeated them on the cross and put them under His feet, after canceling the debts that were ascribed in the decrees against your life, He has given you authority as a member of the royal family and royal priesthood of the kingdom of God, His wealth, power and blessings is your potion, and you rule in the heavens with Him.

Prayer: *I bless the Messiah the Prince, for He is counted worthy of greater glory, for grace and truth came through Him. Let Him empower you with His grace and glory this day in Jesus' name.*

Launching Deeper: Hebrews 2:8, Philippians 3:21, Matthew 11:27, Luke 10:22.

Hebrew Word Study: "shub"—restore, to turn back (Strong's Hebrew: 7725).

March 23

Tzemach Tzaddik

צֶמַח צַדִּיק

The Branch of Righteousness

"Behold, the days are coming," says the Lord, "That I will raise to David a Branch of righteousness; A King shall reign and prosper, And execute judgment and righteousness in the earth.

Jeremiah 23:5 (NKJV)

The personality of Righteousness is the Son of the Righteous Father sent to the earth to live among men. The Son's perfect life upon the earth pleased Him. He gives all believers the power to leave a righteous life; He executes it, sustains, and establishes it. He is the branch of the Lord that bears guiltless fruits and sinless acts. He judges the poor, decides with equity for the meek upon the earth, and wages war against the wicked. Righteousness is His belt, He builds His church with splendor and rules upon his throne, acting in accordance with the Father's will. He showed His righteousness by being obedient to the Father and doing His purpose; He did not do anything by His desire but honored what the Father said by putting on righteousness. He was made perfect and was made the source of eternal salvation to everyone who obeys. You are justified on the accounts of His right standing with God, share and leave in true faith in Him, and know that you are credited with being right with God, not by works or deeds but just by His grace.

***Prayer**: I pray the Branch of Righteousness be exalted in your life and increase His grace upon you.*

Launching Deeper: Isaiah 4:2, 11:1-5, Zechariah 6:12-13, 3:8, Jeremiah 33:15.

Hebrew Word Study: "tsemach"—branch, a sprout, growth (Strong's Hebrew: 6780).

March 24

HaBa'al

באבאאל

The Husband

"For your Maker is your husband, The Lord of hosts is His name; And your Redeemer is the Holy One of Israel; He is called the God of the whole earth" (Isaiah 54:5, NKJV).

As a husband loves, protects the wife and makes the home safely conducive to all, so the Lord assures his people to love and keep them in safety. Adonai is a husband and in a covenant relationship to the people of Israel and to the church, a closest and delicate relation to us. As a husband, he is constantly faithful in all His ways towards Israel, even when they don't remain faithful to Him. When they become unfaithful and adulterous by worshipping foreign gods and sacrificing to idols, He remained perfectly loyal and faithful to bring them to restoration and to fulfill His promises to them; He is the husband to the church forever, giving unto them His righteousness and justice. He shows his devoted love by nourishing and cherishing them continually; As a bridegroom, Christ cleanses the church by His Word and will present her as a glorious, blameless, and Holy bride to the father. He loved and gave Himself as an offering for you and died on the cross; He provides for you, protects you, and keeps His presence with you forever, keeps abiding in Him.

***Prayer:** I pray the Lord gives you His counsel and direct your path, and may His name be great in your life.*

Launching Deeper: Jeremiah 31:32, Jeremiah 3:14, Hosea 2:19.

Hebrew Word Study: "sithrah"—protection, shelter (Strong's Hebrew: 5643b).

March 25

HaRuach Borei

הרא"ה בוראי

The Wind Maker

For behold, He who forms the mountains and creates the wind And declares to man what are His thoughts, He who makes the dawn into darkness And treads on the heights of the earth—The Lord God of hosts is His name.

Amos 4:13 (AMP)

The Hebrew word "ruach" has the same meaning as a spirit, breath, and wind. He is the Maker of the seen and the unseen. The mountains, the stars, animals, and plantations were all made by Him, seen and unseen. The wind, as subtle as it can be, is very powerful as the spirit and breath. He made them all and did all things. The Wind figuratively represents God's power and his presence. In the flood's time in Genesis, the Lord caused the wind to blow and receded the waters, the Lord brought an east wind in the deliverance's time of the Israelites, to bring the locusts as a plaque against the Egyptians, He caused the wind to blow to divide the Red Sea, He commands the wind to do His bidding, God asked Ezekiel to prophesy to the four winds to bring breath to the dry bones (Ezekiel 37:9). When the Lord appears, He will gather His elects in the day of the Lord from the four winds of the earth. He can hold the wind in His palm and restrain it. He will come in the wind on your behalf and bring flesh and life to every dry bone. He will command the wind to be still and bring peace into your life.

Prayer: *I pray, let the Lord command the wind to bring restoration and bring peace and life unto you*

Launching Deeper: Exodus 10:13-19, Psalm 78: 26, Ezekiel 37, John 3:8.

Hebrew Word Study: "ruach"—breeze, breath, spirit, wind, mind (Strong's Hebrew: 7307).

March 26

Ruach Hakkodesh

רוּחַ הַקֹּדֶשׁ

The Holy Spirit

"Do not cast me away from Your presence, And do not take Your Holy Spirit from me" (Psalm 51:11, AMP).

When we pray, and it's difficult to articulate our desired words, and don't even know the right things to ask as we ought to, on our behalf, The Holy Spirit makes intercessions for us with unspeakable groanings, too deep to be uttered according to the will of God for our lives (Romans 8:26). He is the one Who appoints and commissions us into various ministries to fulfill His plan. The Holy Spirit indwells believers: The prophet Joel prophesied that in the last days, the Spirit would be poured upon all flesh, young and old, male and female, rich and poor, no respecter of persons, to empower them to choose to follow the will of God, making His gifting accessible to us. He gives you the ability to tap into the unlimited power of God on earth and have access to His divine counsel and wisdom, helping you to function in His plan. When the spirit came upon Saul, the king, he became another person and began to declare the wonders of God for the nation. You a new man, as the Spirit of the Lord lives in you. You have divine access to His power, His anointing, His wisdom and counsel, His grace and favor, to do great and mighty things in Him.

Prayer: *The Lord will not take away the Holy Spirit from you. The Lord restores unto you the joy of salvation and walks you in the power of the Spirit in Jesus' name.*

Launching Deeper: 2 Samuel 23:2; Acts 8:29; 13:2, 20:28, Revelation 2:7; Romans 8.

Hebrew Word Study: "paneh"—presence, face (Strong's Hebrew: 6440).

March 27

HaVegeleh Razim

הווגלה רזים

The Revealer of Secrets

"The king answered Daniel, and said, 'Truly your God is the God of gods, the Lord of kings, and a revealer of secrets, since you could reveal this secret'" (Daniel 2:47, NKJV).

Humans cannot easily see the eternal plans and purpose of God. It's the Lord who reveals them. To reveal means to disclose and made to bear. The owner of secrets and mysteries is Adonai. He unveils His secrets through visions and dreams, through the interpretation disclosed by His prophets. For mysteries are His, the ones revealed belong to His people. He is the one who uncovers what is most hidden. Visions and secrets are a primary team in the book of Daniel. Daniel received revelations of mysteries in the spirit, things happening concerning his people, and events to happen. He made known unto the king of Babylon mysteries to take place at the end of days. He disclosed His divine intentions for the kingdom and His people through the inspiration of the Excellent Spirit. The Lord does nothing without revealing it to His prophets. He did not hide from Abraham what He was about to do in Sodom. The Lord will show you mysteries and secrets by the Spirit through dreams and visions, keep trusting in Him and receive His divine encounters and revelations.

Prayer: *I pray the Lord reveals more secrets and mysteries unto you by the Spirit.*

Launching Deeper: Deuteronomy 29:29, Amos 3:7, Ephesians 3:9, Colossians 1:15.

Hebrew Word Study "gelah"—to reveal (Strong's Hebrew: 1541).

March 28

MALAKH ADONAI

מַלְאַךְ יְהוָה

Angel of the LORD

"And the Angel of the Lord appeared to him, and said to him, 'The Lord is with you, you mighty man of valor!'" (Judges 6:12, NKJV)

Adonai manifested Himself in a form of an angel to His people, visible and in a bodily form to meet their needs. He appeared unto Moses in a flame of fire amid a bush and called unto Moses and said I am the God of your fathers; I hear the cry of my people. I will deliver them, and He did, the same way He delivered His people In the days of the judges. As Israel frequently falls into sins of rebelliousness, the Lord chastises them and causes them to fall into the hands of oppressors by surrounding nations. They will then call upon Him, and by His compassion, He provides deliverers to save them from their plunders. Oppressors like the Midianite ravaged their crops and harvests, and the Lord appeared unto Gideon in a form of an angel and empowered him as the mighty man of valor to defeat their enemies. The angel received worship, the title Lord, the offering, and the sacrifice that Gideon offered Him, which angels do not. See The angel of the LORD come to your aid in time of challenge, just be willing and obedient, draw nigh to Him, receive His Word and the outpouring of His Spirit, and you will see His deliverance.

Prayer: *I pray let the angel of the Lord take you out of every oppression and make you a person of valor.*

Launching Deeper: Genesis 16:7, Exodus 3:2, Judges 2:1, Judges 6:11-25, 13:3.

Hebrew Word Study: "malak"—a messenger, angel (Strong's Hebrew: 4397).

March 29

AVI-'AD

אֲבִיעַד

Everlasting Father

For unto us a Child is born, Unto us a Son is given; And the government will be upon His shoulder. And His name will be called Wonderful, Counselor, Mighty God, Everlasting Father, Prince of Peace.

Isaiah 9:6 (NKJV)

Earthly fathers are limited in their time of fatherhood to their children, some are limited not only in time but in caring, in providing, in loving and being there as a father, but we have a Divine Father who is ever-loving, ever caring, ever merciful and ever faithful to His children. He is the Everlasting Father, compassionate, slow to anger, and rich in love. His grace and peace are abundant upon His people, and His grace gives us the ability to move away from sin and live in godliness and do His will, paving the way for His perfect peace, which passes all understanding to abide with us. His love brings salvation to all men. He is the great and powerful Father of all upon the earth, and His name is majestic in the world; the heavens proclaim His righteousness, and the earth trembles at His presence. He is mindful of you to provide for you and bears your burdens. The love and faithfulness of the Everlasting Father are imminent in your life and everything you do, and by His power, you will excel in all things.

Prayer: *I pray may you find favor in the sight of the Everlasting Father; let Him do you good and every heart desire.*

Launching Deeper: Isaiah 63:16, 64:8 John 14:18, Exodus 34:6.

Hebrew Word Study: "ad"—perpetuity, lasting future (Strong's Hebrew: 5703).

March 30

Avi
אֲבִי
Defender

"A father of the fatherless, a defender of widows, Is God in His holy habitation" (Psalm 68:5, NKJV).

Sing praises for the Lord, He is your defender. The Lord protects the weak; He gives security to the vulnerable; He encourages his children not to be afraid; he gives assurance of safety and security to His children. He commands His ministering angels to protect His children, and He stands as a guard and defends all those who fear Him. When you cry unto the Lord for help, He sends a savior to defend; He is the strong one who vigorously defends His people and brings rest upon the land. He encamps around those who fear Him and guards them, not allowing the oppressor to have His way upon them. He builds and guards His church so that the gates of hell cannot prevail against it. He will defend you. No one and nothing can snatch you out of His hands. He defends the orphans and widows and frustrates every plan of the wicked against them. He looks down from heaven from His glorious dwelling place to hear your prayers to defend, keep and preserve you.

Prayer: *I pray the Lord keep and defend you always and execute justice for you.*

Launching Deeper: Isaiah 31:5, Ephesians 6:13, Psalms 20:1, 59:1, 2 Kings 19:34.

Hebrew Word Study: "ganon"—defend, cover, surround (Strong's Hebrew: 1598).

March 31

MACHSEH

מַחְסֶה

Fortress / Shelter

"I will say of the Lord, 'He is my refuge and my fortress; My God, in Him I will trust'" (Psalm 91:2 NKJV).

In the ancient world, city walls served as a defense for those who lived in and out of the city. Guards are station on the walls to keep watch against invaders. The people in the city rely on these symbols to keep them safe, but absolute trust and loyalty in the Lord is a great defense for the believer. The Psalmist proclaimed the Lord as His fortress, His fortified place, and stronghold. In His fortress, He hides you from every dangerous hazard, in His fortress you are shielded from hidden traps. He Himself is your wall, His presence is your fortress; it's the bunker in times of chaos. He destroys every enemy that tries to scale over your wall of protection. He is close to those who trust in Him to hide them in His secret place and always ready to help. If there is an attack on the city, the Lord will hide you in His safe place, you are secured from any assault. The Lord destroys fortresses of the enemy built against your life and demolishes their strongholds, He will keep you safe in His Fortress, and no evil can break through your defense.

Prayer: *I pray, let the Lord send fire upon their hidden places of the adversary and let them be devoured in Jesus' name.*

Launching Deeper: Psalms 91:9, 94:22, 142:5, 144:2, Proverbs 18:10, Jeremiah 16:19.

Hebrew Word Study: "machseh"—my refuge; "metsudah"—my fortress (Strong's Hebrew: 4268).

April

But I will reveal my ame to my people, and they will come to know its power. Then at last they will recognize that I am the one who speaks to them.'" (Isaiah 52:6 NLT)

April 1

El HaGemulah

הגמולה

God of Recompense

Because the plunderer comes against her, against Babylon, And her mighty men are taken. Every one of their bows is broken; For the Lord is the God of recompense, He will surely repay.

Jeremiah 51:56 (NKJV)

Recompense is the LORD'S prerogative, something He administers or assigns His messengers to execute. He pays back and takes revenge on the wicked, He declares, "vengeance is mine and I will repay" (Romans 12:19). Recompense belongs to Him. He is merciful and loving to those who fear Him, but those who hate and reject Him, He is not slow to punish and destroy them. He pays them back according to their deeds and rewards them according to their works. The Lord commands us not to recompense ourselves but to wait on Him to deliver and leave judgment in His hands for in His justice. He will pay those who afflict you with affliction and give you rest from every trouble. In times of persecution, the Lord will pay those who persecute His children in the last days. His wrath will come upon them. He has appointed a day of judgment against the wicked. Wherever you have suffered any wrongdoing by the enemy, He will continue to plead your cause. He is the God of equity. He will render recompense on your behalf and trouble those who trouble you.

Prayer: *I pray the Lord breaks the bows of the mighty on your behalf and gird you with His strength.*

Launching Deeper: Deuteronomy 32:41-43, Job 34:11, Proverbs 24:12, 20:22, Isaiah 1:24.

Hebrew Word Study: "shalem"—to be complete, fully repay, fulfilled (Strong's Hebrew: 7999).

April 2

YASHAR

יָשָׁר

Upright One

"The way of the just is uprightness; O Most Upright, you weigh the path of the just" (Isaiah 26:7, NKJV).

See a one-year-old baby with the help of a parent, learning how to walk; the baby grips the father's hands and try to take each step one after the other as the father leads, it might be rough, but as long as the baby's hand is gripped to the parent, he will never fall, if the baby is tired he lifts him, That's the way the Upright One leads us if it gets tough, he lifts us up, if there are obstacles on the way, He removes them. Moses asked the Lord to show him His way so He might know Him. The Lord said His presence would go with Him (Exodus 33:13). To know the way of the Lord is to walk with Him. He will have to walk with you to show you the way. Living in His presence and being obedient to His word is how you walk with the Upright One. He takes the lead, and you follow, and He directs the steps you should take; if the path is rough, He straightens up the way. Follow the steps of the Upright God and know His ways. "I will bring the blind by a way they did not know; I will lead them in paths they have not known. I will make darkness light before them, And crooked places straight. These things I will do for them, And not forsake them" (Isaiah 42:16). He will not abandon you but will lead you to the fulfillment of His promises.

Prayer: *I pray the Upright One lead and guide you on unfamiliar paths and level the ground. Let Him do this for you.*

Launching Deeper: Psalms 25:4,5, 27:11, Psalms 37:7, 23-26, Isaiah 52:12, 57:2, Jeremiah 10:23.

Hebrew Word Study:"yosher"—straightness, upright (Strong's Hebrew: 3476)

April 3

Melekh HaKavod
מֶלֶךְ הַכָּבוֹד
King of Glory

"Lift up your heads, O your gates, And be lifted up, you everlasting doors! And the King of glory shall come in" (Psalm 24:7, NKJV).

As David brings the ark of the covenant from Obededom's house, the procession is accompanied with people rejoicing, playing musical instruments, and offering sacrifices, the King of glory returns as the Lord Mighty in battle, entering through the gates after triumphant warfare against His enemies, He conquered and vanquished every foe. The Mighty warrior marches through the gates, the ark of His presence comes through the ancient doors in His glory. He ascends on high and leads away captives and receives gifts for them. He's giving you victory today. The gates of the nations are open unto you, and the Lord will fill this house with treasure and His glory, the latter glory will be greater than the former, and He's given unto you peace and prosperity. Doors of favor and abundance, doors of good health and wealth are your portion this day offer your sacrifice of praise and thanksgiving unto Him and rejoice in your continuous victory, Amen.

***Prayer:** As the presence of the Lord comes, pray arise O Lord and let every enemy be scattered and those who hate you flee in Jesus' name.*

Launching Deeper: Psalms 29:2,9, 68:16-18, Numbers 10:35,36, Haggai 2:7-9, Isaiah 26:2.

Hebrew Word Study : "tera"—gate, gatehouse, place, location (Strong's Hebrew: 8651).

April 4

MELECH HAMELACHIM

מלך המלך

King of Kings

"And He has on His robe and on His thigh a name written: KING OF KINGS, LORD OF LORDS" Revelation 19:16 (NKJV).

Fiery eyes with His head full of crowns, bloody robe, and sharp sword out of His mouth to strike the nations, ruling with iron. Christ is the king and the ruler in the monarch of all the kings of the Earth. His kingship and scepter are to maintain righteousness, execute justice, rule amid His enemies, and continue to reign until He puts all His enemies under His feet and destroys dominion, powers, and authorities. His kingdom is from heaven and is given to Him by the Ancient of Days, dominion and authority is given to Him, and by that, every country, every tribe, every people, every system, every language, every culture, every race will submit to His kingship and dominion forever; His kingdom can never be destroyed. He revealed and presented the kingdom of God to humanity and comes in power with signs and wonders and blessings for believers. His kingship is of righteousness, peace, and joy in the Spirit. By His power, He subjects all things to Himself, and at the mention of His name, all knew bow to Him, and all tongues confess He is Lord to the glory of the Father. Exalt His name and lift Him up as the King of Kings and let every situation in your life bow to His name.

Prayer: *I pray the King of Kings be blessed, let Him decree justice for you, reign in your life, and bring joy and peace.*

Launching Deeper: Revelations 17:14, Daniel 7:14, Hebrews 1:8, Psalms 72:11, 98:6.

Hebrew Word Study: "mishtar"—rule, authority (Strong's Hebrew: 4896).

April 5

Elohim Bileti Nitann Lashinuy

אלוהים כרטיס ניטאן לשיאנוי

Unchangeable God

"For I am the LORD, I do not change; Therefore, you are not consumed, O sons of Jacob" (Malaci 3:6, NKJV).

Unto man change is inevitable, it's a condition of life; however, our God is unchangeable, and this gives us the assurance to depend on him. We keep trusting in Him for His promises concerning our lives. He does not change on His purpose for His people nor change His mind like a man. Creation will pass away, but the Unchangeable God remains forever faithful, the same yesterday, today, and forever. There is no variation or change or shifting shadows in Him, the One who is, who was and who is to come, the First and the Last. Know that everything the Unchangeable God has said about you would surely come into fulfillment. His promises are yea and amen and do not lie. His purpose for your life will stand and will not change. His people are not destroyed, for He remembers His promise to have mercy upon them. He will do you good, protect you and keep His eye on you.

Prayer: *I pray His strength, power, and grace for you will not change. Keep trusting in Him.*

Launching Deeper: 1 Samuel 15:29, Psalm 102:26, Hebrews 6:18, Hebrews 13:8.

Hebrew Word Study: "shana"—to change (Strong's Hebrew: 8132).

April 6

SHOMER HABRIT

שומר הברית

Covenant Keeping God

Therefore, know that the LORD your God, He is God, the faithful God who keeps covenant and mercy for a thousand generations with those who love Him and keep His commandments.

Deuteronomy 7:9 (NKJV)

Covenant is an agreement or a contract with certain conditions between two parties. Some are marriage, business, and our relationship with Elohim. His everlasting covenant and devotion to us go to generations to generations of those who fear Him. He does not grow weary of His covenant. His loving kindness is endless, His mercy never fails, His compassion is forevermore. He works everything together for our good to enact his covenant with us. When He begins a wonderful work, He will always perfect it. Our Covenant Keeping God renews his faithfulness every morning. He does not allow the enemy to exact upon His people; they are blessed, and nothing can change it, nothing can change His blessings for you, what He has blessed no one can curse. He said this about David, that His covenant with David will He not break nor alter the thing that has gone out of His lips concerning Him; He had sworn by His Holiness that He will not lie to David. He will not lie to you as He has promised. Keep your part to rely on Him, and He will keep His promise to bless you.

***Prayer:** I pray the Lord shows you loving kindness and keep His covenant of blessings unto all your generations.*

Launching Deeper: Philippians 1:6, Romans 8:28-32, Lamentations 3:22:23, Nehemiah 1:5, 9:32, Deuteronomy 7:12, Psalm 89:34,35.

Hebrew Word Study: "berith"—covenant (Strong's Hebrew: 1285).

April 7

AVIR YA'AKOV

אֲבִיר יַעֲקֹב

Mighty One of Jacob

"You shall drink the milk of the Gentiles, And milk the breast of kings; You shall know that I, the Lord, am your Savior And your Redeemer, the Mighty One of Jacob" (Isaiah 60:16, NKJV).

There is a special favor that the Lord has caused to rest upon the nation Israel for the continuity of the covenant with Jacob, the nations will give onto them valuable possessions, and they will be nourished and flourished by their riches and abundance, and also submit to them. The mighty One of Jacob promised a time of glory for his people. They were highly honored and reverenced for keeping His Word. Their expectations were not cut off but were fulfilled and satisfied. The mighty One of Jacob shows forth his goodness in keeping His promise with Jacob that He will bless him, He will increase him, He will multiply him and cause him to eat the good of the land. This He will give to the believer His favor, the light of His presence, the workings and abilities of His grace, answering your prayers, establishing His promises, and giving onto them riches in heavenly places. He will empower you with the spirit. For He is your savior and redeemer who never leaves you nor forsakes you but gives onto you the joy of His salvation.

Prayer: *I pray, be satisfied with the richness of the nations and prosper in their favor.*

Launching Deeper: Isaiah 49:23, Revelation 21:24, 26, Exodus 6:7, Isaiah 14:1.

Hebrew Word Study: "goyim"—nations; "goy"—people (Strong's Hebrew: 1471).

April 8

Sar Shalom
שַׂר-שָׁלוֹם
The Prince of Peace

For unto us a Child is born, Unto us a Son is given; And the government will be upon His shoulder. And His name will be called Wonderful, Counselor, Mighty God, Everlasting Father, Prince of Peace.

Isaiah 9:6 NKJV

Peace is a sense of inner tranquility, absence of chaos and fear. There is no true peace without the presence of the Prince of Peace. Jesus is our principality of peace. He took up the chastisement that brought us peace. Through His blood, we reconciled and made peace with the Father. He is the one who declares, "Peace I leave with you, My peace I give to you; not as the world gives, do I give to you. Let not your heart be troubled, neither let it be afraid" (John 14:27, NKJV). When the storm rages, He declares, "peace be still." As long as He is in the boat, peace cannot be disturbed. We see the manifestation of His presence in His mighty power to still every raging storm that lifts itself up. Let that be your declaration today, take up the authority and say, let there be peace and let peace be still, let the Lord replace any life of oppression and affliction, every nervousness, every fear, every emotional impulse, distracting thoughts and uncertainties with His perfect peace that passes all understanding and be rest assured He is with you in the boat. Be still and know that He is God.

***Prayer:** Receive the divine inner tranquility, let the presence of the Prince of Peace overcome every presence of restlessness and every demonic presence.*

Launching Deeper: Ephesians 2:14-18.

Hebrew Word Study: "yeled"—child, youth (Strong's Hebrew: 3206).

April 9

NACHAH

נחמה (נה)

The Guide

The LORD will guide you continually, And satisfy your soul in drought, And strengthen your bones; You shall be like a watered garden, And like a spring of water, whose waters do not fail.

Isaiah 58:11 (NKJV)

When it was time for Abraham's son Isaac to marry, he sent forth his servant Eliezer to go into his family to find a wife for him. Eliezer obediently set off on the journey to the house of Abraham's brother and got the right person there for Isaac. In his journey, he relied on the God of Abraham to guide him along the way. He was not sure exactly what was going to happen, but his faith and trust in the Lord's guidance paved the way to make his journey successful, and He praised the Lord. In the journey of the Israelites to the promised land, there was no map or GPS guiding them, but the Lord's guidance took them through the way. As the Guide, He guided them by the pillar of cloud and by a pillar of fire. By His guide, they camped and set off at His command. His rod and staff are always there to guide us to take away every fear of evil along the way. He guides with counsel, with wisdom, and with understanding in life's matters; He promised to never leave us or forsake us. He will always guide, satisfy us and strengthen us to be like a well-watered garden that our waters will never fail on the journey to the promised land.

***Prayer**: I pray the Lord lead you in the path of righteousness for the sake of His name and guide you in your decision-making with His counsel.*

Launching Deeper: Genesis 24:48, Exodus 15:2, Numbers 9:20, Deuteronomy 26:17, Psalm 73:24.

Hebrew Word Study: "tamid"—continuity (Strong's Hebrew: 8548).

April 10

Ma'on

מָעוֹן

Refuge / Dwelling Place

"Lord, You have been our dwelling place in all generations" (Psalm 90:1, NKJV).

A Prayer of Moses, the man of God. Lord, You have been our dwelling place in all generations.

The Lord is a sanctuary for His people, a secured retreat and a place of renewal and restoration, and a stronghold. He is a place for the believer to always be refreshed. Your Dwelling Place will command safety for you by His everlasting arms and drive away the enemy. Adonai is your Refuge Who provides shade from the sun and protection from any deadly trap. His mighty Arm drives away every harm and makes sure that flying arrows of the day will not touch you. Although challenges can arise at certain places, He will make sure you are untouched because you have made Him your Refuge and live in His presence. You're established in his favor. You will increase in His power and multiply in His blessings. You continue to live in His strength and in His mercy to receive His grace. No evil, no curse can come close to you; wickedness can't get through the door to hurt you. He has given command to His angels to escort you every step of the way to the place of safety, and you will experience the everlasting peace of God.

***Prayer:** I pray the Lord be your habitation and be kept safe in His secret place in Jesus' name.*

Launching Deeper: Psalms 91:1,9, 71:3, Exodus 33:14-19, Deuteronomy 33:27.

Hebrew Word Study: "ish"—man (Strong's Hebrew: 376).

April 11

TSUR YISRAEL

צוּר יִשְׂרָאֵל

Rock of Israel

"The God of Israel said, The Rock of Israel spoke to me: 'He who rules over men must be just, Ruling in the fear of God" (2 Samuel 23:3, NKJV).

The patriarch Jacob established the nation Israel, and David as an anointed king established the kingdom of Israel. The title Rock of Israel is highly outstanding in the course of David. This name signifies David and Israel's total dependence on God for protection and deliverance. There was no other rock like the Rock of Israel who saved them. He is greater above any other gods. When enemies come against Israel, The Rock empowers them to subdue their adversaries; He gives them skills and military strength to fight in battles, providing all kinds of arsenals to give them victory and dominion. They could triumph and break out into praises and joyful noise most of the time. The Lord is giving you every weapon needed for every battle. He will teach your hands to war for conquest over evil forces. Sickness can be an enemy, but He is your perfect health; lack can be an enemy, but the Rock is your provider when every other help fails. He will help you and give victory for you to break forth into joyful praise and give Him all the glory.

Prayer: *I pray in time of trouble the Lord keeps you in His pavilion because you always desire to stay in the presence of the Lord.*

Launching Deeper: Isaiah 44:8, Psalm 78:35, Habakkuk1:12.

Hebrew Word Study: "ganan"—to cover, surround, defend, protect (Strong's Hebrew: 1598).

April 12

TSUR OLAMIN

צור אולאמין

Rock of Ages

"Trust [confidently] in the Lord forever [He is your fortress, your shield, your banner], For the Lord God is an everlasting Rock [the Rock of Ages]" (Isaiah 26:4, AMP).

Buildings made of rocks last longer, some can last for hundreds of years. They can be exposed to atmospheric agents in time and still stand strong for hundreds of years. Rocks stand for security and stability; they are an embodiment of strength, safety and protection. Throughout Moses' mission of leading the Israelites to the promised land, nations that rose against them were totally defeated by their Rock. He declared, "their rock is not as our Rock" (Deuteronomy 32:31). The Rock of Ages gave them a firm foundation on which the nation was built, the Rock of Ages fought for them, giving them a permanent refuge and a permanent trust. Their experience shows there was no other god they could trust and find refuge. The Rock of Ages is your permanent strength, your everlasting hope, your source of existence, and One who provides your abilities to fulfill destiny. On Him, everything rests since the foundation of the earth. He is the Rock of Ages whose ways are perfect and undefeatable. The everlasting Strong One Is your Rock.

Prayer: *I pray The rock of Ages be your firm foundation and permanent strength. May no storm overshadow you as He is your Rock.*

Launching Deeper: Deuteronomy 32:4,15,31,33, Isaiah 17:10, 32:2.

Hebrew Word Study: "batach"—to trust (Strong's Hebrew: 982).

April 13

Roeh

רֹעֶה

Shepherd

"The Lord is my shepherd; I shall not want" (Psalm 23:1, NKJV).

David, the king, was once a shepherd in the wilderness. In his experience as a king and as a shepherd, he protected them from lions and from bears, he would fight for them and put his own life at risk for the flock. He will do everything to keep them safe and alive. The Lord is your Divine Shepherd. You are His child. He makes sure you are secured. Those who seek Him lack nothing. He gives grace and withholds no good thing from them; The Divine Shepherd preserves your life. He will lead you through His perfect way to bring you to an expected end and be led to a pasture that flourishes, full of His goodness by His divine provision. He will protect you by His righteous right arm and destroy every work of the enemy against you with His restoration and His grace and glory upon you. His perfect provision is yours. His perfect protection is yours, His perfect peace is yours, His perfect restoration is yours, and His perfect guidance is your portion, be nourished in His flourishing pastures.

***Prayer**: I pray you will lack nothing and will receive every good thing prepared for you.*

Launching Deeper: Psalms 23, 28:9, 34:10, Hosea 4:6, John 10:1, 1 Peter 2:25, Revelation 7:17.

Hebrew Word Study: "tob"—a good thing. Benefit, welfare (Strong's Hebrew: 2896b).

April 14

SHILOH
שִׁילֹה

"The scepter shall not depart from Judah, Nor a lawgiver from between his feet, Until Shiloh comes; And to Him shall be the obedience of the people" (Genesis 49:10, NKJV).

By the direction of the Spirit of God, Jacob apportioned the blessings of the Lord of the covenant upon his twelve children. Each one and his role and destiny. Judah was to be the head, and with kingship lineage, his siblings will give him respect and bow to him, he will rule over them, the symbol of rulership will abide with his descendants until it comes to the One that is to be sent, the peaceful One and Whom all will gather unto and come and find perfect rest, Shiloh, the Messiah, and the everlasting King, to whom all will gather and bow to His righteousness and give Him all the glory. Shiloh is the long-awaited deliverer in the old testament, that kings and kingdoms are allowed to rule until the One who has the right of ownership of kingdoms and governments and authorities and dominions and principalities, a promised Seed, and a sign of expectancy to the people of the earth and a Savior to give hope. Like Hannah found an answer to her prayers at Shiloh, so you will find rest and restoration and will not be disappointed. He will give you peace and answer you when you call upon His name.

Prayer: *I pray let Shiloh come to your aid and arise on your behalf and bring you to His place of rest in Jesus' name.*

Launching Deeper: Psalms 72:8-11, 60:7, Isaiah 11:10,12,13, 42:1,4, 62:11.

Hebrew Word Study: "bo"—to come in, come, go in (Strong's Hebrew: 935).

April 15

KOKHAV MIYA'AKOV

כּוֹכָב מִיַּעֲקֹב

Star from Jacob

"I see Him, but not now; I behold Him, but not near; A Star shall come out of Jacob; A Scepter shall rise out of Israel, And batter the brow of Moab, And destroy all the sons of tumult" (Numbers 24:17, NKJV).

It was a journey that Balaam was not supposed to take, but he could not refuse the reward given by Balak for this mission. When he arrived at Peor, the Lord reminded him that His children are blessed and can't be cursed. Balaam declared blessings and foresaw the Star of Jacob, the Messiah, the Lord Jesus Christ. He could be seen from afar, a star radiating in beauty and splendor of His glory and triumphed over His enemies. He is the star that shines as lights in our hearts and shines through the dark and difficult times. His light never fails and shines to destroy the powers of darkness. He is the star that shines and lightens the path of life, helping us to navigate our way through life and gives us energy, strength, and peace. As the stars shine in the night, so the eyes of the Lord keep watch over His children to guard and protect. He has transferred his light into our lives to shine unto others and to draw them closer to His kingdom of light as the star that caused the wise men to come to the baby Jesus so let the world see the Star of Jacob, the light of salvation, and let them call upon the name of the Lord.

***Prayer**: I pray as you journey through life, let the Lord preserve you wherever you will be and whatever you do in Jesus' name.*

Launching Deeper: Isaiah 9:2, Isaiah 42:6, 49:6, Genesis 27:29,40, 2 Samuel 8:14.

Hebrew Word Study: "qum"—to arise, stand up (Strong's Hebrew: 6965).

April 16

'Even Yisrael

אֶבֶן יִשְׂרָאֵל

Stone (or Rock) of Israel

"But his bow remained in strength, And the arms of his hands were made strong By the hands of the Mighty God of Jacob (From there is the Shepherd, the Stone of Israel" (Genesis 49:24, NKJV).

The weather was warm that day, and it was getting late into the night, and Jacob was so weary on his journey; he found a stone and used it as a pillow to rest on. As he fell asleep, he saw the Lord in a dream, and the Lord confirmed and renewed the covenant of blessings and divine protection upon him and his descendants. After finding rest upon that stone, he set up the stone as an altar and anointed the place and named it "Bethel"—the House of God. The stone that supported him to find rest birthed the assurance of the covenant of God and his fathers, an everlasting covenant renewed by the Stone of Israel to bring fulfillment of the promise and the blessings. The Stone of Israel is bringing you help this day and as a sign of divine establishment for your life. In 1 Samuel 7, Samuel set up a stone in Mizpah and named it Stone of help. He declared it was the Lord who had helped the nation to conquer and subdued the Philistines. He will not leave you defenseless and restless. He is making the strength of your hands empowered and will never leave you until the promise is fulfilled in your life.

Prayer: *I pray the Stone of Israel be your defense and helper. Let Him comfort you and nourish you.*

Launching Deeper: Genesis 28:1-15, 1 Peter 2:6, Deuteronomy 32:4, Psalm 118:22, Isaiah 28:16.

Hebrew Word Study: Eben (Even) Ezer—The Stone of Help (Strong's Hebrew: 68, 5828).

April 17

Peleh Yo'etz

פֶּלֶא יוֹעֵץ

Wonderful Counsellor

For unto us a Child is born, Unto us a Son is given; And the government will be upon His shoulder. And His name will be called Wonderful, Counselor, Mighty God, Everlasting Father, Prince of Peace.

Isaiah 9:6 NKJV

Ahithophel's counsel was very prudent and highly regarded by David and his kingdom but was not always dependable. It failed with Absalom, The counsel of the Lord is trustworthy. He is marvelous in giving true wisdom and advice to men. His good and wise admonishment brings fulfillment in life. By the counsel of His will, He has predestined us and chosen us to receive His glory. When we seek His counsel, heed to His voice, attend to His Word and astounding teachings, we possess hidden treasures of wisdom and knowledge without measure, and He gives to all men. The Wonderful Counsellor will direct you to fulfill your destiny and direct you through His right path. For He knows the counsel of the Father and makes them known to His children. In every situation, seek His counsel. He is the author and giver of understanding and wisdom. No one teaches and preaches like He does. Follow His directions to be successful and fulfilled in life.

***Prayer**: I pray by His wonderful counsel excel in all you do, hope in Him, and be the praise of His glory.*

Launching Deeper: Jeremiah 32:19, Isaiah 28:29, Exodus 1:11, Revelation 3:18.

Hebrew Word Study: "chokmah"—wisdom, skill (Strong's Hebrew: 2541).

April 18

Atik Yomin

וְעַתִּיק יוֹמִין

The Ancient of Days

I watched till thrones were put in place, And the Ancient of Days was seated; His garment was white as snow, And the hair of His head was like pure wool. His throne was a fiery flame, Its wheels a burning fire.

Daniel 7:9 (NKJV)

Sometimes you marvel how rulers of certain nations hold on to power for years as if their positions and authority would never end, but you see them fade off and are remembered no more as time passes by. Daniel had a revelation of the self-existing and timeless God. He saw the throne of The Ancient of Days, He appears like lightning, the hair of His head as white as wool and snow, the purity and perfection of His sovereignty beyond eternity, with the host of heaven standing before Him and thrones cast before Him, He rules and reigns as the Lord of the heavens and the earth. He makes the clouds His chariot and walks upon the wings of the wind. Fire and flames are His ambassadors and the winds as His commanded messengers. His throne established in the heavens, and the earth His footstool. The Ancient of Days knows the end from the beginning, and His will is the ultimate cause of all things; no plans of His can be thwarted. He sits upon His blazing throne, and His sovereignty is over all creation and over all situations of your life. He has predestined you before time to glorify and bless and favor you.

***Prayer**: I pray the Ancient of Days brings to judgment anything that will rise up against you and gives you favor in all you do in Jesus' name.*

Launching Deeper: Daniel 7:13,22, Psalm 90:2, Ezekiel 1:26, 2 Chronicles 18:18, Psalm 104:2.

Hebrew Word Study: "korse"—a throne (Strong's Hebrew: 3764).

April 19

KABOD

צור אולאמין

My Glory

"But You, O LORD, are a shield for me, My glory [and my honor], and the One who lifts my head" (Psalms 3:3, AMP).

It is an honor to be called a child of the Most High God and a privilege to have the Adonai as your source of glory, your trust, and confidence. He is the one who transforms the believer's life and brings honor to him, the Christians' glorifier. Glory "kabod" means weight in the Hebrew language. That is the eternal weight of His glory that would come upon you. That weight of His glory puts price and value upon your life. It is the abundance of His wealth and His treasure. The presence of His glory saturates your life with perfection and makes you honorable. We give Him all the praise for His glorious presence that fills the earth, and by His glory, we receive prosperity upon the land, by His glory and His power He causes the richest of the nations transferred to His children, for all will see the hand of God upon your life and will see the distinction and call you by a new name. He is your Glory, and the glory of your latter shall be greater than your former.

Prayer: *I pray the Lord surrounds you with the shield of grace and the covering of His glory.*

Launching Deeper: Deuteronomy 10:21, Exodus 34:29-35, Isaiah 62:2, Zachariah 2:5, Isaiah 61:6.

Hebrew Word Study: "rum"—to be high or exalted, rise (Strong's Hebrew: 7311).

April 20

ELOHEI ZECHARTI

אלוהי זכרתי

The God of Remembrance

"Then I will remember my covenant with Jacob, and I will remember my covenant with Isaac and my covenant with Abraham, and I will remember the land" (Leviticus 26:42, ESV).

It's difficult to find a mother who has forgotten her newborn baby in a day or at any time, but it's still possible for this to happen; some even abandon them completely. She might get involved in something that might take her mind off the child. But this the Lord said He would never do. He will not forget His people. The Lord is always mindful of them and remembers his covenant with his children; He does not forget His promises and will never forget His covenant. The God of Remembrance is always faithful to His children to a thousand generations of those who walk in His ways. He remembers to provide for them as He promised in the covenant, to give them a place, and established them as He promised. The God of Remembrance remembers to show them His compassion, faithfulness, and kindness. He remembered Sarah and Rachel and blessed them with the fruit of the womb, for He is faithful in all His ways and to His nature to fulfill what He says; he is constant and never changing. People might forget their promises and even contract agreements, but He is not a man to forget and alter His word. He will remember you and bless you. He will remember to deliver you as He remembered and favored Noah.

Prayer: *I pray let the Lord establish you in His blessings and remember you always, for He has inscribed you on His palm.*

Launching Deeper: Genesis 9:16, 22:15, Exodus 2:24, 6:5, Psalms 105:8, 106:45, Judges 2:1.

Hebrew Word Study: "berith"—covenant (Strong's Hebrew: 1285).

April 21

HaChomah Esh

חכמה אש

The Wall of Fire

"'For I,' says the LORD, 'will be a wall of fire all around her, and I will be the glory in her midst'" (Zechariah 2:5, NKJV).

A word of assurance was given to Zachariah, the prophet for God's people, the message was that no matter how desolate the land of Israel looks now, there is still hope. It will again be inhabited with people, life will resume to normal as the Lord has intended. He will be A Wall of Fire around her as a sign of protection. He will be within them as His glory and will help them. His glory will radiate in your life, and all people will see and bless the name of the Lord. You should see the mountain surrounding Jerusalem as a sign of the Lord's protection and preservation from any invasions of the evil one. His consuming fire will not spare your adversaries if they dare come near. He is the glowing flame of fire that blazes in the night to give you security, for He is great among His people, and He establishes His salvation as a wall of safety and their place of rest where they are secured. So the Lord will continue to protect and preserve you with his protection of fire, and the goodness of His glory will dwell with you

***Prayer**: I pray His glory dwell with you like a canopy of protection and a blessing.*

Launching Deeper: Haggai 2:9, Zechariah 2:11, Ezekiel 42:20, 38:14, Isaiah 60:18, 32:18, 31:9.

Hebrew Word Study: "sabib"—circuit, roundabout (Strong's Hebrew: 5439).

April 22

YHWH

יהוה

Jehovah

"And God says again to Moses, 'Thus you say to the sons of Israel: YHWH, God of your fathers, God of Abraham, God of Isaac, and God of Jacob, has sent me to you; this [is] My Name for all time, and this [is] My memorial, to generation [and] generation.'"

Exodus 3:15(LSV)

The word LORD, when spelled with capital letters, stands for the divine name, YHWH, which is here connected with the verb *hayah*, "to be" He is called according to His actions. When He judges the creatures. He is Elohim, and when He has mercy with His world, He is YHWH. He is the origin of all that exists and all possibilities, the origin of life. He is the one that implants life into mortal bodies, the soul, and the spirit, given both physical and spiritual life by the redemption of Christ. YHWH is the one Who causes things to be and the impossibilities to be possible. When Moses doubted the deliverance of the Israelites from Egypt, the Lord assured Him He is the "I Am" the "to be," He will cause that deliverance to be at every cause. He brings things into existence for His name to be a memorial and His remembrance unto all generations. When it seemed impossible for His people to possess the promised land because of the giants and the nations greater and mightier than them, He caused the possessions to be. They subdued the nations and took full possessions, He fulfilled His promises to be, YHWH will cause things to be for you, He will bring all expectations into existence for your life, and you will see fulfillment in Jesus' name.

Prayer: *I pray the Lord deliver your lands into your possession and cause your to conquer the giants completely in Jesus' name.*

Launching Deeper: 1 Kings 20:28, 2 Chronicles 6:10, Zechariah 10:12.

Hebrew Word Study: "natsal"—to deliver oneself, be delivered (Strong's Hebrew: 5337).

April 23

JEHOVAH-RAPHA

יְהוָה רֹפְאֶךָ

"And said, 'If you diligently heed the voice of the Lord your God and do what is right in His sight, give ear to His commandments and keep all His statutes, I will put none of the diseases on you which I have brought on the Egyptians. For I am the Lord who heals you.'"

Exodus 15:26 (NKJV)

Healing is a benefit our God, Jehovah Rapha, gives unto us. He is our source and author of healing; He preserves His people in good health, in body, soul, and spirit. He preserves them from diseases and plagues like the coronavirus and other pandemics. In times of afflictions, He takes away sicknesses and evil diseases, for He forgives them of their iniquities and blesses their food and water. When praying and asking for his healing, faith is very important; it releases results quickly. Jesus healed the sick wherever He went. He was willing to transform their lives by hearing their prayers and healing them. He fulfilled what Isaiah prophesied about Him: that he took our infirmities and carried our diseases; He bore the burdens of pain in His body, by the wounds in His body, His feet, and His pierced hands we are healed. By these wounds, the blind receive sight, the lame walk, the leper are cleansed; the deaf hear, and the dead are raised up and total healing of the nations.

Prayer: *I pray whatever that would cause diseases in your bodies; let His healing power touch you and His blessings cause nothing to affect you in Jesus' name.*

Launching Deeper: Isaiah 53, Psalm 103:2,3, Matthew 11:5, Mark 1:32-34.

Hebrew Word Study: "arukah"—healing, restoration (Strong's Hebrew: 724).

April 24

Ruach Mechayyeh

רוח משיח

The Quickening Spirit

"And so it is written, The first man Adam was made a living soul; the last Adam was made a quickening spirit" (1 Corinthians 15:45, NKJV).

Wherever the Spirit of the Lord dwells, there is freedom from restraint or control of evil, life emancipates from spiritually yoked, and bond to a life full His Spirit, a life unbounded, unfettered, and discharged from any guilt of sin and resurrection from the dead to life. The Quicken Spirit brings a life full of His strength and power, a work of the Father, the Son, and the Holy Spirit. Paul said if the Spirit who raised Jesus is in us, He will also quicken our mortal bodies to be empowered in His grace to fulfill what we are called to do in His service. He gives this quicken to whomsoever he wills, to those who believe in him, and in whom He dwells. The Quickening Spirit revives us when we abide in Him, and He abides in us, making us free from the power of sin, and to live a life pleasing unto Him. For in us, He worked His power to transform us and even subdues all things unto Himself. His breath in us produces the life-given spirit to help us function in faith and worship. He will quicken your spirit to meet God's requirement for your life. Despite every weakness and limitation, He will provoke the anointing upon your life to do mighty things and also revive the mortal bodies of all believers in the resurrection's day unto eternal glory.

***Prayer:** I pray may the Lord strengthen and receive His divine enablement to accomplish His purpose for your life.*

Launching Deeper: John 5:21, 6:57, Romans 8:2, Philippians 3:21, Colossians 3:4, John 1:4, John 4:10,14.

Hebrew Word Study: "naphach"—to breathe, to blow (Strong's Hebrew: 5301).

April 25

HADELET

הדלת

The Door

"I am the Door; anyone who enters through Me will be saved [and will live forever], and will go in and out [freely], and find pasture (spiritual security)" (John 10:9, AMP).

The believers' access to God is through faith in Jesus Christ. Jesus is the point of entry to God's kingdom, a place of safety, provision, and blessings. In Him, we have peace with God and access to his throne room of grace. Jesus is always standing at the door of our hearts and knocking. If we hear His voice and open, He would come in and dine with us, always cautioning us to be ready. He is the True Shepherd who enters through the door, way of life and the door to salvation, the access into the presence of the Father, a privilege into His throne room of grace; He is the shepherd's door in which the flocks walk through into greener pastures and are protected and led to springs of living water. Through the door, you find shelter. He defends you as the gatekeeper and sustains you; He feeds and nourishes your soul and spirit with sound, rich and true doctrines of His word.

Prayer: *I pray the Lord open heavenly doors unto you and gives you access to heavenly treasures.*

Launching Deeper: Romans 5:1,2 Ephesians 2:18, 3:12, John 14:6, Acts 17:27.

Hebrew Word Study: "daleth"—the door (Strong's Hebrew: 1817).

April 26

Kokhav HaShachar

אַיֶּלֶת הַשַּׁחַר

The Bright Morning Star

"I, Jesus, have sent My angel to testify to you these things in the churches. I am the Root and the Offspring of David, the Bright and Morning Star" (Revelation 22:16, NKJV).

Human sight can see the planet Venus as a star; it is the most dazzling of all the stars, rising early in the morning hours, it's seen in the skies glowing steadily. Christ, the Morning Star, shoots forth to introduce redemption and grace in the darkest times of human life and leads many into a day of salvation and righteousness. Radiating the glory of the Father in the perfection of His brightness to shine like Him in His glory. The Morning Star of Joy, one that springs forth hope, rises in the hearts of many and transforms their hearts and lives with the lights of peace, goodness, grace, and love. The light of the Morning Star is the glorious light of the knowledge of the glory of God in the radiance of Jesus. By the power of its brightness, the magi followed the star, traveling miles upon miles to see the newborn king. Let the light of the Morning Star continue to shine upon you to manifest his light to the lost world and to lead your path to victory overcoming every darkness in Jesus' name.

Prayer: *I pray in the multitude of His mercy, let Him hear you, in the truth of His salvation, let The Morning Star deliver you.*

Launching Deeper: Isaiah 11:1, Matthew 2:2, Numbers 24:17, 2 Peter 1:19, Revelation 2:28.

Hebrew Word Study: "helel"—a shining one (Strong's Hebrew: 1966).

April 27

ED HANE'EMAN

טקסט מקור

Faithful and True Witness

"And to the angel of the church of the Laodiceans write, These things say, the Amen, the Faithful and True Witness, the Beginning of the creation of God" (Revelation 3:14, NKJV).

Our Lord Jesus bears witness of the Great Father, His ministry, the miracles, His teachings, and His death on the cross bears witness of the truth and prophecies written about Him. He spoke what He had knowledge of and testified of what He has seen. He is faithful, meaning He's trustworthy in all He does. Jesus is the eyewitness of the revelation of the Father. He remains competent in doing His will and approves what the Father approves. The Father's assignment onto Him was to bear witness that He is the one Whom the Father sent, and He faithfully executed His mission by preaching the good news of the kingdom in His service and making atonement for the sins of the people. He is faithful to fulfill all His promises; He is faithful in his promise of giving salvation on to all that believe, He's faithful to His children to strengthen them and to protect them from every work of evil. He is faithful in providing for you and pouring His Spirit upon you to do His will in your life.

Prayer: *I pray let Him work His promises unto you, for faithful is He that has called you, and He will do it for you.*

Launching Deeper: Psalm 89:37, John 3:11, 1 Thessalonians 5:24, Revelation 3:14, 1:5.

Hebrew Word Study: "ed"—a witness (Strong's Hebrew: 5707).

April 28

MELITZ YOSHER

מליץ יושר

Advocate

"My little children, these things I write to you, so that you may not sin. And if anyone sins, we have an Advocate with the Father, Jesus Christ the righteous" (1 John 2:1, NKJV).

A mediator in the courts of heaven, the only one and Faithful advocate between the Father and man, the intercessor who lives to make intercession for us after we have been reconciled to Him, through the death of Christ. He's at the right hand of the Father on our behalf, by His grace making peace for us, making intercessions for transgressors and to bring us salvation and righteousness, and also sustaining us through the power of the Spirit of God. Through Him all things were made and through him all things exist, for He is a mediator of the new and better covenant with a better promise of eternal inheritance, as the sacrifice, He offered himself upon the altar, and as a priest, He makes atonement for the sins of the people. The Advocate continued to plead for us in this world so that our faith fails not and that we hold on to our callings. He pleads our cause and brings us divine help, and presents our needs before the throne room of grace, silencing the voice of the accuser granting us our heavenly goodness.

Prayer: *I pray the Lord be your advocate and bring His will to be fulfilled in your life.*

Launching Deeper: 1 Timothy 2:5, Romans 8:34, Isaiah 53:12, Hebrew 7:25, 9:24.

Hebrew Word Study: "paga"—to intercede, to meet, to encounter (Strong's Hebrew: 6923).

April 29

EVEN PINNAT YIKRAT

אפילו משטחים יקרט

Chief Cornerstone

"Therefore, it is also contained in the Scripture, 'Behold, I lay in Zion A chief cornerstone, elect, precious, And he who believes in Him will by no means be put to shame'" (1 Peter 2:6, NKJV).

The dependable and reliable stone in a foundation of a building is the cornerstone. It gives the building the stability to thrive through the times and seasons. The stone is a symbol of the basis of faith in Jesus and the church. He is the Living Stone chosen by God and rejected by the builders, rejected by men as the Cornerstone. This stone will crush every worldly rulership and will become a mountain, exalted above every other, established to fill the whole earth, depicting the knowledge of the Lord which occupies the earth as waters. The stone will crush every evil system that tries to lift itself above the knowledge of God in your life. It will fill your life with establishment and progress. He was rejected, mocked, despised and rejected, treated with disdain and crucified, a mark of ingratitude, but he that believes in Him will not be confounded, If your trust is in the Cornerstone, you are firmly established, for He is prominent and indispensable, sure security for you and all that is yours. He will establish you as His dwelling place, full of His glory and blessings.

Prayer: *I decree the Lord cause all you do be prosperous. As the Chief Cornerstone continues to be with you, keep trusting in Him and be established in His land.*

Launching Deeper: Matthew 21:42-44, Isaiah 28:16.

Hebrew Word Study: "eben"—a stone (Strong's Hebrew: 68).

April 30

HaAleph HaTav

האלף הטב

The Beginning and The End

"'I am the Alpha and the Omega, the Beginning and the End,' says the Lord, 'who is and who was and who is to come, the Almighty'" (Revelation 1:8, NKJV).

We see in Genesis, the beginning, God first before everything followed. He is the most significant of all and knows the end. He sustains all that is in between the beginning and the end, demonstrating His power from the beginning to the end of time. He calls for the generations right from the beginning of time, there is no God like him; he's the one who was who is and who is to come; he is the author of life, of all creation and all that exists and will bring all to a glorious conclusion. Faithful is He that starts a splendid work in your life. The Lord Jesus has begun something wonderful. He called you into His marvelous light of liberty from the yoke of sins and knew His agenda for your life. He is awesome, faithful and merciful, and wonderful to begin working and putting everything together for your life and faithful to accomplish it to what is expected. Remember, your expectations will not be cut short. He is omnipotent and all-powerful to execute His promises for your life.

***Prayer**: I pray let the Alpha and Omega bring you to a wondrous completion of all His promises for your life.*

Launching Deeper: Isaiah 41:4, 44:6, 48:12, Revelation 1:4, 11, 17, 2:8, 21:6.

Hebrew Word Study: "resith"—beginning, chief (Strong's Hebrew 7225).

May

Because he has set his love upon Me, therefore I will deliver him; I will set him on high, because he has known My name.'
Psalms 91:14 NKJV

May 1

Sar HaChayyim

שר הים

Prince of Life

"And killed the Prince of life, whom God hath raised from the dead; whereof we are witnesses" (Acts 3:15, KJV).

The Prince who gives repentance to Israel and gives forgiveness of sins is the Master and principality of life; The Father granted the Son life so He can give life to all men. Prince of Life is the light of life and the resurrection springing forth grace. The spoken Word, which when declared gives life to the souls of men, for the One who has the power of life, has power over His own life to put it down and take it back again. The eternal wisdom of God, which was hidden from the people of darkness, has been revealed and its abundant and everlasting life, for in Him we live and move. We walk in his ways so we may live and increase in the blessings he has given to us. We stay in His presence and walk with Him so that His goodness and His mercy and His grace will always abide with us. The whole duty of man in life is to fear God and keep his commandments and believe in his son Jesus Christ, the Prince of Life for grace and eternal life.

Prayer: *I pray you receive His abundant life in all aspects of your life, share and be a witness of His goodness and favor.*

Launching Deeper: Galatians 2:20, John 1:4, John 3:16, 4:10,14, 5:26, Acts 2:32, 5:31.

Hebrew Word Study: "edah"—testimony, witness (Strong's Hebrew: 5713).

May 2

Tikvah Hameashsheret

תקווה שמשרת

The Blessed Hope

"Looking for the blessed hope and glorious appearing of our great God and Savior Jesus Christ" (Titus 2:13, NKJV).

His promise unto all men is the hope of eternal life, the sure expectation in the Lord's presence. He is our hope, the one who saves in time of distress, and in Him and the power of His word, will all nations, all tribes, all people, every soul put their hope. He will fill them with joy and peace as they put their trust in Him. In the Blessed Hope, they have hope in the resurrection and eternal life given to all. He was raised from the dead as the first of those who fall asleep so that all who believe in Him will have life in eternity; in this hope we live and walk in His obedience and receive the promises of the heavenly blessings in store for us, and have also become heirs of the promise. The Blessed Hope is a steadfast anchor to the soul, a hope that will not put us to shame, given us safety and security, well established, so that we overflow in joy and peace to touch other lives.

Prayer: *I pray the Blessed Hope be your refuge and your anchor, be established firmly in His joy, peace, and blessings.*

Launching Deeper: Psalm 71:5, 1 Timothy 1:10, Romans 8:24,25, 5:2, Titus 3:8.

Hebrew Word Study: "tiqvah"—expectations, hope (Strong's Hebrew: 8615).

May 3

LECHEM HASHEM

לך השם

The Bread of God

"For the bread of God is He who comes down from heaven and gives life to the world" (John 6:33, NKJV).

One of the disciples told Jesus that two hundred denarii worth of bread would not be enough for the people. They had gathered around Jesus to listen to Him preaching and seeing the signs and wonders that He performed. A little boy's snack, bread, and fish were enough for Jesus to feed them. He took it and thanked God, and it became a miracle of multiplication right there. They kept on following Him for more bread, but He taught them they should not strive for food that will perish, but food that will endure eternal life, food that results in everlasting life is what matters. Jesus is the bread from the Father given to the world, given to anyone who believes in Him. They will receive sustenance in their lives and have abundant life. The providence of the Father is to cater for the totality of man, the spirit, soul, and body, the essentials of life, food, water, and shelter. He provides the bread from heaven whom His children will feed on, who will nourish the spirit by His teachings and doctrines that bring comfort and strength to the believer.

Prayer: *I pray His Bread from heaven satisfies your soul and spirit and be blessed by Him.*

Launching Deeper: John 6:32-58, 3:13, 8:42, Psalm 105:40, Nehemiah 9:5.

Hebrew Word Study: "oklah"—food, nourishment, eating (Strong's Hebrew: 402).

May 4

HA CHOSON

הא צ׳וסון

The Bridegroom

"Then the kingdom of heaven shall be likened to ten virgins who took their lamps and went out to meet the bridegroom" (Matthew 25:1, NKJV).

Marriage is celebrated in almost every culture of the world. There is a great deal of preparation for the wedding ceremony, sometimes a great amount of money is spent on every aspect of the ceremony, the clothing, the tokens, the location, the group of companions, assigned attendants and the banquets, all are very important in anticipation of the bride and groom. Christ, the bridegroom of the church is preparing the place for the grand banquet, a great supper for his bride the church, and they that prepare themselves to come and partake. At the banquet, there's the sound of music, harpers, trumpets, joy, and celebration. Christ, the Bridegroom rejoices over His bride, His church, and takes delight in His people. He is devoted to the bride to redeem her from the bondage of slavery, refines her, and presents her blameless and spotless to the Father. As we wait for the Bridegroom, let our spiritual garments be spotless, and our lambs always be kept burning for Him.

Prayer: *I pray be always ready for the coming of the Bridegroom and keep your light shining.*

Launching Deeper: Luke 12:35, John 3:29, Judges 14:10, Isaiah 62:5.

Hebrew Word Study: "kallah"—bride, daughter-in-law (Strong's Hebrew: 3618).

May 5

LECHEM HACHAYYIM

לך היי

The Bread of Life

"I am the bread of life" (John 6:48, NKJV).

Bread is a very common food, mostly enjoyed by lots of individuals all over the world. Water and bread can sustain a person for a long period. In the wilderness, the nation of Israel was sustained by bread rained down from heaven as they journeyed. Christ declared Himself as the Bread of Life, the life sustainer, the food that satisfies the cravings of the soul, the spiritual nutrients the spirit of man needs to survive and live. As food keeps the physical body healthy, so Jesus gives Himself the word, His teachings to keep our spiritual lives healthy and our hearts healthy. The Bread of Life, His Word, is the gospel of life that preserves and keeps our spirit and soul strong, refreshed, nourished, and flourishing. He is the real manna from heaven that whoever eats will not die. As you partake of Him and keep the faith continually, let the bread of life assimilate into your spiritual life and bring satisfaction to every craving and yearnings. Let Him enable you to stand strong. His love, power, support, good health, grace, and mercy help you to fulfill destiny and sustain you for all times.

Prayer: *I pray as you take in the bread of life, His body, receive abundant life and prosperity in your body, soul, and spirit.*

Launching Deeper: John 6:31-35, Exodus 16:4, John 6:35,51, Psalm 78:24,25, 1 Corinthians 10:3.

Hebrew Word Study: "matar"—to rain (Strong's Hebrew: 4305).

May 6

HaMigdal Azaz

המגדל עזאז

The Strong Tower

"The name of the LORD is a strong tower; The righteous run to it and are safe" (Proverbs 18:10, NKJV).

A tower is a structure that is higher above its surroundings or stands apart from all other buildings and noticed from afar. It's also a place of security, a fortress, a representation of the Lord to His people. He is the Strong Tower where the righteous finds refuge and is safe from troubles and afflictions of this world. The name of the Lord gives security as the tower does, the righteous runs into it, and they are secured and lifter above all challenges which overwhelm in its appearance. He calls upon the name of the Lord, and a standard is lifted for him above every battle that comes up. The Strong Tower is the deliverer, the stronghold which saves the believer from any trouble, a tower of strength against the enemy, our trust in the Strong Tower subdues the enemy from under us and sets us securely high, as you have known His name as the mighty haven for your life, you shall not fear any evil but keep your confidence in the Lord, He will deliver you and set His love upon you.

***Prayer**: I pray be secured in His High tower, and your children find refuge in Him.*

Launching Deeper: Psalm 91:14, 2 Samuel 22:3,51, Psalm 18:2, 27:1, Genesis 17:1, Proverbs 14:26, 29:25.

Hebrew Word Study: "oz"—strength, might (Strong's Hebrew: 5797).

May 7

NECHAMAT YISROEL

נחמת ישראל

Consolation of Israel

"And behold, there was a man in Jerusalem whose name was Simeon, and this man was just and devout, waiting for the Consolation of Israel, and the Holy Spirit was upon him" (Luke 2:25, NKJV).

The time of redemption for Israel was long-awaited. They anticipated the presence of Adonai and His kingdom, His presence to comfort them and take away every distress from them. He will come with strength to rule over Israel and recompense the people, gathering and caring for them. He is coming to proclaim good news to the oppressed, to heal the brokenhearted, to declare those in captivity free and liberated from every bondage, decreeing favor upon their lives and vengeance against their enemies. The old prophets had declared that the Messiah will bring consolation to the nation Israel and when He was born, Simeon and Anna, filled with the Spirit, perceived who He was and praised Yahweh and spoke about the Child to the people thanking the LORD for fulfilling His Word, that now the comforter of Israel has come. He is having mercy upon you to deliver and comfort you, sing for joy and let the sounds of thanksgiving be, every site of ruin is restored, Zion will be consoled.

***Prayer**: I pray the Lord console and comfort you, bringing liberation to all areas of your life in Jesus' name.*

Launching Deeper: Isaiah 49:13, 51:3, 66:13, 61:1-2, Mark 15:43, Luke 1:6, 2:38.

Hebrew Word Study: "nabi"—prophet, a spokesman, speaker (Strong's Hebrew: 5030).

May 8

SHEMESH TZEDAKAH,

שמש צדקה

Sun of Righteousness

"But to you who fear My name The Sun of Righteousness shall arise with healing in His wings And you shall go out And grow fat like stall-fed calves" (Malachi 4:2, NKJV).

The sunlight has wonderful health benefits to the human body. The exposure of the rays, according to studies, lowers blood pressure, improves bone health, improves brain functions, heals some skin diseases, and boosts children's growth, just to mention a few physical healings we may know. Jesus, our Sun of Righteousness, shines His light of grace and blessings, as the Sun rises, it shows the time of the Lord's deliverance and healing for His people, as it shines at every direction, nothing under the sun hides from its rays, so the Lord will shine on every kind of situation and radiate His light of good health and preservation. The Sun of Righteousness is the one who delivers your soul from the darkness of pits and causes your life to see light as you walk in the light of the living, His Sunlight is healing every disease and sickness. Afflictions are being removed out of your life today, burning out every agent of weakness in your body, His healing virtue is radiating to your soul, spirit, and body. He is the Sun and shield giving grace and glory unto your life.

Prayer: *I pray let the Sun of Righteousness arise on you to make you radiate His glory in your world.*

Launching Deeper: 2 Samuel 23:4, Psalms 61:5, 84:11, Isaiah 30:26, 35:6, 60:1, Jeremiah 30:17.

Hebrew Word Study: "zarach"—to rise, come forth (Strong's Hebrew: 2224).

May 9

Chemdat kol HaGoyim

חמדאת קול הגויים

The Desire of all Nations

"'And I will shake all nations, and they shall come to the Desire of All Nations, and I will fill this temple with glory,' says the Lord of hosts" (Haggai 2:7, NKJV).

There are the shakings and the shiftings of the nations. Kingdoms and governments have been shaking throughout the ages and times, some falling and some rising, until Shiloh comes and brings peace to all nations. The Lord declares through the prophets that out of Judah would come one who through Him all the nations are to be blessed including the gentile nations, for to Him shall obedience of the nations be. The Desire of the Nations comes in His glorious power as a king of the nations announcing peace, His dominion from sea to sea, and as the river to the ends of the earth, bringing joy to all people. He is the peace that the nations desire in a time of chaos, wars, and epidemics across the world. The Desire of All Nations brings healings and comfort, so they will glorify God for His mercy and praise Him, in Him they hope as He rises to rule over them to declare the good news of liberty and deliverance, and in Him, the yearnings of the heart of people will be satisfied with grace, blessing, and hope.

***Prayer**: I pray let the kings of the earth bring you wealth and His glory fill your house.*

Launching Deeper: Isaiah 60:4,7, Ezekiel 31:16, 44:4, Romans 15:9-15, Galatians 3:8, Luke 2:10.

Hebrew Word Study: "raash"—to quake, shake (Strong's Hebrew: 7494).

Avi HaRuchot

אבי הרוכות

Father of Spirits

"Furthermore, we have had human fathers who corrected us, and we paid them respect. Shall we not much more readily be in subjection to the Father of spirits and live?" (Hebrews 12:9, NKJV)

God is the creator of all spirits, the One who forms and originates every spirit both with flesh and without flesh and sustains the existence of them all. His inspiration gives understanding to them. The spirit of man is a lamp with which the Father of Spirits searches out his inmost being. He made the realm of spiritual beings. Angels do the biddings of the Father. He created Lucifer and the fallen angels, thrones, dominions, rulers, and authorities and has the authority and power over all spirits. At His command, He cast evil spirits out of people, redeeming the souls and spirits of men and establishing an eternal relationship to the ones He saves. Christ has disarmed spiritual rulers and authorities and triumphed over them on the cross for you. The Holy Spirit of God gives you the ability to test every spirit, to distinguish between spirits if it's sent of God by the spirit's confession that Jesus Christ has come in the flesh. Be empowered and walk and live by the Spirit of God.

Prayer: *I pray the Father of Spirits restores your spirit and soul into a life of prosperity.*

Launching Deeper: Numbers 16:22, Proverbs 20:27, Isaiah 38:16, Zechariah 12:1.

Hebrew Word Study: "basar"—flesh (Strong's Hebrew: 1320).

May 11

Ro'el Yisroel

רואל ישראל

Shepherd of Israel

"Give ear, O Shepherd of Israel, You who lead Joseph like a flock; You who dwell between the cherubim, shine forth!" (Psalm 80:1, NKJV)

The Lord shepherds His people and carries them, He gathers them like lambs in His arms and leads. He feeds them with good pasture that is on the high mountains, the richness of the land of Canaan flowing with milk and honey. He nourishes them with abundance, providing security for His people and causes them to lie down in perfect peace. He will do that to reveal His might and strength, His faithfulness and loving-kindness for the sake and glory of His holy name, so His name will not be profaned before the nations. As the Shepherd, let Him place you in high places and satisfy you with His goodness, and His showers of blessings come on you and keep you safe in the promised land. You will not be ashamed, for the people of His flock are His pasture. He will give you rest and take away every form of uncertainty as He guides you to greater glory and grace.

Prayer: *I pray the Shepherd of Israel supply all your needs and cause you to never lack.*

Launching Deeper: Philippians 4:19, Genesis 49:24, Psalms 79:13, 23:1, 28:9, 50:2, Isaiah 40:11.

Hebrew Word Study: "raah"—to pasture, tend, graze (Strong's Hebrew: 7462a).

May 12

KOL MELO ELOHIM

קול מלו אלוהים

The Fullness of The Godhead

"For in Him dwells all the fullness of the Godhead bodily" (Colossians 2:9, NKJV).

Of the fullness of Christ have we all received all things that pertain to life, With the presence of the Spirit of God in us, we have the knowledge of the Father, for He is pleased to have his fullness dwell in Christ so that through Christ we all will be reconciled to the Father. In His fullness, we have received peace and grace upon grace and truth, knitting us together in love and onto all richness of the full understanding of the mystery of God. In His fullness, we have been made complete and worthy of pleasing Him and making us fruitful in all good works and to continue to increase in the knowledge and fullness of the Godhead. We have all the spiritual blessings in heavenly places, and to know the love of Christ which leads us to the unity of faith and to His perfection, in the fullness of Christ He has made us reconciled and restored in our inheritance and blessings.

Prayer: *I pray you receive honor, grace and strength, and power in His fullness in Jesus' name.*

Launching Deeper: John 1:14,16, 2:21, Isaiah 7:14, Colossians 1:19, 2:2,3,.

Hebrew Word Study: "shem"—a name (Strong's Hebrew: 8034).

May 13

Eloah Osai

אלוה אוסאי

God my Maker

"But no one says, Where is God my Maker, Who gives songs in the night" (Job 35:10, NKJV).

"The Maker," who made your spirit, soul, and body, is more than able to make all provisions for your sustenance. Elihu speaks in Job's case that men go through challenges and distress and can call on people and other gods but do not seek their Maker. He is the God of all souls and spirits, be it spirits of natural men or the supernatural, angels and fallen angels, they all live unto Him. He gives mortal body's life and its providence. The Father's gracious act toward humanity is displayed in Christ Jesus. He continues to bring restoration even when there is no hope. But the nature of man that forgets his source and Maker and falls into false promises of pagan gods and abandons the worship of God when in trouble. My Maker made provision for salvation when man sinned and fell short of the glory of God. Call upon your Him as the patriots called upon Him and made altars through their journeys. He alone is your Maker, who gives you rest and His perfect peace in the night and gives you songs of victory and of praise.

Prayer: *I pray in the night hour, in time of distress, remember the mercies of your Maker never fail, let Him answer you out of the thunder cloud.*

Launching Deeper: Isaiah 51:13, Psalms 77:6, 42:8, Job 27:10, 21:14, 4:17.

Hebrew Word Study: "asah"—do, make (Strong's Hebrew: 6213a).

May 14

Elohei kol Nechamah

אלוהי קול נחמה

God of All Comfort

"Blessed be the God and Father of our Lord Jesus Christ, the Father of mercies and God of all comfort" (2 Corinthians 1:3, NKJV).

Job received comfort from the community and family after he went through his distress. It's needed when there is a challenge. The mountains will break forth and rejoice, for the Lord has comforted His people; with the comfort received in times of trouble, the people of God can comfort others. Though challenges may come, the Lord is always with them. His word and promises comfort in time of affliction. The God of all Comfort exchanges their sorrows with His comfort, gladness, and love. In time of loneliness, He is there to motivate and encourage you as a friend you can trust and rely upon. Anytime you get worried about a situation, let His word strengthen you, take away anxiety and present your request to Him with prayer and supplication, and allow His peace to overshadow you. The God of all Comfort answers prayers when we call upon Him and always near to heal the broken-hearted. He comes to the aid of the contrite in spirit and revives their heart. He abounds in loving devotion and compassion and binds up the wound of the broken in heart.

Prayer: *I pray receive all comfort in all areas of life and let the Lord provide and strengthen your spirit.*

Launching Deeper: Isaiah 49:13, 2 Corinthians 1:3-4, Psalm 23:4, Psalm 71:20,21, Isaiah 40:1.

Hebrew Word Study: "chazaq"—to be or grow strong, strengthen (Strong's Hebrew: 2388).

May 15

Shemesh Mogen

שמש מוגנ

Sun and Shield

"For the Lord God is a sun and shield; The Lord will give grace and glory; No good thing will He withhold from those who walk uprightly" (Psalm 84:11, NKJV).

He is the Sun that enlightens and directs the ways of the believer and radiates His glory upon his life; You are to shine His light and glory when it comes upon you. His light shines in our hearts to give us illumination of Him and to shine forth the knowledge of the glory of God; even kings will come to the bright light of your sunrise, His radiating love and glory. The Lord, the Sun and Shield will give you warmth and comfort. You will miss nothing good from above. He will cause your life to yield its increase and fruitfulness like plantings that grow in the sun's richness and bring good health to your body. He is your shield as a defender. A shield is an armor used to fend missiles away from the user and blows away any form of offensive weapon. As a pillar of cloud and a pillar of fire, the Lord stood between Israel and the Egyptians when they followed them, they could not come close. He stood as a shield against their enemies and protected them. As a shield, the Lord goes before you and guards your back, no evil will come close to you, and His glory continues to shine upon you.

Prayer: *I pray the Lord be exalted in your life; He is the strength and grace of your life.*

Launching Deeper: Exodus 14:19-20, Isaiah 52:12, Isaiah 58:8, Genesis 15:1, Psalm 3:3, Isaiah 31:5.

Hebrew Word Study: "tob"—a good thing, benefit, welfare (Strong's Hebrew: 2896b).

May 16

Elohei Dovid Aviv

אלוהי דוד אביב

God of David

"Go and tell Hezekiah, 'Thus says the Lord, the God of David your father: 'I have heard your prayer, I have seen your tears; surely I will add to your days fifteen years'"

Isaiah 38:5 (NKJV)

The prophet Isaiah came to Hezekiah to deliver the message that he will be healed, for Hezekiah had prayed that the Lord would remember Him and heal him completely from his sickness. By the sure mercies of David by Adonai, Hezekiah was granted his request. For the sake of the name of the Lord, and for the sake of David, the Lord delivered him. As a king, Hezekiah did what was right in the eyes of the Lord as his father, David. The God of David was with Hezekiah as He was with him and fulfilled his promise, he made to Him. He lacked no one to sit on the throne; David was anointed by God to be Israel's great king; The Lord loved him as a man after His heart, the blessing of the Lord was upon his life, The God of David will protect and defend you as you trust Him in all you do. Always enquire from the Lord about your decisions, and He will use you to conquer more territory as He did for David. Anything that lifts itself against your life will fail. Let The God of David establish you in His presence with His goodness and mercies.

Prayer: *I pray the Lord gives you the grace to do what is in your heart for Him and let Him be with you.*

Launching Deeper: 2 Samuel, Psalms 89, 119:9, Proverbs 8:17, 2 Chronicles 34:3.

Hebrew Word Study: "shema"—to hear (Strong's Hebrew: 8086).

May 17

HaTzur

צור

The Rock

"He is the Rock, His work is perfect; For all His ways are justice, A God of truth and without injustice; Righteous and upright is He" (Deuteronomy 32:4, NKJV).

There is no God like our rock. He is the Rock that cares for His people. Man-made images crafted and worshiped profit nothing. They are made of wood and stones and cannot see or hear when people call them to care or protect them. These idols put them in shame, they are disappointed and frustrated, but the Lord who is our Rock, He will not put you to shame when you put your trust in him, He is worthy to be praised, Your refuge and fortress, He is the strong and mighty one Who abides forever, always faithful to His promises and delivers His people in times of trouble, He is the Rock that spring out water for His people in abundance in the terrifying wilderness and made sure they never thirst; the Rock who trains your hands to war and fingers to do battle against forces of darkness, and subdues enemies under you, and provide for you to never lack or be in need of any good thing, He will keep you strong.

***Prayer:** I pray the Lord be your refuge and cause you to pursue a thousand and ten thousand to flight.*

Launching Deeper: Numbers 20:8, Exodus 17:6, Numbers 20:10-13, Deuteronomy 8:15.

Hebrew Word Study: "misgab"—a secure height, retreat, stronghold (Strong's Hebrew: 4869).

May 18

HASHEM SHOFET HAKOL

השם שופה הקול

God, the Judge of All

"To the general assembly and church of the firstborn who are registered in heaven, to God the Judge of all, to the spirits of just men made perfect" (Hebrews 12:23, NKJV).

He executes His righteousness and authority as the judge of all. The inhabitants of the heavens witness God's character as the Righteous Judge who operates to see His intentions and purpose established as pre-determined. He sits enthroned in eternity for justice upon the earth and judges the world and the people with righteousness and with equity. He will defend the oppressed and will bring justice to the afflicted, and will not forsake them. The Judge is deeply concerned about His children, for He requires a reward for disobedience and injustice. When God the great Judge judges the earth, the earth trembles; for everything that man does, he must give an account to the God of the earth. He presides in the heavenly courts and settles disputes among people and among the nations. The Judge of all is impartial, compassionate, and truthful. He is holy and all-powerful in judgment and searches the heart of men and reveals secrets; He judges not only the people but also the angels and fallen angels, and no one can escape His judgment. He will judge your enemies and reward them with destruction in Jesus' name.

Prayer: *I pray the Lord arises on your behalf and silence the voice of the accuser. As you lift your soul to the Lord, let Him be your great Judge and show you abundant mercy.*

Launching Deeper: Psalms 50:1,6, 76:8-9, Isaiah 33:22, 66:16, James 4:12, Psalm 75:7.

Hebrew Word Study: "din"—judgment (Strong's Hebrew: 1779).

May 19

Tzur Yeshua

צור ישועה

Rock of Salvation

But Jeshurun waxed fat, and kicked: Thou art waxen fat, thou art grown thick, thou art covered with fatness; Then he forsook God which made him, And lightly esteemed the Rock of his salvation.

Deuteronomy 32:15 (KJV)

When children of God forsake and reject Him, they also abandon every wonderful thing ascribe to Him as their cause of joy, peace, blessings, wisdom, strength, and comfort. After God being a Mighty Savior, a deliverer, and Rock of salvation to Israel, the nation is found abusing the blessings and the goodness of God, provoking Him to jealousy by sacrificing to strange gods. They forsook the Rock, which gave them salvation and new birth as a nation from the oppression of Egypt. After He blessing and enriching your life, you should not forsake Him when you grow fat on His blessings. The security of salvation is by continually abiding in Christ. You should not stray away and sin willfully by disdaining Him, regarding His blood, something not important, and also denying the Holy Spirit. Stay in His goodness and favor. It is your source of salvation that brings eternal life, and remember what Joshua said, "you know in all your hearts and in all your souls that not one thing has failed of all the good things which the Lord your Rock of salvation spoke about you." Joshua 23:14. Every word of God for your life will never fail, it will come to fulfillment in Jesus' Name.

***Prayer**: I pray may you continue to abide in Him and delight in His great goodness.*

Launching Deeper: Psalms 95:1, 89:26, Deuteronomy 32, Jeremiah 2:31, 5:28,

Hebrew Word Study: "shamen"—to grow fat (Strong's Hebrew: 8080).

May 20

EL SIMKHAT GILI

שמחת גילי

God My Exceeding Joy

"Then I will go to the altar of God, To God my exceeding joy; And on the harp I will praise You, O God, my God" (Psalm 43:4, NKJV).

The joy of the Lord is our strength. He is the source of the believer's joy and gladness. When His path of life is revealed unto us, we are filled and cheered with joy in his presence, and there is nothing that can be compared to that joy, its full of His everlasting pleasures and blessings, we express our thanksgiving to Him in our instruments of praise when we come to His altar; He is our exceeding great joy, and He rejoices in the success of His covenant people. All we can give to His significant benefits and His precious blessings is to call upon His great name and sing praises and be joyful in His house, for He has broken our chains of captivity and heal all diseases and redeemed us. Our Exceeding Joy has delivered us by His goodness and His compassion. He has clothed us with the garment of praise, the garment of salvation, and His righteousness. He has restored us and caused His face to shine upon us continually, so we rejoice in His mighty acts toward us and offer unto Our Exceeding Joy, our sacrifice of praise and thanksgiving.

Prayer: *I pray the Lord fills your heart with His great joy and grant you blessings with joy in His presence.*

Launching Deeper: Psalm 37:4, Nehemiah 1:11, 12:43, Isaiah 61:10, John 15:11.

Hebrew Word Study: "simchah"—joy, gladness, mirth (Strong's Hebrew: 8057).

May 21

MELECH HAYEHUDIM

מלך ההודים

King of the Jews

"Saying, 'Where is He who has been born King of the Jews? For we have seen His star in the East and worship Him'" (Matthew 2:2, NKJV).

The Magi set out their journey to look for the great king who was to come from the Jews according to prophecies of Isaiah. A son and of the royal descent of David, the Jews had waited so long for Him, and now He is here as the king to save the entire world. He is born in Bethlehem, and He's being sought after by men from the east; this brought fear to the rulership of Herod. By the miracles and the wonders he performed, many of the Jews believed in Him, and on the day of the feast, He rode on a donkey to Jerusalem; they took Palm branches and went out to meet him, they shouted, "hosanna blessed is the one who comes in the name of the Lord blessed is the king of Israel" For this reason, He was crucified, and on the cross, He was declared king with an inscription upon the cross to imply even though He was betrayed and crucified and was not recognized by them as king, He was still king, reigns and continued to rule from the cross and also at His resurrection, He continues to rule over the universe His kingship is everlasting.

Prayer: *I pray for you, let great people who are divinely sent locate your star and bring you gifts and favor.*

Launching Deeper: Numbers 24:17, Jeremiah 23:5, Matthew 27:11, John 18:37, Mark 15:26.

Hebrew Word Study: "kokab"—a star (Strong's Hebrew: 3556).

May 22

MOSHEL

משהל

Governor

"And thou Beth-lehem, in the land of Juda, art not the least among the princes of Juda: for out of thee shall come a Governor, that shall rule my people Israel" (Matthew 2:6, KJV)

The Son of God, the Christ, rules as a shepherd. His kingdom is not of this world, for this reason He was born. There were prophecies that out of Bethlehem shall come forth the governor who would rule over His flock of Israel. His arm establishes His rulership over the earth. Jesus is the shepherd Who rules, the governor who will deliver the sheep from bondage of sin and leads them through eternal life, the governor who protects and feeds his people, the benevolent provider, and a great and mighty defender. He takes care of those that the Father has entrusted unto Him; He preserves His church and empowers them; He breaks in pieces the governor of the world and those who rise against Him. As governor, many bring their glory to Him and worship Him. He brings together those that have scattered to the fold of the kingdom, and displays His love and mercy to those without help, and sacrifices Himself for them. His government for you has the increase of endless peace, justice, and righteousness.

***Prayer:** I pray the Lord as your Governor lead you to springs of living water.*

Launching Deeper: 1 Chronicles 5:2, Isaiah 9:7, Isaiah 40:10,11, Micah 5:2, Revelation 3:14.

Hebrew Word Study: "mashal"—to rule, have dominion, reign (Strong's Hebrew: 4910).

May 23

NATZRI

נצרתית

The Nazarene

"And he came and dwelt in a city called Nazareth: that it might be fulfilled which was spoken by the prophets, He shall be called a Nazarene" (Matthew 2:23, KJV).

When Nathanael head from Phillip that the one of whom the prophets and Moses wrote about, the Messiah has been found; He doubted if good can come out of Nazareth, this implies that Nazareth might be a village not appropriate for the Messiah to originate, a place out of nowhere, not recognized, despised and looked down upon, people from there might not be regarded. A Nazarene is resident and a native of Nazareth, a title of Christ, from a place where no one could expect that something good can come out, but became the town of the King of Kings and the Lord of Lords, where He will be born, and His name is associated with. God takes the foolish things of the world to confound the wise, something great is going to come out of you that people did not expect, a place not regarded is where the Lord will make you great, and His glory be seen up your life. The Nazarene will make you great in Jesus' name.

Prayer: *I pray for you that the Lord use you mightily, and something great comes from you to glorify His name.*

Launching Deeper: Matthew 21:11, Mark 1:9, 24, Luke 1:26,26, 2:39, John 1:45,46,

Hebrew Word Study: "yasha"—to deliver (Strong's Hebrew: 3467).

May 24

Rebbe

האדמו"ר מגור

Master/Teacher

"Then a certain scribe came and said to Him, 'Teacher, I will follow You wherever You go'" (Matthew 8:19, NKJV).

An Honorable title given to Jesus, The Rabbi, the Distinguished Teacher who proclaims with authority the teachings and the Words of the kingdom of God. His disciples addressed Him as Rabbi, the Teacher. He was known in the synagogues of Galilee as a teacher and a preacher of the gospel of the kingdom and healing sickness and diseases among the people. Many wondered how He attained such wonderful knowledge without studying. He then responded that He was anointed to teach by the One who sent Him with His Word, the Father. Jesus never spoke of His own. He spoke in the power of the Holy Spirit. He was commanded to say what to say and how to say it. John reminded believers that they remain in the teachings of Christ. This will prove we have the Father and the Son in us. The teachings of the Rabbi admonish us to live in holiness and in righteousness and to obey His Word. His teachings were lessons drawn from parables and day-to-day life, full of His life and Spirit, which brings His blessings upon your life.

***Prayer:** I pray you keep the teachings of the Great Rabbi and, by His authority, grow in power.*

Launching Deeper: Luke 9:57, 1 Corinthians 16:6, Mark 12:32-34, Luke 9:57,58.

Hebrew Word Study: "sopher"—enumerator, scribe (Strong's Hebrew: 5613).

May 25

BEN HAADAM

בן האדם

Son of Man

"And Jesus said to him, 'Foxes have holes and birds of the air have nests, but the Son of Man has nowhere to lay His head'" (Matthew 8:20, NKJV).

John 20:31 is one statement that communicate the Father's endorsement, commission, and empowerment of Jesus as the chosen king and the Son of God. This states the position, the authority, the majesty of Jesus, God in the flesh, by believing, eternal life is obtained "But as many as received Him, to them He gave the right to become children of God, to those who believe in His name" (John 1:12, NKJV). This title depicts the human nature of Christ and the servanthood of His ministry, as Daniel saw in His vision that the Son of Man appeared to execute authority and judgment upon the earth and to give eternal life. With Word from the Father, the Son of Man goes to sow the seeds in the heart of men; those who receive from Him receive everlasting life. Which will cause you to bear an abundant increase in all areas of life, Son of Man as a servant came to serve and not to be served, He went through suffering and death but resurrected, and ascended into glory and seated at the right-hand side of the Father, where you are seated with Him in power.

Prayer: *I pray that you will rejoice and be glad in your days. Let the favor of the Lord my God be on us.*

Launching Deeper: Daniel 7:13-14, Matthew 20:28, Mark 10:45, Ezekiel 2:1.

Hebrew Word Study: "laqach"—to receive, to take (Strong's Hebrew: 3947).

May 26

PACHAD YITZCHAK

פצ'אד יצחק

The Dread and Fear of Isaac

"The God of Abraham, the God of Nahor, and the God of their father judge between us." And Jacob swore by the Fear of his father Isaac" (Genesis 31:53, NKJV).

Jacob could see how his father, Isaac, feared and dreaded in the presence of the Almighty God. The Lord provided the lamb for the sacrifice instead of Isaac and answered the prayers of his father Abraham, and provided a wife for him. Isaac's prayers were answered when his wife Rebecca was barren. The Lord opened her womb, Jacob and his brother Esau were born. The Lord confirmed his covenant with Isaac and blessed him, Isaac sowed in the land of Gerar, and His God whom he feared and dread made him prosperous on the land. He continued to be prosperous until he became very prosperous. Isaiah 8:13 notes, the Lord of Host should be our source of fear and dread and not man, for fear of man is a snare, Him only we should fear and worship. Just a thought of the work of His hands put you in a state of awe and dread. His covenant with you is not to forsake you. Like Jacob, if you will not forsake Him, He will bless you and make you prosperous until you become very great upon the land, He has planted you and be a blessing unto others. Serve Him with awe and reverential fear and see His glory.

Prayer: *I pray you will not be afraid of any man, but the fear of the Lord will rest upon you to walk in His ways.*

Launching Deeper: Isaiah 8:13, Genesis 31:42, 14:22, Deuteronomy 6:13.

Hebrew Word Study: "pachad"—dread (Strong's Hebrew: 6343).

May 27

Echad Gadol Haetzah

אחד גדל הצה“ה

The One Great In Counsel

"You are great in counsel and mighty in work, for Your eyes are open to all the ways of the sons of men, to give everyone according to his ways and according to the fruit of his doings"

(Jeremiah 32:19, NKJV).

We see the presence of the Word, His counsel throughout the scriptures. By His great counsel, He led and taught His people to walk in His ways and reveal the glory of God. His counsel brings life that transforms the spirit of a man from the bondage of sin to eternal life by the Holy Spirit. The spoken counsel, the Word of power, brings growth, like the branches that abide in the vine, our spiritual connection with the Word is what matters. If life is fruitless, it needs to be connected to the source of productivity and success, His counsel by the Word. God commanded Joshua that the book of the law should not depart from His mouth. The law should be His counsel that directs His path and help make decisions by that He will be prosperous in everything He does. The Vinedresser cultivates and maintains grapevines and does the daily pruning, a sense of purging and spiritual cleansing through His counsel. Jesus declared, "You are already clean because of the word which I have spoken to you" (John 15:3, NKJV). Abiding in His great counsel will make your life meaningful, fruitful, and prosperous.

Prayer: *I pray your life be fruitful and prosperous in all ways as you abide in His great counsel.*

Launching Deeper: Isaiah 9:6, 28:29, 40:13, Proverbs 8:14.

Hebrew Word Study "etsah"—counsel, advice (Strong's Hebrew: 6098).

May 28

OHR HAAMITTI

אוזן האמיתי

The True Light

"That was the true Light which gives light to every man coming into the world" (John 1:9, NKJV).

John the Baptist bear witness of the True Light, the Christ, the presence of God in our midst, the True light is the salvation of the world, the revelation and knowledge of God to His people, they will have full knowledge of Him by the True Light, many gave some sort of light in falsehood, many false lights had shown up, but Jesus is the only true light, all others lead to darkness without Christ, the true light that shines the path to the Father, distinguishing Him from others, the light of truth brings enlightenment into your life, it unveils the righteousness of God in Christ. Christ in your life reveals the glory of the Father, through the promise of the Holy Spirit, you can overcome sin and the oppression of darkness, and His will manifest to you; by walking in His ways and obeying His Word to live life to its fullest, in success, in power, and in His grace, the True Light replaces ignorance and brings knowledge and grace of God into your life.

Prayer: *I pray be radiant as a lamp shining unto others with His glory.*

Launching Deeper: Luke 11:36, 1 John 2:8, 1 John 4;7, 6:32, 7:12, 12:46, 14:6.

Hebrew Word Study: "emeth"—firmness, truth, faithfulness (Strong's Hebrew: 571).

May 29

SEH HaElohim

ש"ה האלוהים

The Lamb of God

"The next day John saw Jesus coming toward him, and said, "Behold! The Lamb of God who takes away the sin of the world!" (John 1:29, NKJV).

When the time of deliverance came for the Israelites to leave Egypt to the promised land, every family was commanded to offer a lamb without blemish on the fourteenth day of the month and the blood of the lamb to be on the doorpost and lintel of their houses, the blood preserved their lives from the angel of death that came against the firstborns of the Egyptians, commemorating the Passover, a symbol of His grace, the blood of the lamb that redeemed and set us free from His judgment. The sacrificial offering ordained and given by the Son to bear the guilt of the sins of the world is not for Jews only but to everyone. The Passover lamb that atones for your transgressions and buys His children back from spiritual slavery, every tribe, and nation. His death is the epic fulfillment of the Passover. The innocent and glorious Lamb with seven eyes is upon the throne and worthy. He executes judgment against the wicked and represents the bridegroom of the Church. The blood continues to speak better things for your life and keeps you in His covenant blessings and peace all around you.

***Prayer:** I pray to be preserved by the blood and have the fullness of Him.*

Launching Deeper: Exodus 12, Revelation 5:6, 1 Corinthians 5:7, Hebrews 4:15, 7:26, Revelation 22:1-3.

Hebrew Word Study: "seh"—lamb, a sheep (Strong's Hebrew: 7716).

May 30

Moshi'a HaOlam, Go'el HaOlam

מושיה האולאם, גול האולאם

Savior of the World

And they told the woman, "We no longer believe just because of what you said; for [now] we have heard Him for ourselves and know [with confident assurance] that this One is truly the Savior of [all] the world."
John 4:42 (AMP)

It is astounding to meet someone you don't know, and you talk with the person for a few minutes, and the person tells you something that happens to you yesterday, a believer would say that's a prophet, the Samaritan woman had the same impression about Jesus and went to tell the people in Samaria, and when they met Jesus and heard His Word, they testified themselves and said indeed, this is The Savior of the world. The Savior promised by the Father whose assignments were to see the lost in the world find salvation, for there is no other name given under heaven in which men can have salvation except in Christ the Lord. All that believe in Him receive forgiveness of sin and reconciliation to the Father. He is the door of salvation and eternal life. By his death and resurrection, He has called many into the kingdom of light and has illuminated the way for the world to know the Father. He saved the world by destroying the works of the evil one and delivering humanity from the power of sin and the wrath of God. You are justified and have eternal life; He is concerned about all you are thinking about. Your needs and desires are before Him to meet them and bless you, keep spreading His knowledge in your world.

***Prayer**: I pray as you search Him daily; let Him empower you to do great for Him.*

Launching Deeper: 2 Timothy 1:10, Romans 7:21-25, Titus 3:6, 2 Peter 1:1.

Hebrew Word Study: "shaar"—a gate (Strong's Hebrew: 8179).

May 31

HaOhr HaOlam Hazeh

הוהר האולאם חזה

Light of the World

"Once more Jesus addressed the crowd. He said, 'I am the Light of the world. He who follows Me will not walk in the darkness, but will have the Light of life'" (John 8:12, AMP).

The Light of the world continues to shine through the darkness. The Lord Himself will be your everlasting light. He will bring you out of every darkness, and you will see His goodness upon those who fear His name. He is like the rising of the sun upon their lives. In time of gloom, He rouses Himself to illuminate the way. When we trust in Him, we are transformed from darkness to light, from the gloominess of falsehood of the devil to the light of truth and knowledge of God. We are enlightened to have the power to discern falsehood and truth. His light in you shines outward and imparts others the revelation of the word you received. Those who walk in darkness will see the glorious light of the knowledge of Christ, for light cannot be hidden under a basket. A God-fearing and obedient life in these times is an armor of light to the lost world. The light makes visible all things. He's light demands you radiate His image and His glory risen upon your life, let Jesus in you shine in the world.

Prayer: *I pray your light breaks forth like the morning, and the light of His glory guard your rear.*

Launching Deeper: Romans 13;12, Ephesians 5:13, Isaiah 58:8, John 1:4-9, 9:5.

Hebrew Word Study: "or"—a light (Strong's Hebrew: 216).

June

The name of the Lord is a strong tower;
The righteous run to it and are safe.'
Proverbs 18:10 NKJV

June 1

Ro'eh HaTov

רועי טוב

Good Shepherd

"I am the Good Shepherd. The Good Shepherd lays down His [own] life for the sheep" (John 10:11, AMP).

The Good Shepherd enters through the door to the flock, and the flock knows Him and recognizes his voice. He does not abandon the sheep. When danger approaches, He is concerned to deliver them. The sheep trust Him to follow his instructions and follow His directions. The Lord will bring the other flock which has not joined, and they will also hear His voice, and all will be one big fold. All believers from around the world, both Jews and gentiles, into His redemptive fold. He laid down His life for you as the Good Shepherd and offered Himself as a ransom. He does what's in your best interest to make sure you do not lack and will do everything to keep you in safety so that the wolf, the enemy will not have you, for the enemy comes to steal, kill and destroy the sheep, but Christ, the Good Shepherd, has come that you would have life and have it overflowing. The Good Shepherd poured upon you His love and took your punishment for your sins. He gave you His gracious life and carried you close to His heart as He gently led you.

Prayer: *I pray as you follow the steps of the Good Shepherd, be fed in His greener pasture, and be satisfied in His abundance.*

Launching Deeper: Matthew 26:31, 9:36, Matthew 18:12-14, John 10:14-15, Romans 8:36.

Hebrew Word Study: "tub"—good things, goods, goodness (Strong's Hebrew: 2898).

June 2

HaDerech, HaEmes, and HaChayyim.

הארץ, העמקים והחיי"ם

The Way, the Truth and the Life

"Jesus said to him, 'I am the [only] Way [to God] and the [real] Truth and the [real] Life; no one comes to the Father but through Me'"(John 14:6, AMP)

Pilate then asked Jesus the big question, "What is truth?" And it can also be a question you would ask. If you want to know what truth is, like Pilate, Truth is a personality, it has a set of distinctive traits and characteristics, and it exists. It's unchangeable, it's eternal, it's above the human mind, it's the person of Jesus. He is the truth of God and the source of truth, the truth that gives light to the path and leads you to the right way When the soldiers took Jesus to Pilate, He was wondering why they brought Him. He interrogated Jesus to know more about him and know who He really is. He asked Jesus if he is the king of the Jews, Jesus answered, " ...You say rightly that I am a king....and for this cause I have come into the world, that I should bear witness to the truth. Everyone who is of the truth hears My voice" (John 18:37, NKJV). The truth is the Word of God, His way that leads you to His eternal Life. He is the word and the word that is the lamp unto your feet and a light for your path and gives you the knowledge.

***Prayer**: I pray His name defend you, walk in His ways, trust in His truth, and live in His life.*

Launching Deeper: Isaiah 35:8,9, Matthew 11:27, John 8:32, 15:1, 1:4, Acts 4:12.

Hebrew Word Study: "nephesh"—a soul, living, life (Strong's Hebrew: 5315).

June 3

ELOHEI KEDEM

אֱלֹהֵי קֶדֶם

Eternal God

"Abraham planted a tamarisk tree in Beersheba and called there on the name of the Lord, the Eternal God" (Genesis 21: 33, AMPC).

Abimelech, king of Gerar in the land of the Philistines, recognized the power and blessings of God upon Abraham's life and acknowledged that God was with him in all things, so He asked that Abraham will deal with Him well and be kind to Him and His posterity. When Abimelech's people tampered with the well that Abraham had dug, Abimelech told him and made a covenant to establish him as owner of the well; they swore an oath and called the place Beersheba, planted a tamarisk tree, and called upon the name of the Lord as the Eternal God. One Who will be the God of him and his descendants forever, and to many that will believe and be blessed through him, for He is the eternal God Whose love extends to all. His wisdom is eternal, His power is eternal, His righteousness and grace are eternal, and He never changes. He fulfills His promises and His Word to His children, see Him fulfill His Word in your life.

Prayer: *I pray no one will take what the Lord has put in your hand; your well of blessings will not be stolen.*

Launching Deeper: Psalm 90:2-4, 2 Peter 3:8, 1 John 1:1-2, Romans 16:26, Jeremiah 31:3.

Hebrew Word Study: "olam"—long, duration (Strong's Hebrew: 5769).

June 4

Adonai and Elohai

אדוני ואלוהי

My Lord and My God

"Thomas answered Him, 'My Lord and my God!'" (John 20:28,AMP)

Sometimes it's difficult to believe when you have not seen what you believe, but that is the pedestal to walk with God. You walk with Him seeing nothing about Him, but yet everything around is still about Him. He is all and in all. This was the situation of Thomas when the disciples told him they had seen the Lord after His resurrection. He had come to visit them and had revealed Himself to them and blessed them with His peace and the Holy Spirit; Thomas said unless he sees, he will not believe. The next time Jesus appears in their midst, Thomas now calls Him My Lord and my God, He recognizes that Jesus is the Lord God; He is the Master who reigns over the powers of darkness; He is your Lord God who has overcome for you to receive victory without sweat and live in His power and His glory.

Prayer: *I pray be blessed as you believe, there will be a manifestation of all His promises for your life.*

Launching Deeper: John 20:16-31, 5:23, 9:35-38.

Hebrew Word Study: "kol"—the whole, all (Strong's Hebrew: 3605).

June 5

HAKADOSH TZADDIK

הקדוש צדיק

The Holy and Righteous One

"But you disowned and denied the Holy and Righteous One and asked for [the pardon of] a murderer to be granted to you" (Acts 3:14, AMP).

Have you been in a situation when no one believed something good could come out of you, and when God turned things around for the best, you hear questions about how you could come this far? When it happens, you recount how the Lord has seen you through. Peter and John were in the same situation and were before the people giving a narration of the great things the Holy and Righteous One has done. The one whom they crucified but rose and ascended and granted His power to all those who believe. He has healed this man. The man had no hope but had great faith in the name of Jesus. Faith in Jesus can transform the lame to leap for joy, the hopeless to be hopeful, and the fruitless to be fruitful. This is the testimony the Righteous One has giving you, they've seen you getting a job, opening your own business, getting a new house, your children graduating and doing great in their career, and everyone wondering how you made it because no one expected you could make it this far, but you held on and kept the faith, just wait this is just the beginning more testimonies are on the way receive it!

***Prayer:** I pray as you have waited patiently on the Lord. Let Him set you on a solid foundation and establish you in greatness and prosperity.*

Launching Deeper: Isaiah 48:2, Isaiah 51:13, Acts 4:27, 7:52.

Hebrew Word Study: "echad"—one (Strong's Hebrew: 259).

June 6

Hu Adon Kol

הו אדון קול

Lord of All

"You know the message which He sent to the sons of Israel, announcing the good news of peace through Jesus Christ, who is Lord of all" (Acts 10:36, AMP).

In other to defuse Peter's mindset of being anti-gentile, God gave a vision of a sheet of unclean animals for Peter to kill and eat, and he wondered, but it was just a symbol to tell Peter that gentiles are not unclean, He accepts all of them into His kingdom, and He is Lord over them all. There is no kind of Lord for the Jews and a kind for the gentiles but Only One Lord of all, everyone in all nations and every kindred who believe in him. There's no difference between the Greek and the Jew, and no distinction. He is in all who put their trust in Him. So all goodness in His Lordship is available to many that come to Him. Through Him, all things were made, people and all that is in the universe. He is outstanding, and there is no God, no one holy like him. His name is everlasting, his throne is established forever. The Lord of all is majestic and powerful and arms himself with strength. He is mighty to save all entrusted to Him. His light shines in our hearts and transcends unto every aspect of our lives, and Lord, above anything that comes your way.

Prayer: *I pray let the Lord who shows not partiality favor you among many and make you distinct.*

Launching Deeper: Romans 10:12, Acts 2:36, 5:31, Psalm 2:6-8, Psalm 85:9,10.

Hebrew Word Study: "kol"—the whole, all (Strong's Hebrew: 3605).

June 7

Moshiach Yehoshua Adoneinu

מושיח יהושע אדונינו

Jesus Christ our Lord

"For the wages of sin is death, but the free gift of God [that is, His remarkable, overwhelming gift of grace to believers] is eternal life in Christ Jesus our Lord" (Romans 6:23, AMP).

Paul always greets the churches in the name of our Lord Jesus, His grace and peace be unto all who love Him. This depicts the relationship the church has with our Lord. He is your Master as a believer; He is Lord over your life; The master over your spirit, soul, and body. Our Lord Jesus is our great teacher. He teaches and directs us in His Word. His instructions in the word mold our life in His perfection admonishes us to do His will and excel in His service. For in our Lord, we are more than conquerors and have victory by the Father, and by what He has given unto us, His aroma and glory of knowledge in us spreads everywhere we are. By His grace, our Lord Jesus became poor, so we might be rich. He has given His life as a ransom for us, and His blood has preserved us and called all unto a holy call, not our deeds but for His own purpose and plan for our lives through the gospel.

Prayer*: I pray our Lord Jesus will be with your spirit, soul, and body. His grace and peace cause to do great.*

Launching Deeper: 2 Corinthians 2:14, Romans 8:37, 2 Timothy 1:8, Corinthians 15:57.

Hebrew Word Study: "teshuah"—deliverance (Strong's Hebrew: 8668).

June 8

CHOKHMAT ELOHIM

צ׳וקהמט אלוהים

The Wisdom of God

"But to those who are the called, both Jews and Greeks (Gentiles), Christ is the power of God and the wisdom of God" (1 Corinthians 1:24, AMP).

The wisdom of men cannot assimilate the acts of the great God, they are senseless in His sight, for He is exquisite and remarkable in counsel, and His understanding is above comprehension, unsearchable and untraceable are His ways. Christ Jesus is the wisdom of God. He shows the extraordinary and mysterious plan of God the Father, which He determined before ages of time for His glory, to save man from His sins. This plan of God is not the priority of men, but being redeemed and having eternal life through Christ is the significant thing in life. Christ has become His wisdom unto us, and we are wise as we believe and have the fear of God in him, and have become servants and stewards of Christ. In Him are the hidden treasures of wisdom and knowledge that we can find. Through that, we will be equipped in our callings and will not drift away in deception of the enemy. By the wisdom of Christ and His Word, we are encouraged in heart and joined in His love.

Prayer: *I pray the Spirit of His wisdom rest upon you, and let things work for your good.*

Launching Deeper: Proverbs 8:1,22-30, Colossians 2:3, Luke 11:49, Romans 1:7,16, 8:28.

Hebrew Word Study "tebunah"—an understanding (Strong's Hebrew: 8394).

June 9

Gevurat Hashem

גבורת השם

Christ, Power of God

"But to those who are the called, both Jews and Greeks (Gentiles), Christ is the power of God and the wisdom of God" (1 Corinthians 1:24, AMP).

The Greek word for power is "dynamis" referring to the miraculous acts of the Almighty to deliver His children from the powers of sin and wrath of judgment, for the exaltation of His name upon the earth and to show forth His greatness. He is all-powerful, the possessor of control over creation, over nations, over system, over governments. His power is known in the wonders of old, what He accomplished in the lives of the Israelites, how He delivered them in wars and possessions of nations and lands. That generation will always commend His magnificent deeds to the next generation, He does anything, and no purpose of His can be thwarted, nothing can annul His plans, His name is who He is, and it's mighty in power, through faith in the power of God we are made alive in Christ and have grace and mercy of God, and by His power, we receive healing from all diseases, He has transferred that power unto us His children and has exalted our horns in Jesus' name

Prayer: *Receive the power of God to do great things in His kingdom.*

Launching Deeper: 1 Corinthians 1:18, Romans 1:4, 1:16, Mark 10:27, Psalm 93:1, Mark 14:36, Job 42:2.

Hebrew Word Study: "koach"—ability (Strong's Hebrew: 3581).

June 10

ADON HAKAVOD

אדון הקב"ד

Lord of Glory

"None of the rulers of this age recognized and understood this wisdom; for if they had, they would not have crucified the Lord of glory" (1 Corinthians 2:8, AMP).

The Jewish and Roman officials who carried out the crucifixion of Christ did not realize the depth of the task they were executing on the Lord of glory. By divine ordination, Christ's suffering was God's way of bringing redemption to the world. If the enemies had known that it would win more lives to God's kingdom, they would have abated their act, but thank God they carried it on, and now we are all counted as God's children. As a Child of God, the Lord Jesus is your glory and the lifter up of your head. Christ is the Lord of Glory, the radiance of the Father, and represents the nature of Him, His reflection, and the image of His goodness. He is the one who sustains everything by the power of His Word; He can sustain you by the power of the same word that made the heavens and the earth. You will see the manifestation and tangibility of the word in your life. The Lord of Glory is the light that shines out of the darkness, shines in your heart, and dwells within you. The tabernacle presence of the Lord of glory is with you always. His reflection will radiate His glory in every aspect of your life.

***Prayer**: I pray the Lord of Glory reveals secrets of His riches in His glory unto you and all areas of your life.*

Launching Deeper: Psalm 24:7, Matthew 13:22, Acts 7:2, 1 Corinthians 1:20, 26, Ephesians 1:17.

Hebrew Word Study: "tipharah"—beauty, glory (Strong's Hebrew: 8597).

June 11

SHAMA TEPHILLAH

שאמה תפילה

Hearer of Prayer

"O You who hear Prayer:, To You all mankind comes" (Psalms 65:2, NKJV).

A time of offering incense to the Throne room of the Father is the time of prayer, and He has made a promise to hear individual or corporate prayers and for their needs. Whether in a group, the church or a nation, as Moses interceded for the nation Israel for the Lord to spare them in their disobedience, the Lord had mercy and did not eradicate them. Hannah went before the Lord to pray and cried unto Him for a son. The Lord heard her cry and through the Priest Eli, The Hearer of Prayers, met her need and fulfilled His promise by giving her the prophet Samuel. He answers prayers of deliverance and healing of the sick, and as Jesus said, whatever we ask if we believe; He is faithful to answer and hear us; He is always the covenant-keeping God who never fails, as we pray in good relationship with Him, He will attend to the voice of your cry and bring answers, He regards and listens to the cry of the destitute and does not despise their prayers and their calls. Call on Him in every time, and with mercy, He will respond as He listened to Hannah, Daniel and Nehemiah.

***Prayer**: I pray the Lord draw nigh unto you as you call upon Him.*

Launching Deeper: Psalm 145:18,19, 3:4, Genesis 35:3, Exodus 15:23-25, 1 Samuel 1:27, 1:10-20, Psalm 99:6.

Hebrew Word Study: "tephillah"—prayer (Strong's Hebrew: 8605).

June 12

RUCHANIT TZUR

רוחנית צור

Spiritual Rock

"And all [of them] drank the same spiritual drink, for they were drinking from a spiritual rock which followed them; and the rock was Christ" (1 Corinthians 10:4, AMP).

Paul encouraged the Corinthians to have faith in Christ and not to be swayed by idolatry. The Rock that provided meat and water for the Israelite in the wilderness is Christ as a type, the bread of life and river of life that refreshes our spirit. The rock supernaturally supplied water of life and never stopped flowing to quench their thirst. It followed them along the way, meaning He was always ready to serve and attend to his people. Christ, the Rock was smitten in His death and tortured, poured out rivers of redemption, eternal life, grace, mercy, and every spiritual blessing that sustains every believer in the wilderness of life, and continue till all appear in the glorious presence of the Father. Job declares the rock poured upon him the anointing oil for his existence, from the Rock, received the oil that will keep the fire in your lamp burning, that same oil for your health, and for your greatness in your life. His perfect accompanying presence, where He shows you the path of life and gives you the fullness of joy, at the right hand of the Father where Christ is exalted, you will find pleasures forever.

Prayer: *I pray bend down to listen and answer me quickly when I called to you and pour upon you rivers of joy.*

Launching Deeper: Psalm 105:4, Exodus 17:6, Numbers 20:11, Psalm 78:15,20.

Hebrew Word Study: "mayim"—waters, water (Strong's Hebrew: 4325).

June 13

Adam Haacharon

אדם השרון

Last Adam

"So it is written [in Scripture], 'The first man, Adam, became a living soul (an individual);' the last Adam (Christ) became a life-giving spirit [restoring the dead to life]" (1 Corinthians 15:45, AMP).

Adam was put in the garden of Eden to take care of it and be the progenitor of humanity. As he was given the command by the father to do his will, where he failed, Jesus Christ the last Adam came to fulfill the purpose and will of the Father. Through the first Adam's sin of disobedience that contaminated humanity, judgments pronounced was pardoned by the death of Christ and by the gift of God's grace we have eternal life, condemnation was turned around by the last Adam to bring justification and glorification to all believers. Adam was made out of dust and returned to dust after sin, but Christ, the last Adam, came from heaven and was of the Spirit and a life-giver. As we had the image of the first Adam, so do we have a new image of the last Adam, which is the image of the glory of the Father. In Christ, you have the citizenship of heaven, and He has the power to transform your body to His glorious body when He returns.

Prayer: *I pray receive His abundant life, be free in your spirit and be quickened and empowered by His Spirit.*

Launching Deeper: 1 Corinthians 15:46, Romans 5:14-19, Philippians 3:20,21.

Hebrew Word Study: "neshamah"—breath (Strong's Hebrew: 5397).

June 14

Demut of Hashem

דמות השם

Image of God

"Among them the god of this world [Satan] has blinded the minds of the unbelieving to prevent them from seeing the illuminating light of the gospel of the glory of Christ, who is the image of God" (2 Corinthians 4:4, AMP).

The manifestation of the Father is in the Son, the identity and character of the Father is in Christ Jesus, the image of the Father. He has made the Father who is invisible in the natural now known to everyone who believes in the Son. The essence of the Father is represented in Him by the power of His word, all you wish to see in God is demonstrated in the Son, the light that radiates the knowledge of the glory of God who wants us to conform to the image of Christ, and as we become like Christ, we become what we were made to be—the image of God as it was from the beginning, God's intention that we all be in His image through the infilling of the Holy Spirit, our image is renewed and restored by our faith in Him. Jesus presents the good news of the kingdom of God through His grace in preaching, teaching, healing and discipling. You have grace in Jesus, that's rested upon you, it lightens up your spirit into the power of the Holy Spirit as a believer, the flaming fire kindles into a flame of zeal in you to do the work of God.

Prayer: *I pray, let the image of Adonai and His perfection overshadow you.*

Launching Deeper: John 1:14,18; 12:45; 14:9,10, 2 Corinthians 4:6, Isaiah 60:1,2.

Hebrew Word Study: "tselem"—meaning, image (Strong's Hebrew: 6459).

June 15

HaAhuv

השוב

The Beloved

"To the praise of His glorious grace and favor, which He so freely bestowed on us in the Beloved [His Son, Jesus Christ]" (Ephesians 1:6, AMP).

That morning on the brinks of the Jordan, Jesus came from Galilee to be baptized by John. When John saw Him, he proclaimed, "That's the Lamb of God who takes away the sins of the world." John knew he was not worthy to baptize Jesus, but Jesus cautioned him that, in order for all righteousness to be fulfilled, he needs to be baptized. John obeyed. After that, a voice from heaven was heard, saying, "This is my beloved son in whom I am well pleased," and that was a decree by the Father, declaring He shall bring the people to a right relationship with God because he has given out his life even unto death and has been numbered with sinners. The beloved bore the transgression of many people and has also interceded for them. The Beloved brings justice to the nations in faithfulness, and the nations wait upon him for his teachings of power and authority, in the Beloved Son, the grace of God has been bestowed upon us and His love spread upon humanity, for the Father loved the Son even before the foundation of the earth, His love overshadows you, His love protect you and His love fulfills His covenant with you.

***Prayer**: I pray you will rest safely in Him as He shields you upon His shoulders.*

Launching Deeper: Deuteronomy 33:12, Psalm 2:7, Isaiah 52:15, 53:12, John 17:23,25.

Hebrew Word Study: "yadid"—beloved (Strong's Hebrew: 3039).

June 16

Rosh Antien

ראש אנטין

Head of the Church

He is also the head [the life-source and leader] of the body, the church; and He is the beginning, the firstborn from the dead, so that He Himself will occupy the first place [He will stand supreme and be preeminent] in everything.

Colossians 1:18 (AMP)

The authority and leadership of the church is Christ. He who empowers the church to grow in strength. He has canceled the records of inductiveness that were written against us legally in the Spirit demanding our payment. Christ, as the Head of the Church, paid our spiritual dept on the cross and has filled us with himself, when we were raised with him through our faith in the mighty work of God the Father. By this, we are alive, and our trespasses are forgiven, for he has put everything under his feet and has made him head over everything with the fullness of Himself who fills all things. He rules with power over the Church and directs them to fulfill God's mandate and His intentions. As the church obeys Him, He reveals Himself to them as the cornerstone and builder. The gates of hell do not prevail against it and match on with authority. As the head of the Church, He provides the needs of the Church, leading them to springs of living water, and causes it to grow as a body and always live to intercede and present the body of Christ guiltless before the Holy God.

Prayer: *I pray the Lord blesses you forever above all and equip you to do greater works in His kingdom.*

Launching Deeper: Ephesians 4:15, 5:23 -27, 1:10, Colossians 2:19, John 13:13, Ephesians 4:11, Psalm 89:27.

Hebrew Word "bekor"—firstborn (Strong's Hebrew: 1060).

June 17

Bekor Mesim

בקור מסים

Firstborn from the Dead

He is also the head [the life-source and leader] of the body, the church; and He is the beginning, the firstborn from the dead, so that He Himself will occupy the first place [He will stand supreme and be preeminent] in everything.

Colossians 1:18 (AMP)

Originator prophets of all other religions have died and never rose again, none of them are alive, but Christ is the first to resurrect from the dead; the Father raised Him as the first from the dead, the personality of resurrection is Christ, anyone who believes in Him will also resurrect and live forever. He is the firstborn of all and the highest above the kings of the earth and proclaims salvation to all people. Through the first man, there was death, the same way through the Son of God comes the first to come out of death and to never die again. He is preeminent in resurrection and leading His Church to have eternal life and to have a hope of future glory. There will be a glorious body that will be given to believers who have conquered at the end. He gets the power to bring into existence eternal for the soul and body all to be in perfection to the glory of the Lord. There is a resurrection for you and for your life.

Prayer: *I pray the Lord will cause you to rejoice and fill you up with His power to bring freshness and newness into your life.*

Launching Deeper: Romans 8:29, 1 Corinthians 11:3, 12:27, Ephesians 1:22.

Hebrew Word Study: "qum"—to arise, stand up (Strong's Hebrew: 6965).

June 18

Reshet Bri'at Hashem

רשת בריעת השם

The Origin of God's Creation

"To the angel (divine messenger) of the church in Laodicea write: These are the words of the Amen, the trusted and faithful and true Witness, the Beginning and Origin of God's creation" (Revelation 3:14, AMP)

The primary source of all creation is Christ Jesus, for by Him everything is made, the seen and unseen. All in heaven and upon the earth, dominions and powers were all made through Him, and creation is held together by Him, the one from the beginning and the principal. He was with the Father in the beginning and had the presence and the glory. By Him, out of the ruins, a new creation was established and came into existence. By His spoken Word, all creation is sustained and maintained by His power. By Him, man is created new from His new birth to bring into the perfection of His glory. A new birth of the spirit and soul, a new creation wiping away the past, so all that believes in Him, has been given the power to become sons of the Most High and the promise of a new heaven and a new earth, where the righteous will dwell and leave eternally in the presence of the Lord. Live a continued relationship with him and keep yourself by the power of the Spirit to be spotless and blameless and holy in Him.

Prayer: *I pray the Lord does something new. All former troubles be wiped out in Jesus' name.*

Launching Deeper: Proverbs 8:22, Colossians 1:5, Revelation 4:7, 19:11, 21:6, 22:13.

Hebrew Word Study: "Bara"—to shape, to bring about, to create (Strong's Hebrew: 1254).

June 19

Zera Dovid

זארה דוד

Seed of David

"Remember that Jesus Christ of the seed of David was raised from the dead according to my gospel" (2 Timothy 2:8, KJV).

Prophecies upon David's life established the covenant of the Lord for Him and for His seed. It's declared there will be one who would execute judgment and bring justice upon the earth. The Lord Jesus came as an offspring of David to fulfill what He promised and, as part of His covenant, a king who would cause the kingdom of God to be established forever and also establish the name of the Lord upon the earth. The Seed of David is giving the throne of his father David to keep the lamp of the kingdom burning. In Jesus' ministry, many times, the people called Him "the Son of David" those who sought Him for healing and for mercy called upon Him and said, "Lord, Son of David, have mercy upon me." When He was entering into Jerusalem in triumph, they cried out to Him, "Hosanna to the son of David!" This shows that he truly came in the flesh and was truly a man with human nature and with all the flaws of men; He left without sin but obeyed the law and lived in righteousness to please the Father.

Prayer: *I pray the Lord cause you to triumph as the Seed of David triumphs in his time.*

Launching Deeper: Jeremiah 23:5, 33:15, John 7:42, Ezekiel 37:24-25, Revelation 5:5.

Hebrew Word Study: "kun"—to be firm, to be established (Strong's Hebrew: 3559).

June 20

SHECHINAH ZOHAR HASHEM

השכינה זוהר השם

Brightness of His Glory

Who being the brightness of his glory, and the express image of his person, and upholding all things by the word of his power, when he had by himself purged our sins, sat down on the right hand of the Majesty on high.

Hebrews 1:3 (KJV)

A lot of mansions in the Father's house, Jesus is still preparing a place for His people to take them with Him. As Jesus said this, the disciples wondered where He was going and asked Him to show them the way; He said He's going to the Father,Philip wondered and said, "Lord show us the Father, and that will be enough." Jesus declared if you have seen me, you have seen the Father. Well, He speaks the words of the Father, He does the works of the Father and shows forth the radiance of the Father, the brightness of the glory of the Father is seen in Him, The glory of the power of God is displayed, for Elohim is glorified in Him for whatever He does, the glory of His wisdom is seen in Him, the glory of the strength and mind of God is seen in Him. He is the light of glory of the gospel and a representation of God. Let the brightness of His glory radiate in your life and glow in His power.

Prayer: *I pray His light shines in your heart to reveal the knowledge of His glory in your life.*

Launching Deeper: John 14:9, 2 Corinthians 4:4, Colossians 1:17.

Hebrew Word Study: "helel"—a shining one (Strong's Hebrew: 1966).

June 21

Rosh Mekhonen Yeshua'at Hashem

ראש מחונן ישועת השם

Captain of Salvation

"For it became him, for whom are all things, and by whom are all things, in bringing many sons unto glory, to make the captain of their salvation perfect through sufferings" (Hebrews 2:10, KJV).

Through Christ's suffering, he has been made perfect in obedience to bear the sins of many and also lead them to the way of salvation, by a perfect sacrifice offered by the perfect high priest, Who was concentrated and placed in the position to be a savior to mankind and also gained for them the promise of the Father. By being concentrated in his suffering, he is able to support and have mercy on those who go through suffering, leading us as the Captain of Salvation to the blessings of the Father, leading us as a Captain of Salvation to the perfect peace of God and eternal and abundant life. Christ as the captain, leads us into all truth. His teachings have been granted unto us. The grace and the ability and the strength to do His will and also to fulfill the plans of the Father in us by the Spirit. He is the commander of your soul and the host of those who have been redeemed and elected to give them the glorious life that has been prepared for them that they believe.

***Prayer**: I pray the Caption of the Lord's Host arise and stand on your behalf.*

Launching Deeper: Hebrews 6:20, 12:2, Joshua 5:14,15.

Hebrew Word Study "tsaba"—army, warfare (Strong's Hebrew: 6635).

June 22

MEKHONEN SHLEIMUT EMUNAH

מחונן שלימות אמונה

Author and Finisher of Faith

Looking unto Jesus the author and finisher of our faith; who for the joy that was set before him endured the cross, despising the shame, and is set down at the right hand of the throne of God. Hebrews 12:2 (KJV)

He is the source of our faith; we follow His example and a matchless way of life that distances him from others who lead a life of faith in the Old Testament. We are the followers of His faith; we look up to Him and put our trust in Him, and keep on believing in Him more than any other treasure or riches, for He rewards those who believe in Him and diligently seek Him. Well, He never changes. He is the object and perfecter of our faith, For He was faithful in His assignment and displayed His faith in the Father who sent Him from the beginning of His ministry on earth. And has now become the Pathfinder of our faith. He continues to lead us to the path of righteousness to the end of our faith, which is the salvation of our souls. Keep on looking up to him, turning aside everything that distracts and causes you to drift away from him by the power of the Holy Spirit. By His strength, you are able to stay on course and focus on Him, the perfector of your faith.

Prayer: *I pray the Lord strengthens your faith to greater heights and remove every block of unbelieve.*

Launching Deeper: Hebrews 5:9, 6:1, 7:11,19,28, 9:9, 10:1,14.

Hebrew Word Study: "betach"—security (Strong's Hebrew: 983).

June 23

HaOmein

האומין

The Amen

"And unto the angel of the church of the Laodiceans write; These things saith the Amen, the faithful and true witness, the beginning of the creation of God" (Revelation 3:14, KJV).

To Him be all the glory and all power, and so be it. Let it be as it has been obtained, for all the promises in Him are yes, and through Him, it's Amen. All to the adoration of the Father, as we glorify Him for what He has done, His mighty works. Christ is the Amen. He is the Sovereign of our faith, so be it of the power of God in our lives. The Amen meaning, the manifestation of all the promise and the fulfillment and what executes the Agenda of God Almighty. The Lord does so according to His word. The Lord does so according to the grace He's giving to us. His might and strength. And from Grace to Grace, let His peace be as he intended for us and let His glory be as he intends for us. The manifestation of His power, for faithful, is he that has given the promise, and He is faithful to bring it to pass. If anyone trusts in anything, let Him trust in the one who is Yes and Amen. The fulfillment of every blessing of the Father is accomplished through Christ, who is true, and Amen. Let His Word for your life manifest.

Prayer: *I pray the Lord does something new in you and perfect all that concerns you.*

Launching Deeper: Isaiah 65:16, Revelation 7:11-12, 19:4, 22:20-21, Philippians 4:23, I Corinthians 16:24.

Hebrew Word Study:"malak"—a messenger (Strong's Hebrew: 4397).

June 24

HaAryeh Shevet Yehudah

אריה שבט יהודה

The Lion of the Tribe of Judah

"And one of the elders saith unto me, Weep not: behold, the Lion of the tribe of Judah, the Root of David, hath prevailed to open the book, and to loose the seven seals thereof" (Revelation 5:5, KJV).

John ran tears when there was no one in the capacity to unfold the mysteries in the book. The angel told John the Lion of Judah has prevailed; He has conquered and qualified to open the scroll to unravel divine secrets and agenda for His creation. He prevails to be outstanding in all His ways. No other creature can open or can accomplish what the Lion did. The lion is a symbol of the tribe of Judah and the symbol of sovereignty, courage, strength, and of power. The blessings of Jacob upon his children show how He likened Judah to that of a lion. It crouches to go after His prey, and no one dares to rouse Him. He conquers and triumphs over His enemies; He subdues and prevails over the powers of evil. Jesus represents the lion-like characteristic of a great and courageous ruler. He is mighty to save and strong to redeem. As a lion, He protects and preserves the church, and if the enemy lifts up himself against you, He's able to lift up a standard of protection and avenge your enemies. Through the Lion of Judah, we have access to the Divine mysteries of His kingdom, full of grace and love and peace.

Prayer: *I pray the Lord unravels unto you things which must shortly come to pass, and let the Lion of Judah roar on your behalf.*

Launching Deeper: Genesis 49:9, Revelation 3:21, 5:4, Numbers 24:9, Hebrews 7:14.

Hebrew Word Study:"amets"—to be stout, strong, bold, alert (Strong's Hebrew: 553).

June 25

Hashem-Yireh

השם-ירכא

The Lord Who Provides

"So Abraham named that place The LORD Will Provide. And it is said to this day, "On the mountain of the LORD it will be seen and provided" (Genesis 22:14, AMP).

We are to recount his divine providence and mercy. He provides for the needs of creation, especially His children who are created in His own image. They have the covenant rights of unlimited provision. They have access to heaven's treasury open unto them whenever the need arises as in Ephesians 3:20: "Now to Him who is able to do exceedingly abundantly above all that we ask or think, according to the power that works in us." We recount His abilities to cover the needs of men—both physical and spiritual blessings—"The eyes of all look expectantly to You, and You give them their food in due season. You open Your hand and satisfy the desire of every living thing." (Psalm 145:15,16). In His providence, His eye is always upon His children. In their straits and distresses, He avails His help in season and out of season, and that is what we recite and recount, for there shall surely be a performance of His promises to His children. If I had not taken the step to the mountaintop, I would not have had the experience of Him. That was a tough operation and a process, but, at the end, I have Him as my provider.

***Prayer:** I pray the Lord cause you not to lack but to be satisfied in His provisions in all seasons.*

Launching Deeper: Genesis 22:8,13, 32:30, Exodus17:15.

Hebrew Word Study: "maqom"—a standing place, place (Strong's Hebrew: 4725).

June 26

HASHEM NISSI

השם ניסי

The Lord Our Banner

"And Moses built an altar and named it The LORD Is My Banner" (Exodus 17:15, AMP).

At Rephidim, the Amalekite came to fight the Israelites, Moses commanded Joshua with his troops to fight whilst He went to the mountain and lifted the staff unto the Lord. They had victory as long as Moses' hands stayed up. They eventually overwhelmed the Amalekites and defeated them. Moses was commanded by the Lord to write a memory and build an altar and called the name "The Lord is My Banner." Banners are to stay up, it is an ensign used by a leader as a standard for the battle. When we lift Him up, He gives us victory over every challenge. The lifting up of our hands with the staff becomes the channel of His divine strength and might being poured upon His people for accomplishment and success. The revelation of Him also gives a promise and an assurance of what He can and will do. He is your Banner, and as you lift Him up, you win the battle. The banner is the prayer. If the flag is down, it's not good news. When the flag is up, it means we are winning. Lift Him up as your Banner and lift up your hands to the holy place and bless the Lord!

***Prayer:** I pray His banner over you be lifted and bring you victory wherever you will be in Jesus' name.*

Launching Deeper: Exodus 17, Psalms 134:2, Numbers 2:2, 17, Psalm 74:4.

Hebrew Word Study: "mizbeach"—an altar (Strong's Hebrew: 4196).

June 27

HaDaqar Echad

הדאקאר אחד

The Pierced One

"And again another Scripture says, 'They shall look on Him whom they pierced'" (John 19:37, NKJV).

God promised to make His children, without exception, immune from all diseases, He will take away their transgression from them. He was pierced for their iniquities, and His wounds bring healing. The sufferings of His body remove every disease and restore us from sicknesses to good health. He heals their spirit, soul, and body, forgiving every iniquity upon obeying the voice of the Lord, with no exception to emotional healing. The Pierced One heals the brokenhearted and binds wounds, Healing and delivering the oppressed of demons, healing from constant afflictions that cause them to generate sickness, certain situations, and troubles. He provides health and revelation unto abundance of prosperity. He will bless your bread and bless your water, for He is the Source of your strength, Jesus had mercy upon the sick and healed them completely, and all will lift up their voices and praised the name of the Lord, for He was anointed and filled with the Spirit to deliver and heal through His pains.

Prayer: *I pray He will not lay on you any kind of plaque that came upon the Egyptians but will put upon every enemy.*

Launching Deeper: John 19:37. 20:25-27. Psalm 22:16, Isaiah 53:5, Psalm 147:3, Jeremiah 33:6, 3 John 1:2.

Hebrew Word Study: "daqar"—to pierce, pierce through (Strong's Hebrew: 1856).

June 28

HASHEM SHALOM

השם שלום

The Lord our Peace

"Then Gideon built an altar there to the LORD and named it The LORD is Peace. To this day it is still in Ophrah, of the Abiezrites"(Judges 6:24, AMP).

"Peace" and "peace be unto you" is a biblical term of friendly greetings and a statement of farewell to demonstrate a friendly disposition. "Shalom Aleichem" a Jewish greeting meaning "May peace be unto you," "Wellness and prosperity be your portion." Anxiety and restlessness come when we lose focus on the fact that God is in absolute control of every situation. "You will keep him in perfect peace. Whose mind is stayed on You, Because he trusts in You (Isaiah 26:3, NKJV). To the believer, peace is the calmness you have when you put your trust in Him in times of challenges. The Lord our peace has an everlasting covenant with us, a covenant of peace, in that peace He establishes us in His presence, in that peace He causes us to increase, and gives us liberty. His covenant of peace gives you perfect rest, alleviates divine wrath, and establishes you in His kingdom of joy and prosperity.

Prayer: *I pray the Lord grants you His peace in every aspect of your life, the completeness of His perfect peace.*

Launching Deeper: Genesis 9:13. Exodus 13:21-22, Psalm 37:11, Isaiah 41:10.

Hebrew Word Study: "batach"—to trust (Strong's Hebrew: 982).

June 29

ADONAI TZIDKEINU

אדוני צדקינו

The LORD our Righteousness

In His days Judah will be saved, And Israel will dwell safely; Now this is His name by which He will be called; 'The LORD Our Righteousness'"(Jeremiah 23:6, AMP).

He is the perfect God, His sovereignty is righteous, and it's eternal. He reigns in righteousness and works in righteousness. In Christ, we have become the righteousness of God, and by the help of the Spirit, believers continue to live and have a right standing with the Almighty. He is the Holy God who fellowships with His people through their sacrifices and obedience to His righteous laws. For in Him alone are righteousness and strength and execution of justice. He takes away sins and makes atonement for their iniquities, for the righteousness of his people is of him. He chooses and anoints His people to minister to Him, sanctify themselves to stand in His presence, and stretches forth His hand against His enemies. There is the proclamation that the dwelling of God is with humanity, He Himself will be with them, and they will be His people, He dwells with them with all his power and His glory, and in His righteousness. In Him, all the fullness of deity dwells, and there is the restoration of the relationship between man and the Lord.

Prayer: *I pray His breastplate of righteousness protects you continually.*

Launching Deeper: Jeremiah 33:16, 2 Corinthians 5:21, Romans 5:17.

Hebrew Word Study:"tsaddiq"—just, righteous (Strong's Hebrew: 6662).

June 30

Hashem Maariskem

השם מאריסקם

The Lord Your Dread

"The LORD of hosts, Him you shall hallow; Let Him be your fear, And let Him be your dread" (Isaiah 8:13, NKJV).

The prophet Isaiah cautioned God's children not to fear the kings of Assyria and those that threatened them, but their object of fear, their dread should be the Lord God almighty, for fear of man is a snare, they should keep trusting the Lord of Hosts, and He will be a place of refuge and a sanctuary to them that fear His name. He tests His people for them to fear His name and keep them from sinning. He chooses His dwelling place for His name to be there and not any other name, not on the earth or underneath the earth, for at the mention of His name, every knee shall bow and tremble at His presence. All creation stands in awe of His presence. He is our dread. No one can stand in His sight when His wrath is poured; He has given us His covenant of grace and life that we will not shift from trusting and depending on Him, for there is none like the great I Am.

Prayer: *I pray the covenant of the Lord will be with you, and He will be your dread and not man.*

Launching Deeper: Malachi 2:5, Psalm 76:7, Genesis 31:52, Numbers 20:12,13, Isaiah 26:3,4.

Hebrew Word Study: "arats"—to cause to tremble (Strong's Hebrew: 6206).

July

And on that day you will say: "Praise the Lord , call upon His name; Declare His deeds among the peoples, Make mention that His name is exalted. (Isaiah 12:4 NKJV)

July 1

HASHEM SHAMMAH

השם שמעה

The Lord Who is There

"All the way around shall be eighteen thousand cubits; and the name of the city from that day shall be: THE LORD IS THERE" (Ezekiel 48:35, NKJV).

We see the manifestation of the presence of the Lord in the universe. We see that He is in here with us. "We give praise and thanks to You, O God, we praise and give thanks; Your wondrous works declare that Your name is near and they who invoke Your name rehearse Your wonders.". When we rehearse His wondrous deeds, He descends by an open token of His presence and manifests His glory amid His people. At the presence of the Lord, there is always shaking and shifting; nature aligns to His will, the mountains are set on fire, the earth trembles, "Tremble, O earth, at the presence of the Lord, at the presence of the God of Jacob, who turned the rock into a pool of water, the flint into a fountain of waters (Psalm 114:7-8, AMPC). We rehearse His presence that goes with us through every desert and turns the dry land into fountains of living waters, that nourishes us and causes us to flourish. He makes the difference when He is there.

Prayer: *I pray the Lord will not forsake you for His namesake. He will be there for you and in you to bless your ways.*

Launching Deeper: Isaiah 12:6, 14:32, 24:23, Jeremiah 3:17, 8:19, 14:9, 33:16.

Hebrew Word Study: "ayar"—city, town (Strong's Hebrew: 5892).

July 2

HaShem Zimrath

השם זמרת

The Lord, My Song

"Behold, God is my salvation, I will trust and not be afraid; 'For YAH, the LORD, is my strength and song; He also has become my salvation'" (Isaiah 12:2, NKJV).

The Lord is my tune and my melody; we express our praise and worship to His name in songs of joy; He has become our salvation, and His right hand does great wonders for His children. When the Egyptians pursued the nation of Israel to the red sea as the Lord hardened their hearts, He became a pillar of fire and stationed between the Egyptian army and the armies of Israel. He hastened His people to cross as they feared what was going to happen. As the Egyptians pursued, Moses gave them assurance that they should stand still and see the salvation of the Lord. They will never see the Egyptians anymore as Pharaoh and his troops followed, Moses stretched his rod at the Lord's command, and the waves covered the Egyptians. By His mighty hand, He led the Israelites to cross the red sea with such splendid victory and delivered them from their enemies. They sang the songs of triumphed gloriously; they ascribed all praises to His name in joyful songs and exalted His name as The Mighty Man of war who has drowned the chariots of Pharaoh in the sea, and His mighty hand dashed their enemies to pieces. He will cause you to sing victory songs as He goes ahead of you to pave the way.

Prayer*: I pray let your heart rejoice in the Lord, and He exalts your horn against your enemies.*

Launching Deeper: Exodus 15, 1 Samuel 2:1, Psalm 118:14, Isaiah 26:1.

Hebrew Word Study: "oz"—strength, might (Strong's Hebrew: 5797).

July 3

HaTzur kol Levavi

צור קול לבבי

Strength of My Heart

"My flesh and my heart fail; But God is the strength of my heart and my portion forever" (Psalms 73:26, NKJV).

When the soul is in distress, the heart is failing, when there is anguish in the spirit, and there is no hope, you don't know what to do, where to go, and who to look up to, who to call in a state of despair. The Psalmist lifted up his eyes and cried unto the Lord for help, the one who made the heaven and the earth. He called upon the name of the Lord, the strength of his heart, and the strength of his spirit. When his heart fails within him, and he is discouraged, and fear of uncertainty grips him, he recognized that the Lord is the one who protects him, and his portion is the Lord who would answer his prayers and deliver him out of every trap of the enemy. He is the one who we put our hope in. Who would quicken your spirit, empowers you and strengthen your heart and strengthen your soul? He is the rock of your heart. The strength of your heart and your fortress in every time of challenge, the one who will defend you for you not to be moved.

Prayer: *I pray be fruitful in all good work and continue to increase in the knowledge of God.*

Launching Deeper: Psalms 40:12, 38:10, 22:14, 84:2, 119:81, 142:5.

Hebrew Word Study: "lebab"—inner man, mind, heart, will (Strong's Hebrew: 3824).

July 4

Avi Hakavod

אבי חב"ד

Father of Glory

"That the God of our Lord Jesus Christ, the Father of glory, may give you the Spirit of wisdom and of revelation in the knowledge of him" (Ephesians 1:17, ESV).

The most glorious Father, the author and giver of all glory and all glorious things, unto Him all glory is due. When we look at the works of His hands, the mighty acts, we stand in awe of Him; we become overwhelmed by such glory and power. The worth and beauty of His Glory make us tremble. Daniel was overwhelmed with the power and glory of the Father, from whom he received the gift of all wisdom, possession of knowledge, quick understanding and intelligence, the fullness and the excellency of the Spirit. He allowed nothing or no one to take these precious qualities away from Him. The fear of God was upon Him, and God gave him the Spirit of wisdom. The Father's wisdom brings you favor and strength, causing you to make wise decisions that lead to success. His covenant with you is to be your God and for Him to live in you. A walk with the Father in obedience to His Word and instructions will lead you to a fruitful, victorious, and glorious life.

***Prayer:** I pray be filled with the knowledge of his will in all wisdom and spiritual understanding.*

Launching Deeper: Proverbs 2:6, 1 Chronicles 29:11, Psalms 24:7,10, 29:3, Ephesians 1:3.

Hebrew Word Study: "chakham"—to be wise (Strong's Hebrew: 2449).

July 5

Avi HaOhrot

אבי הלוט

Father of Lights

"Every good gift and every perfect gift is from above, coming down from the Father of lights, with whom there is no variation or shadow due to change" (James 1:17, ESV).

In the beginning, the Father declared the light to come into existence. When there was voidness and darkness, God spoke the Word to penetrate through the deep shadows, and the brightness of His glory appears as light. Darkness cannot comprehend the great light of God. The intention of darkness is to make what the Lord pronounced useful to be void and useless, unfruitful and unfulfilled, but the Father always commands fulfillment. The intention of the wicked is to make your living and purpose not to come to accomplishment, your gifts, talents, and potentials and everything useless and void, as the enemy was able to divert the divine plan for Adam and also tried to divert Jesus' plan, He will fail in bringing unfruitfulness into your life, it will not stand, you have the Father of light shining upon you His brightness through life in Christ, He will never cease shining through you, it's great enough to keep every form of darkness away from you.

***Prayer**: I pray His light shine upon your life, and your life declares His glory.*

Launching Deeper: Genesis 1:2-5, 14,15, Deuteronomy, 4:19, Psalm 19:1-8.

Hebrew Word Study: "kabod"—abundance, honor, glory (Strong's Bible 3519).

July 6

Avi HaRachamin

אבי רחמין

The Father of Mercies

"Blessed be God, even the Father of our Lord Jesus Christ, the Father of mercies, and the God of all comfort" (2 Corinthians 1:3, KJV).

The compassion and sympathy of the Father never come to an end. He works in mercy and demonstrates His love unto us. As a Father has mercy upon His children, He knows who we are. He's mindful of us that we are dust. He removes our sins from us and takes away our transgressions by His mercies. He has inscribed His children on the palm of His hands and will never forget them. The Father of Mercies is gracious. He remembers His covenant and redeemed them by His mercies; He lifts them and carries us in all our days. At the throne of grace, we receive rich mercies, and we find favor in our time of need. We are alive in Christ and by his grace. He has delivered us from the wrath of judgment, washed us by His blood into new birth, and renewed us in the Holy Spirit. When we cry for mercy in times of challenges, the Lord hears our cries, delivers us, and hides us in the secret place of His presence. He watches over you wherever you will go and will keep you until he fulfills His promises and shows you mercy.

Prayer: *I pray the Lord respond to your prayers with mercy.*

Launching Deeper: Psalm 86:5,15, Daniel 9:9, Micah 7:18, Romans 15:5.

Hebrew Word Study: "rab"—much, many, great (Strong's Hebrew: 7227a).

July 7

HaShliach

ה שליך'

The Chief Apostle

"Therefore, holy brethren, partakers of the heavenly calling, consider the Apostle and High Priest of our confession, Christ Jesus" (Hebrews 3:1, NKJV).

"Apostolos" in Greek is the one who has been sent with a delegated authority, in this verse our Lord Jesus is described as the Chief Apostle. He is the one whom God sent to us to preach and teach the salvation message of God and also atone for our sins. He was made like a man so He can be the merciful and faithful high priest who gives us access to the Father. The Chief Apostle leads the Church to the future glory prepared for them. He completely obeyed the Father's call and will, which became His ultimate price paid for our sins to have salvation and eternal life. Anyone who receives Him receives the Father who sent Him, and whoever listens to Him, listens to the Father. Whoever rejects the Chief Apostle, also rejects the Father, whoever believes in Him also believes in the Father. As believers and as ambassadors, our commission is to receive the Word of our Chief Apostle, receive the bread of life, receive the light of the world. When we accept and believe Christ, we can also share with others to be saved and have eternal life.

Prayer: *I pray you will hold firmly to the faith He has called you into and keep your focus on Him for His strength and grace.*

Launching Deeper: Matthew 18:5, 25:40,45, Luke 9:48, John 5:23, 12:44, Philippians 2:10,11.

Hebrew Word Study: "aman"—to confirm, to support (Strong's Hebrew: 539).

July 8

Tzadik Avdi

צדיק עבדי

Righteous Servant

"He shall see of the travail of his soul, and shall be satisfied: by his knowledge shall my righteous servant justify many; for he shall bear their iniquities" (Isaiah 53:11, KJV).

He achieved success as a humble servant of the Lord. He fully obeyed the Father to fulfill what was written concerning Him and His assignment. When His assignment was completed, the Father exalted and lifted Him high and above. By His obedience, He made it possible for many from all walks of life, from every nation, every tribe, and language, to be counted righteous before the Father as they walk and live by the Holy Spirit. For He bore our sins and redeemed us. As a servant, He put away His kingship to serve humanity and went to the cross as a sinner and died. As a sign of servanthood, He emptied Himself in obedience to the will of the Father. God delights in Him, and He is glorified by this attitude. He served and finished His task, and this character admonishes believers to follow and walk in His steps. In His words, anyone that wants to be great should be a servant and be in the service of the Father.

Prayer: *I pray as you serve as the servant of the Lord, let the Lord gird you with strength, and pour His Spirit upon you in Jesus' Name.*

Launching Deeper: John 17:4, John 19:30, Philippians 2:9-11, 1 Peter 2:21, Isaiah 53.

Hebrew Word Study: "ebed"—slave, servant (Strong's Hebrew: 5650).

July 9

KOHEN GADOL

כהן גדל

Great High Priest

"Seeing then that we have a great High Priest who has passed through the heavens, Jesus the Son of God, let us hold fast our confession"(Hebrews 4:14, NKJV).

The High Priest served us as an advocate between the people and Adonai. Aaron was the head and the first of the chief priests, whose office was established when the nation of Israel was formed. They would come to the temple to meet the Lord and served in various forms that were critical to the people of Israel and their worship to the Most High. The high priest made atonement for the sins of the people with various sacrifices outlined in the law of Moses. In the time of Christ, through His death, He served as our Great High Priest; He has made atonement for our iniquities, for our sins, and our transgressions with His own blood. His priesthood is eternal in the order of Melchizedek and appointed by God. As a divine High Priest in the throne room of grace, He was perfect to perform the perfect sacrifice once and for all before the Father. He is our mediator in the most holy place, presenting a sacrifice for the sins of the entire world and has made us perfect and has drawn us closer to the Father more than ever, always interceding for you and helping you stay close to the Lord.

Prayer: *I pray the merciful and faithful High Priest continues to make intercessions for you as you hold fast the profession He has called you into.*

Launching Deeper: Hebrews 2:17, 5:5-6, 3:1-2, 7, 1 Peter 3:22, 2 Corinthians 9:13.

Hebrew Word Study: "kaphar"—appease (Strong's Hebrew: 3722).

July 10

Bechor Yoresh Kol

בכור ירש קול

Heir of All Things

God, who at various times and in various ways spoke in time past to the fathers by the prophets, has in these last days spoken to us by His Son, whom He has appointed heir of all things, through whom also He made the worlds.

Hebrews 1:1-2 (NKJV)

The Son of God inherits all things as the firstborn and the head of divine agents, being above prophets and other forces in the spirit. The Father has put all things in His hands. After His resurrection, He declared that He has inherited all authorities in heaven and on the earth to save many and also execute judgment. For by Him, all things were made and exist, for the Lord has put everything subjection under Him, including the nations as His inheritance. Through the grace of God, believers have also become heirs by faith and are partakes of the blessings of the covenant, and also become co-heirs with Christ. As heirs of the glory of the Father, we have received salvation and everlasting life in the kingdom of God. In this, we always thank Him and give praise for qualifying us to share the inheritance of the saints who are in the light. You have an inheritance of favor, grace and strength, and heavenly blessings in the Lord.

Prayer: *I pray let not your inheritance be taken away from you, be fruitful and increase in it in Jesus' name.*

Launching Deeper: Matthew 28:18, Luke 19:12, John 3:35, Hebrews 1:6.

Hebrew Word Study: "yarash"—to take possession of, inherit, dispossess (Strong's Hebrew: 3423).

July 11

HaNer

המנורה שלי

My Lamp

"For You are my lamp, O LORD; The LORD shall enlighten my darkness" (2 Samuel 22:29, NKJV).

Caravans at the East carry lamps and torches in the night. Each person carries his own torch or lamp, so they don't fall in open holes or stumble upon heaps. The shining lamp of the Lord lightens the paths of the righteous and takes away every fear of uncertainty in the darkness, helping you to keep a focus on the right way and not to drift to the wrong paths of danger. His commandment help see blockades on your path so you don't fall. The Lord is the Lamp, and His Word is the Lamp. He is the Word as the lamp unto our feet, which gives directions in time of doubt, and support in discomfort. The Lamp gives guidance and instructions, supporting right decisions in daily lives. There is illumination in Him, the light of the lamp that shines in the world. Following Christ gives you a permanent light in your life. The oil of the Spirit gives the light to the lamp. The oil upon your life stands for the anointing that breaks the yoke. The oil and anointing also keep the fire burning to never cease. The Lamp of His presence and His glory will continue to guide you every step of the way.

Prayer: *I pray let The Lamp of the Lord lead your path and His light shine your way, the lamp guide your feet as you take every step of the way.*

Launching Deeper: Revelation 21:23, Psalm 27:1, 84:11, Job 29:3, Psalm 4:6, 18:28.

Hebrew Word Study: nagah"—to shine (Strong's Hebrew: 5050).

July 12

Bais Metzudot

בייס מזוזות

House of Defense

"Bow down thine ear to me; deliver me speedily: be thou my strong rock, for an house of defense to save me" (Psalms 31:2, KJV).

Anytime the psalmist finds himself in any form of danger, he calls upon the name of the Lord. One of Adonai's nature is a habitation of defense. He is a kind of safety that is never threatened. A mighty stronghold of defense, where His people are hidden, in the shelter of His presence to keep them out of the reach of the evil one. Defense in the High Rock where He hid Moses. As part of His promises and covenant, He will be with His children, help and strengthen and uphold them. He has hidden you in the shadow of His wings. A shade against the heat of the day, and a refuge against the storms of life. Disappointments await those who put their trust in the hands of men, in what they have, in chariots, their wealth, their education and not in God, but those who trust in the Lord become like the mighty oak tree whose roots go deep, they become like Mount Zion which cannot be moved but abides forever.

***Prayer**: I pray the Lord cover you from storms. Your defense in time of distress will never fail you.*

Launching Deeper: Jeremiah 43:10, Isaiah 4:6, 25:4, Psalms 91:1, 83:3, 76:2, 50:15.

Hebrew Word Study: "natsal"—deliver, to be delivered (Strong's Hebrew: 5337).

July 13

HADAR

הדר

Majesty on High

Who being the brightness of his glory, and the express image of his person, and upholding all things by the word of his power, when he had by himself purged our sins, sat down on the right hand of the Majesty on high.

Hebrews 1:3 (KJV)

Many admire earthly royalty for its power and dignity. The Majesty of Christ is high and exalted above the royalty of the earth. He is seated at the right-hand side of the Almighty, the majesty in heaven. All majesty belongs to Him, for all things belong to Him, and He is exalted over all, riches and honor come from him, he is the owner of all power and strength, and he reaches out and give it to whomsoever He wills. He is the greatest and full of splendor, creation, and deeds of the Almighty display His majesty. He's worthy of our praise and exaltation. There is no god like Him, His name and nature are majestic and great, and He's majestic in working wonders. The voice of the Almighty breaks the cedars, and It's full of majesty, the Psalmist declared in Psalm 29. In His majesty, He ministers in the heavenly tabernacle and receives honor and glory from the Father. At his right hand is full of righteousness, At the right-hand side of the majesty in heaven is authority and dominion. His presence and protection are given to you by his right hand.

Prayer: *I pray as you set your eye on Him, be zealous for good deeds and your enemies put under your feet in Jesus' name.*

Launching Deeper: 2 Peter 1:16,17, Hebrew 1:3-4, Isaiah 6:1-4, Ezekiel 1:4-28, Habakkuk 3:3-6.

Hebrew Word Study: "malkuth"—royalty, royal power, reign, and kingdom (Strong's Hebrew: 4438).

July 14

Mikveh Yisroel

מקווה ישראל

Hope of Israel

O LORD, the hope of Israel, All who forsake You shall be ashamed. "Those who depart from Me Shall be written in the earth, Because they have forsaken the LORD, The fountain of living waters.

Jeremiah 17:13 (NKJV)

Adonai is the savior of the people of Israel. He is the hope of their fathers, who delivered them from their enemies and brought them to a promised land when they were in distress and afflicted. The Lord was their hope; they trusted in Him, and He preserves them. Hope is not just expecting something, but the trust and confidence of the faithfulness of God and being expectant in his covenant-keeping power. They were extra expectant in the fulfillment of His promises to them as He directs them in His laws, if they would follow and be obedient, they will see the manifestation of His goodness and His favor and His grace upon their lives, if they forsake Him and walk in disobedience, they will be disappointed, but in every situation, if you will keep on hoping in the power of God as the sure foundation of your existence to take care of you, as you believe in His power to heal you, his power to save you and his power to deliver you, you will eat the good of the land and see His prosperity in your life.

Prayer*: I pray the Lord be your sure confidence and let Him restore unto you double.*

Launching Deeper: Jeremiah 14:8, Psalm 71:5, 1 Timothy 1:1, Isaiah 42:4, Acts 28:20.

Hebrew Word Study: "maqor—a spring, fountain (Strong's Hebrew: 4726).

July 15

MIKDASH

מיקדש

Our Sanctuary

"He will be as a sanctuary, But a stone of stumbling and a rock of offense To both the houses of Israel, As a trap and a snare to the inhabitants of Jerusalem" (Isaiah 8:14, NKJV).

The horns of the altar were symbols of grace and salvation and also a place of refuge. When Adonijah tried to make himself king, the announcement of Solomon overthrew him as the king of Israel, he realized he might be in danger for treason; he ran and took hold of the horns of the altar; it became a sanctuary for him, an asylum for him to find refuge, and Solomon had to spare his life for running to the altar. The Lord Himself is our sanctuary, our Holy abode. The ark of His might, a representation of His presence, is His sanctuary with us. Whenever the patriarchs have an encounter with the Lord, they would build an altar and call upon their Maker, and that place becomes a sanctuary and place of His presence and a place of rescue. His name is The Sanctuary for the righteous. When he calls on the name, He is safe. His name is who He is. The name of the Lord is mighty to deliver. Our trust is in the sanctuary of His name. In Him our Sanctuary, we set up our banner, and He will fulfill all of our petitions.

Prayer: *I pray the Lord be your Sanctuary, let Him be a shelter to give you protection from the heat of the day in Jesus' name.*

Launching Deeper: Isaiah 4:6, 26:20, Psalm 46:1,2, Proverbs 18:10.

Hebrew Word Study: "miqdash"—a sacred place, sanctuary (Strong's Hebrew: 4720).

July 16

Shofet HaChayyim v'HaMesim

חופת הימים נגד הממים

Judge of the Living and the Dead

"And He commanded us to preach to the people, and to testify that it is He who was ordained by God to be Judge of the living and the dead"(Acts 10:42, NKJV).

Christ has the authority and the power given by the Father to execute judgment to all people of the earth with His truth, so that all will honor the Son just as the Father is honored. A day is appointed for all men to appear before the judgment seat of Christ to receive the reward of the things done, in our response to the saving grace in the body, be it good or bad, to them who do not know the Great God and do not accept or believe in Him and obey the gospel of the Lord Jesus, they will be rewarded with everlasting destruction and eternal separation from the presence of God. He judges men's secrets in righteousness. By His resurrection and appearance of His kingdom, He has proven to have the right to judge the living and the dead, and they would give an account of themselves to Him. He is coming quickly, and His day of coming is unknown, so occupy yourself with His service and live a life pleasing, acceptable, and blameless in the sight of the Most High.

Prayer: *I pray the Lord keeps you grounded in His service and keeps you blameless at His coming.*

Launching Deeper: 1 Peter 4:5, 2 Timothy 4:1, 2 Corinthians 5:10, Roman 2:16, 17:31, 1:2.

Hebrew Word Study:"chen"—favor, grace (Strong's Hebrew: 2580).

July 17

Melech HaGoyim

מלך הגויים

King of the Nations

"Who would not fear You, O King of the nations? For this is your rightful due. For among all the wise men of the nations, And in all their kingdoms, There is none like You" (Jeremiah 10:7, NKJV).

The nations of the world will bow to the authority of Christ. He is preeminent in the affairs of men and rules over them, for among all systems are the limits in the kingdoms of the world. There is none like our God, who is the king of all nations. He is enthroned over the nations and gives strength, peace, favor, and blessings for His people; He has declared that the nations will remember and turn to Him, and they will bow down before Him, for all powers and dominion belong so the Lord. The King of the Nations will judge the nations. If they obey His Word, He will relent of His judgment. When the kingdom of the nations, kings, and princes, the great and small, the systems and rulers and authorities and governments a cast down, the kingdom of our God stands forever, for Creation displays His glory and His mighty acts. His sovereignty is universal. He rules in the hearts of the people of the nation who believed in Him, and by His Spirit and His grace, His redemptive power is available to all.

Prayer: *I pray the Lord reigns in your sphere of life, and His power be seen as you go to the nations to tell of His goodness.*

Launching Deeper: Psalms 22:28, 72:11, 86:9, 86:9, Jeremiah 5:22.

Hebrew Word Study: "kol"—all, the whole (Strong's Hebrew: 3606).

July 18

Melech kol Kadoshim

מלך קול קדושים

King of Saints

And they sing the song of Moses the servant of God, and the song of the Lamb, saying, Great and marvellous are thy works, Lord God Almighty; just and true are thy ways, thou King of saints.

Revelation 15:3 (KJV)

The song of Moses is a victory song, celebrated by the people of Israel after the Lord delivered them from the hand of the Egyptians by making way through the sea for them to walk through to the other side. This same song is sung by the Saints who stand in the presence of the Lord to celebrate the victory over the world powers of the ages and how they were persecuted and afflicted by rulers of the world, and now they celebrate the great deliverance of the Lord Jesus, the noble act of the Lord, by His righteousness and His faithfulness in which He said that He would be with them even to the ends of the earth, they kept on praising His name and blessed in His name, singing songs of worship as they behold the mighty power of God and his wonderful ways. His praises go beyond the ends of the earth, the nations ascribe greatness to Him, and He is highly exalted. As a saint of the Lord, remember to magnify His work of deliverance and praise Him in your songs.

Prayer*: I pray the Lord gives you victory and also gives you a triumphant song to celebrate His deliverance*

Launching Deeper: Exodus 15, Deuteronomy 32:3.4, Revelation 4:8, 11:17.

Hebrew Word Study: "zamir"—song (Strong's Hebrew: 2158).

July 19

Elohei Yerushalayim

אלוהים ירושלים

God of Jerusalem

"As for the utensils which are given to you for the service of the house of your God, deliver [those] in full before the God of Jerusalem" (Ezra 7:19, AMP).

The Assyrian King boasted of His conquest over other nations when he came to besiege Jerusalem. Jerusalem is very significant because it is the place where the Lord commanded that the people praise Him, for the temple in Jerusalem is His dwelling place, He chose Jerusalem to put his name and His throne there, and all nations gather onto Him. It is the place where the ark was situated, and the temple constructed and established as a place of worship. In the temple in Jerusalem is where burnt offerings are made upon the altar and where the people bring their contributions, offerings, and tithes. The God of Jerusalem is a mighty God, and there's no one like Him. The inhabitants of Jerusalem are commanded to rise to clothe themselves with strength and splendor, and remove every chain of oppression and continue to praise the name of the Lord. Jesus drove triumphantly into the city of Jerusalem, and where He was crucified and resurrected, He gave the promise of the outpouring of the Holy Spirit, which took place in Jerusalem and in the church. The God of Jerusalem encamps round about His city to protect it. Let Him protect you as He protects the city of Jerusalem.

Prayer: *I pray the Lord be the wall of fire around you and grant you grace and favor within your sphere.*

Launching Deeper: 1 Kings 8:44-51, 2 Samuel 6:1-19, Deuteronomy 12:1-7, 2 Chronicles 32:19.

Hebrew Word Study: "shelem"—to be complete (Strong's Hebrew: 8000).

July 20

OHR YISROEL

אוהר ישראל

Light of Israel

"So the Light of Israel will be for a fire, And his Holy One for a flame; It will burn and devour His thorns and his briers in one day" (Isaiah 10:17, NKJV).

At this time, the Lord decreed to break the yoke of oppression of the Assyrians from the Israelite, the Assyrians pride is broken, their time of judgment has come, and He will arise as the Light of Israel to destroy their enemies. He is the light and savior of Israel, the light that gives comfort spiritually, gives security, and cheers them up, is the same light that blazes to consume every evil when the people of Israel have suffered much, He will come to their rescue. He is your stronghold and will avenge your enemies and cause you to shine. He does not remain silent when His people are being treated unjustly; He fights on your behalf and grants relief to any kind of suppression. Their oppressors will be like thorns and briars, like stubble before the fire, they will be destroyed. His burning anger will be kindled against any works of darkness in your life. The Light of Israel comes as the consuming fire to execute judgment on any challenge that fights you spiritually and brings an end to them. Unto you, He will be your glory and Sun.

Prayer: *I pray the light of the Lord blaze in you to do more for the Lord.*

Launching Deeper: Psalm 27:1, Isaiah 33:14, 60:19, 64:1,2, Psalm 84:11.

Hebrew Word Study: "lehabah"—flame, blade (Strong's Hebrew: 3852).

July 21

Ohr kol HaGoyim

אוזן קול הגויים

Light of the Gentiles

"A light to lighten the Gentiles, and the glory of thy people Israel" (Luke 2:32, KJV).

The season of snow falling upon landscape brings the beauty of nature. There is a kind of brightness that is exhibited all around, places are covered with snow. There is a kind of veil that the Lord talks about spreading over the nations, a covering of darkness and ignorance of the knowledge of God (Isaiah 25:7). But the knowledge of God will fill the earth. It will lighten the gentiles out of darkness, to give understanding not only to the Jews but also to the Gentiles and bring them into the knowledge of His saving power. His everlasting purpose to save all human race into the kingdom of God is fulfilled. They will be lead into the wonderful light of God; His righteous words will rest upon the nations. His mercy, faithfulness, and justice will be their portion, and they will be unto Him a kingdom of priests. They will know Him and know His ways, they will be His people, and He will be their God, chosen as His inheritance and to prosper them. As you walk in His light of righteousness, let Him exalt your horn continually and rejoice in Him.

Prayer: *I pray a prayer of intercession that many across the nations all over the world would come to the knowledge of the power of God through Christ.*

Launching Deeper: Matthew 4:16, Ephesians 4:18, Isaiah 42:6.

Hebrew Word Study: "goy"—nation, people (Strong's Hebrew: 1471).

July 22

Elohei Tzidki

אלוהי צדקי

God of My Righteousness

"Hear me when I call, O God of my righteousness! You have relieved me in my distress; Have mercy on me, and hear my prayer" (Psalms 4:1 NKJV).

Yeshurun is a symbolic name, meaning "the righteous (Yashar) people" "the upright one, true and just one" an aspiring character of Israel, His beloved and chosen ones, and by His divine plan to impute His righteousness unto all people through the redemptive work of Christ, taking up our sins upon Himself and dying on the cross for us. Just by believing in Him turns me once a sinner to be right with the God of my Righteousness. He accepts me as righteous and calls me the upright one. He wants His children to walk in His just ways and be partakers of the divine nature, the nature of perfection and holiness being imparted unto us as we identify with Jesus Christ. I have become holy and perfected unto Him. I will not only be called the upright one but will also call upon His name as the God of my righteousness. I bow to Him in worship and praise His righteous deeds. The God of my Righteousness is powerful, great, and holy and has given us the privilege to be called justified and righteous in His sight.

Prayer: *I pray the God of your Righteousness turn to you, be gracious to you, and be your support.*

Launching Deeper: Psalms 11:7, 24:5, 41:12, 17:6.

Hebrew Word Study: "qara"—to call, to proclaim (Strong's Hebrew: 7121).

July 23

OHR HACHAYYIM

אוזן ים

Light of Life

"Then spake Jesus again unto them, saying, I am the light of the world: he that followeth me shall not walk in darkness, but shall have the light of life" (John 8:12, KJV).

There is a light that shines from Zion. From the light, He teaches His ways and His laws that transform lives from darkness to the lives of light. The knowledge of God in Christ gives us the life which blazes into the great light in us that forces of darkness could not extinguish. The light has come upon people living in spiritual darkness of death. He who believes in the light and has the light will himself be the light that will show forth from him and emit rays of the glory of Christ into the lives of others. His salvation extends to the ends of the earth. Let the light life that abides in you show forth to your world and attract souls to the kingdom of God. His light redeems the soul so they can live to see His light. Christ will proclaim illumination. He proclaims truth; he proclaims the glory of God and knowledge of God to the lost world. When you walk in the light and live the light life, you have His grace and power to emit the splendor of His glory.

***Prayer**: I pray as you live the light life. Let His divine illumination come upon you and His glory rest on you.*

Launching Deeper: John 12:33-36, Psalm 50:2, John 1:4-9, 3:19, 9:5.

Hebrew Word Study: "or"—to be or become light (Strong's Hebrew: 215).

July 24

YAASEH RATSON

יאסה ראטסון

The Fulfiller of Our Desires

"He will fulfill the desire of those who fear Him; He also will hear their cry and save them" (Psalms 145:19, NKJV).

The Almighty knows what is in our heart; our needs and wants are always before Him. Those who delight in Him see Him granting their heart desires. The condition is to set Him as your delight, and you will find your great pleasure in everything about Him. Find your pleasure in seeking and serving Him, and be satisfied anytime you come to His presence and enjoy His company. David said, "One thing that I desire is to dwell in His presence all the days of my life and behold His beauty......." (Psalm 27:4) that is finding contentment in Him when this is upon your heart. He is more than able to fulfill your desires when you lift up your face to Him and call upon Him at all times. He grants your request and will not withhold the supplications of your lips. The Fulfiller of your desires will not withhold any good thing from you. The Lord will hear your cry and save you. He is all-powerful and all-knowing of our hearts, keep abiding in Him and His Word and see Him do all things.

***Prayer**: I pray the Lord grants the desires of your heart and brings to fulfillment His promises to you.*

Launching Deeper: Psalm 21:12, John 15:7,16, Psalms 20:5, 43:4, 104:34, Job 27:10 Matthew 7:8.

Hebrew Word Study: "asah"—accomplish (Strong's Hebrew: 6213).

July 25

Oseh HaGadol Ohr

אוסה הגדול אוהר

Maker of the Great Lights

"To Him who made great lights, For His mercy endures forever" (Psalms 136:7, NKJV).

From the time God said, "Let there be light ....." (Genesis 1:3) and caused the lights in the sky's expanse to distinguish between the day and night and to mark the seasons and years the great lights continue to shine as a fixed law of the heavens and the earth. They never break until He gives the command. A representation of His loving devotion that endures forever. He is the source of all lights, the maker of them all and the controller of them, with Him, there is no shifting shadow, He wraps Himself in light like a garment and dwells in His unapproachable light, and still, He cannot be seen, what an awesome radiance of light, from the brightness of His presence. Heavens and the galaxy display the wondrous works of the Almighty; they show forth His handiwork; the great luminaries give life to the universe. They all display the glory of God. His light shines in its perfection upon us and radiates unto us His blessings. As the great lights rise up you each day, let your life be made easier upon the face of the earth, a sign of His goodness and mercy unto you that never fails.

***Prayer:** I pray His great light of His favor and power shine upon you and surround you with His tender mercies.*

Launching Deeper: 1 Timothy 6:16, Revelation 12:1, Job 9:8, Job 37:18, 40:22, Isaiah 40:22.

Hebrew Word Study: "yapha"—to shine out or forth, to cause to shine (Strong's Hebrew: 3313).

July 26

ADON HAKATZIR

אדון הקציר

Lord of the Harvest

"Therefore pray the Lord of the harvest to send out laborers into His harvest" (Matthew 9:38, NKJV).

The Lord God, the father, is the great Sower. He sends forth more laborers in time of harvest. They are the faithful and diligent workers of the field with talents and different ministries in preaching the gospel to the lost that are scattered all over the world. Indeed, the harvest is ripe, there are more souls that need to be reached out with the gospel of truth to give them salvation. He asked us to put the request before Him, which is making intercession for more laborers, more workers in the body of Christ. As Paul asked the disciples to pray that the Word of the Lord would have a free course and the cities across will grow mightily in the Word of God, the knowledge of the glory of God would spread like waters cover the face of the earth. In Revelation 14:15, an angel was asked to swing the sickle, that a time of harvest has come, the crop of the earth is ready to be harvested. When the crops have maturely grown, it means it's ready for consumption. Then it's harvest time, which also means the plantation has been very successful. The Lord Almighty is the Lord of the Harvest. There is the harvest of blessing for you as you continue to do His will.

Prayer: *I pray the Lord of Harvest sends more laborers to His field and increases His grace on His workers in Jesus' name.*

Launching Deeper: Luke 6:12,13, Acts 13:2, 2 Thessalonians 3:1, Psalm 68:11,18.

Hebrew Word Study: "abodah"—labor, service (Strong's Hebrew: 5656).

July 27

Ish Milchamah

איש מילצ'מ

Man of War

"The LORD is a man of war; The LORD is His name" (Exodus 15:3, NKJV).

Let the Divine Warrior rise up and let every enemy be scattered. As He scattered and destroyed the Egyptians who followed the Israelites, he made war against the forces of wickedness and against the principalities of the Egyptians in various forms. He sent forth the plaques and fought against them to deliver his people, and when they had set off to go out to the promised land, they tried to pursue them even when the sea was parted, they continued to follow, Moses declared everyone stands still and sees the salvation of the Lord. The Man of War will fight for you. You only need to be still as they crossed the sea. He turned back the raging sea upon the Egyptians and destroyed them completely. We wrestle not against flesh and blood but against principalities powers and dominion of wickedness in high places, but the man of war will always fight for you. The heavens and the highest heavens belong to the Lord, and He is above. He would answer your enemies by thunder and crush them under his feet every day.

Prayer: *I pray the Man of War arouses Himself on your behalf and causes your enemies to flee.*

Launching Deeper: Psalms 24:8, 45:3, Revelation 19:11-12, Exodus 3.

Hebrew Word Study: "milchamah"—a battle, war (Strong's Hebrew: 4421).

July 28

HaCheleq kol Nachalahi

הכלק עד נח'לאהי

The Portion of Mine Inheritance

"O LORD, You are the portion of my inheritance and my cup; You maintain my lot" (Psalms 16:5, NKJV).

In the allotment of the lands to the Israelites as promised by the Almighty to possess lands of great nations, each tribe received their portion of the lands, but the tribe of the Levites and priest were exempted because the Lord gave Himself as their lot and portion of the lands. The Great and Mighty God has become their inheritance. Everything about Him is for them. If I were to choose, I would choose Him as my portion in the land of the living, for He makes all things that I will ever need and ever hope for. He sustains and maintains them all. There is no other like Him, for His greatness is my inheritance. His blessing and favor is my inheritance, His mercy and goodness is my inheritance, His wisdom and knowledge is my inheritance. I will not be found wanting. His protection and provisions are mine. As the Psalmist chose Him, have the Lord as your portion that no one can take from you.

***Prayer**: I pray the Lord enlages your coast and your territories and maintain for you every blessing given to you as your inheritance.*

Launching Deeper: Psalms 73:26, 119:57, 142:5, 11:6, 23:5,116:13, 21:7-12.

Hebrew Word Study: "cheleq"—portion, tract, territory (Strong's Hebrew: 2506).

July 29

Gibbor Aritz

גיבור אריץ

Mighty Terrible Warrior

But the Lord is with me as a mighty terrible one: therefore my persecutors shall stumble, and they shall not prevail: they shall be greatly ashamed; for they shall not prosper: their everlasting confusion shall never be forgotten.

Jeremiah 20:11 (KJV)

Jehovah appointed Jeremiah as a great prophet in the time of the reign of Jehoahaz. As the Word of the Lord was given to him to proclaim His righteousness for them to turn from their wicked ways, they rebuilt and broke out against Him in persecution even though the Word he gave to Israel came to pass and the cities were besieged by the Babylonians, he cried unto the Lord on their behalf, and He rescued him. The Lord fought for Jeremiah as a mighty warrior. His persecutors did not prevail. They all stumbled and were put to shame. They all became captive to the enemies. The Lord is the great warrior who always fights for His people; He is mighty in battle and mighty to save. If the Mighty Terrible one is with you, who can be against you. He is more terrible than your enemies, than those that come after you. He's more terrible than any challenge and will put them in terror. The Mighty Terrible Warrior would help you and fight the battle. He will strengthen you and defend you.

***Prayer:** I pray the Lord be a brazen wall around you and fight your battles for you.*

Launching Deeper: Psalms 47:2, 65:5, 66:5, Jeremiah 1:8,19, 15:20, 17:18.

Hebrew Word Study: "gibbor"—mighty warrior (Strong's Hebrew: 1368).

July 30

BACHIR

הנבחר

The Elect One

"Behold! My Servant whom I uphold, My Elect One in whom My soul delights! I have put My Spirit upon Him; He will bring forth justice to the Gentiles" (Isaiah 42:1, NKJV).

The one foreknown before the foundation of the world as the Elected Lamb for the atonement of sins of the world. The faithful Father elects the Son and declared, "This is My Son, I have chosen, listen to Him" (Luke 9:35). He is to gather the tribe of Israel to restore and protect them. Though the world despised him, He will be faithful to bring forth justice and will not be discouraged until He establishes justice on earth. He is the elected one to carry out the purpose of the ages to ransom as many as are called, to be the light for the nations, and to give unto them salvation. He is Elected and Chosen to do the great work as a mediator, endowed with the power of the Holy Spirit and called in righteousness to bestow unto you His righteousness. He is elected and kept so you might be kept in Him, elected to be giving as a covenant unto you, to open the eyes of the blind and set captives free from the dungeon to do something new in your life, as you put your trust in Him, have confidence and know you will not be ashamed He will glorify His name in your life.

***Prayer:** I pray the Lord elect and choose you for His special use in His kingdom.*

Launching Deeper: Isaiah 42:1-7, Luke 9:35, Matthew 3:16-17, 12:15-21, 1 Peter 1:18-21.

Hebrew Word Study: "ratsah"—to be pleased with, accept favorably (Strong's Hebrew: 7521).

July 31

Ben Yachid

בן יחייד

Only Begotten Son

"He who believes in Him is not condemned; but he who does not believe is condemned already, because he has not believed in the name of the only begotten Son of God" (John 3:18, NKJV).

He is one of a kind, the only Son of the Father. He is the eternal son and begotten, a representation of the father and sent by him. For He is the one that makes the Father known to those He calls. And anyone who would believe in Him would live and have eternal life. He will not be condemned but raised on the last day. Jesus, as the Begotten Son, followed the instructions and the will of the Father. He did not disobey, and the Father loved the Son and placed all things under his care. The begotten Son was full of grace and of truth and of the glory of God and became superior to angels. For His inherited name is wonderful and powerful beyond all others. By His obedience, He is unique above all, and through Him, we are called and predestined to be sons of God, all to the glory and the praise of the Father. By the Spirit, we have been adopted as His own children and can call Him Abba Father. The Spirit testifies with your spirit, and by the Begotten Son, you have also become His child.

Prayer: *I pray as a child of God be empowered as you believe in Him to do more in your life.*

Launching Deeper: John 3:16, 1:12, 18, Mark 16:16, John 5:24.

Hebrew Word Study: "yeled"—child, son (Strong's Hebrew: 3206).

August

'My faithfulness and My steadfast loving kindness shall be with him, And in My name shall his horn be exalted [great power and prosperity shall be conferred upon him]. (Psalms 89:24 AMP)

August 1

ELOHIM ECHAD V'HECHACHAM

'אלוהים אחד ו'חכם

Only Wise God

"All glory to the only wise God, through Jesus Christ, forever. Amen" (Romans 16:27, NLT).

All Wisdom belongs to the Father, no one is as wise as Him. He is wiser than the wisest, and the nature of wisdom and the originator of wisdom is He. His infinite wisdom is magnificent and above measure. Creation displays depths of the riches of His knowledge and the mighty act of redemption. He revealed His wisdom through Christ, and the expression of the gospel, and in the profound words and teachings of Christ. His wisdom and understanding are pathfinding out, and man's wisdom cannot understand the wisdom of God. The wisdom of His kingdom is revealed to those who receive Him and believe in Him, but to those that do not believe it is hidden in parables, for the wisdom of God would be revealed to rulers and authorities in the heavenly realms through the Church and the Spirit of wisdom given to His children, as given to Solomon and also given to Daniel. The only wise God gives you His wisdom beyond measure in all your decisions of life.

Prayer: *I pray the great and unsearchable riches of Christ, the richness of His wisdom, be given unto you in Jesus' name.*

Launching Deeper: Isaiah 28:29, Psalm 147:5, Jeremiah 10:7,12, Job 9:4, 12:22.

Hebrew Word Study: "bin"—to discern (Strong's Hebrew: 995).

August 2

YOTZER KOL SHOMAYIM V'ARETZ

יוצר רוכב על אופניים שומאים נגד הארץ

Possessor of Heaven and Earth

"And Abram said to the king of Sodom, I have lift up mine hand unto the Lord, the most high God, the possessor of heaven and earth" (Genesis 14:22, KJV).

When Abraham heard that his brother had been taken into captivity in the battle of the Valley of Siddim, he took up his forces to attacked and rescued Lot from the battle. He met the king of Salem, who was Melchizedek, the priest of the Most High, who blessed Him and gave him bread and wine and said, "The Possessor of the heavens and the earth, The Most High has delivered your enemies into your hand" (Genesis 14). For He is all-powerful to save His children. His power fills the heavens and the earth. When the king of Sodom also met Abraham and asked Him to take the goods taking from the war, Abraham referred to Him and said he had taken an oath by the Possessor of the heavens and the earth that He will take nothing from the king, His God is more than able to supply all His needs, and the Lord confirmed His Word concerning Abraham if He possesses the heaves and the earth He can provide you with anything you need He will make sure you do not lack and will perform His work concerning you.

Prayer: *I pray the possessor of the heavens and the earth stand for you and bring you victory in your undertaken.*

Launching Deeper: Isaiah 37:16, 2 Kings 19:15, Genesis 14:18-23, Psalms 115:15, 121:2, 124:8, 134:3, 146:5-6.

Hebrew Word Study: "qanah"—to get, acquire (Strong's Hebrew: 7069).

August 3

NOTZER HAADAM

נוטר הדהם

Preserver of Men

"I have sinned; what shall I do unto thee, O thou preserver of men? why hast thou set me as a mark against thee, so that I am a burden to myself?" (Job 7:20, KJV)

To preserve is to keep safe from destruction. Job in his affliction cried unto the Lord in prayer, in his time of sickness, He cried unto the Lord to preserve him, and He did. He testified that his redeemer lives. The Preserver of Men came to his aid, and he survived. Captivity of human life is sickness, Divine health is living without sickness, and divine healing is being healed by the Lord when one is sick When God's people cried to God as the God of their fathers, He took action and brought them out of their affliction and preserved them, by a Mighty Hand and an outstretched arm with signs and wonders. He keeps them alive. The Lord remembers His covenant with His children, every other thing will fade, but His Word to them stands to keep and preserve them. Anything that is against your joy of life is in captivity. The Lord will preserve you. If He created the heavens and the earth and their host and all things that are in, the seas and all that is in it, if He preserves them all, then He is more than able to preserve and sustain you in all situations.

Prayer: *I pray the Lord gives unto you the mantle of prayer, receive the mystery of prayer that brings the miracles into your life and His power to preserve you.*

Launching Deeper: Numbers 9:6, Psalm 36:6, Exodus 15:26, Job 7:12.

Hebrew Word Study: "natsar"—to watch, guard, to keep (Strong's Hebrew: 5341).

August 4

Tzur Uzzi

צור עוזי

Rock of My Strength

"In God is my salvation and my glory; The rock of my strength, And my refuge is in God" (Psalms 62:7, NKJV).

The Psalmist, David, expresses the stability of God's protection, with his experience as a political fugitive hunted by Saul, hiding in caves and moving from one hiding place to another, David always calls upon the Lord to help, to lead him to a rock no one can reach, a place where his enemies cannot get to him, a higher rock where the Lord will establish His feet never to be moved. As one who was always fleeing for his life, David could easily see how God kept him safe. When He finds a rocky cave to hide, he sees the security of God overshadowing him. When the adversary comes implacably, attacking and trying to destroy you, feel safe and keep your confidence in the Rock of your strength. One thing you should know is your enemies will always stumble and fall at your feet. Storms and challenges of life will be destroyed when they try to get close to you. The Rock of your strength is your firm support. He is the strength of your body, of your mind, and of your spirit, stable protection you can rely upon, a shade in weary times, a protection that is right on time of need.

Prayer: *Let the Lord be your strength and support, and those who pursue you be pursued and be persecuted by the destroying angels of the Lord.*

Launching Deeper: Psalms 61:2, 40:2, 18:2,46. 94:22, 95:1

Hebrew Word Study: "machaseh"—refuge, shelter (Strong's Hebrew: 4268).

August 5

Kapporah

קאפורה

The Propitiation for Our Sins

Whom God set forth as a propitiation by His blood, through faith, to demonstrate His righteousness, because in His forbearance God had passed over the sins that were previously committed.

Romans 3:25 (NKJV)

When man sinned against God and attracted His anger and judgment, there was a need for pardon, a pardon of forgiveness of the sins, by His mercies and love unto us, He sent forth His only son to be the propitiation for our sins and iniquities, to die upon the cross to wipe the punishment and to avert God's anger against us, what a merciful God, a compassionate God who forgives our sins and does not destroy his children. He restrains His wrath and remembers that we are flesh and has reconciled us to Him once again. We are holy in him and unblemished in His presence, the sacrifice of His beloved son atoned for our sins and covered them all for His namesake. Through faith in His blood, His righteousness is shown, not only to us but to the entire world. The people of Samaritan declared when they heard from Jesus themselves and said, they know that He is truly the Savior of the world and no one else, the only propitiation to humanity.

Prayer: *I pray the blood of Jesus speaks better Words and promises for you and yours and mark you for more blessings and favor.*

Launching Deeper: Roman 1:18, 3:25, Ephesians 2:3, 5:10, 8:1,30, Colossians 1:21, Ephesians 2:12.

Hebrew Word Study: "Kaporeth" means "propitiatory" (Strong's Hebrew: 3727).

August 6

Moshi'a kol Bnei Adam

מושיה קול בני אדם

The Savior of All Men

"For to this end we both labor and suffer reproach, because we trust in the living God, who is the Savior of all men, especially of those who believe" (1 Timothy 4:10, NKJV).

As we work together in the service of the Lord, we are partners of grace, and we draw our strength from the spirit of grace, not from our own strength. By his grace, we can do what He has called us to do. The Lord has given us uncommon gifts, different ministries, and different services unto Him to minister in His kingdom. The Savior of all men gives the grace to work out our salvation with fear and trembling, to do His will, and to act according to His good purpose. Let the spirit of grace continue to rest upon us, so we grow from glory to glory. He does not delay in His promises, but He patiently waits for all to receive Him as their Savior. He has given Himself for all, His gifts and power and the heavenly promises as we seek Him for our good and for the sake of our children in which He had promised to give an inheritance and chose them as His own. His name is to be feared. There is no Savior but the Lord Yahweh, who has chosen you to favor and glorified His name in your life.

Prayer: *I pray the Savior of all men, will touch more lives into His kingdom, and many more be used for His glory.*

Launching Deeper: 1 Timothy 2:4,6, Psalm 36:6, Psalm 107:2,5.

Hebrew Word Study: "yasha"—to deliver (Strong's Hebrew: 3467).

August 7

ZERA AVRAHAM AVINU

אפסים אברהם אבינו

Seed of Abraham

"For indeed He does not give aid to angels, but He does give aid to the seed of Abraham" (Hebrews 2:16, NKJV).

As Paul said, salvation is of the Jews, God chose Abraham to bring forth the Redeemer of the world, through His Seed, the entire world would be blessed by the blessing of salvation, a blessing and a promise that was given to him and to every people to show forth the kingdom of God, blessings pronounced upon Abraham by the Priest of the Most High, Melchizedek. Through the lineage of Abraham as the genealogy of Matthew inscribed, the Savior of the world was born by the virgin, a Child and a Son given to the nations, Christ who assumed the nature of seed and taking on a form of a human, not a form of angels, made like His brothers in all ways in order for Him to be merciful and be the faithful High priest to serve God, and to demonstrate the sovereignty of God and His awesome love, grace and mercy to the lost, the helpless, the bound and the ones that are spiritually wayward, to bringing them into the sheepfold and family of God; not to perish, but to have everlasting life.

Prayer: *I pray the blessing of Abraham be established in your life, never to the moved.*

Launching Deeper: Hebrews 2, Matthew 1:1, Genesis 22:18.

Hebrew Word Study: "zera"—sowing, seed, offspring (Strong's Hebrew: 2233).

August 8

HaBen Hamevorakh

הבן המבראך

The Son of the Blessed

"But He kept silent and answered nothing. Again the high priest asked Him, saying to Him, 'Are You the Christ, the Son of the Blessed?'" (Mark 14:61, NKJV).

Before the chief priests and the Sanhedrin, who sought testimonies against Jesus but found no one to do that, they sought for men who would say something bad about him even concerning the law and things he might have done wrong, but all the testimonies did not agree for them to kill him, and they kept asking if He had anything to say about those false testimonies He answered "No," finally they asked if He is the Son of the Blessed and He responded "I AM," He is the Son of Blessed God overall and blessed forever, the Most Blessed One is Himself, He is blessed and is the river of every blessing we can think of, flowing to every creature and all that He has made, proclaiming blessings to everything to be fruitful and multiply, our Lord Jesus is given unto us as an eternal blessing. He is the source of blessings of long life and good health, our peace, prosperity, favor, and victory over enemies, and glorious restorations.

Prayer: *I pray be blessed by the Son of the Blessed and expand your territories to reach others in Jesus' name.*

Launching Deeper: Psalms 2:7, 29:11, 119:12, Numbers 6:26, Isaiah 9:6,7.

Hebrew Word Study: "berakah"—a blessing (Strong's Hebrew: 1293).

August 9

BEN HAELYON

בן האליון

Son of the Most High

"He will be great, and will be called the Son of the Highest; and the Lord God will give Him the throne of His father David" (Luke 1:32, NKJV).

The angel of the Lord came to the city of Galilee to confirm a prophecy to a lady called Mary who was minding her own business, she was greeted as the one favored by God who will kind of greetings it was, but the angel continued to give His Word concerning the one that will be born, He will be great, the established throne and kingship of David will be given unto him. He will reign in Isreal, and his kingdom is endless, fulfilling prophecies of the old testament. The Son of the Most High is appointed as a savior to the nations right from the time he was born. Greatness was seen in Him as a child. Great men traveled from the east to come and have a look as the king born. His great star was identified and worshipped as the born messiah. The Father confirmed His Son as the one in Him. He is well pleased with you, Son of the Most High received honor and glory, and that is what He is given unto you now receive the blessing upon your life.

Prayer*: I decree your star be located by great people. Let them come to you and bring you gifts and favor.*

Launching Deeper: John 11:27, 2 Corinthians 1:19, 3:3, 6:16, 1 Thessalonians 1:9, 1 Timothy 3:15.

Hebrew Word Study: "gaboah"—high, exalted (Strong's Hebrew: 1364).

August 10

BEN ELOHIM CHAYYIM

בן אלוהים ים

Son of the Living God

"Simon Peter answered and said, 'You are the Christ, the Son of the living God'" (Matthew 16:16, NKJV).

At Caesarea Philippi, Jesus asked the disciples what was going on in town about Him, how are people talking about Him, and what they are saying. They gave Him a lot of examples, declaring to Him, Some say he is Jeremiah the prophet, others say Elijah the prophet and John the Baptist," and Jesus asked them who they thought that He was. Apart from all that people are saying, what is their view? Peter did not hesitate, by the divine revelation given to him and declared, He was Christ, the Son of the Living God, upon this rock, the revelation received, the Lord declared He would build His church. The Son of the Living God continues to live because the Father who sent Him lives, demonstrating His special relationship with the Father. He came and did nothing of Himself except what the living Father does, for He loved the Son and showed Him wonderful things, and performed miracles in the life of His children, His goodness, and His mercies. He blesses them and lives among them. They will hear the voice of the Son of the Living God and tremble at His presence. He will preserve and keep you safe and use you to do great things in Him.

***Prayer:** I pray you live in the life of the Living God and show who He is to your environment.*

Launching Deeper: Matthew 11:27, Luke, Psalm 42:2, Matthew 1:16, 16:15, 26:63, John 6:57, 68.

Hebrew Word Study: "chay" means "alive, living" (Strong's Hebrew: 2416a).

August 11

Ruach HaMoshiach

רוח המשיח

Spirit of Christ

"But you are not in the flesh but in the Spirit, if indeed the Spirit of God dwells in you. Now if anyone does not have the Spirit of Christ, he is not His" (Romans 8:9, NKJV).

The spirit of Christ is in us, helping us to cry Abba Father. The spirit of Christ introduces us to the gracious and loving nature of Christ. It is the mind and the Spirit of Christ that gives us the ability and the power to feel free. The spirit helps us to have liberty from the bondage of sin and live in righteousness and gives us His power to pray for the sick and to tread upon the works of darkness and authority over sins. For us to continue His works, He grants onto us the power of resurrection, to not die but live to declare the good works of God. in the spirit of Christ, His holiness is restored unto you, His grace and mercy follow you. You have the joy of Christ; you have the knowledge of Christ; you have the mind of Christ; you have the perfection of Christ; you have the righteousness of Christ; you have the wisdom of Christ; you have the sonship of Christ; you have the eternal life of Christ and seated with Him in heavenly places.

Prayer: *I pray you do great things in Him as He endows you with all His goodness.*

Launching Deeper: John 3:34, Galatians 4:6, Philippians 1:19, Luke 10:19, Matthew 28.

Hebrew Word Study:"Ruach"—breath, wind, spirit (Strong's Hebrew: 7307).

August 12

Ruach kol Etzah Gevurah

רוח קול נצחה גבורה

Spirit of Counsel and Might

"The Spirit of the Lord shall rest upon Him, The Spirit of wisdom and understanding, The Spirit of counsel and might, The Spirit of knowledge and of the fear of the Lord" (Isaiah 11:2, NKJV).

The Holy Spirit is the one that gives counsel to the believer. He is the one that advises and strengthens the believer and gives Him might, and draws him nearer to God. He abides in us and teaches us to know the truth because he is the truth. The spirit of counsel is poured upon us as he rested upon Christ, and out of us would flow rivers of living waters. He assures us that we are the children of God. He equips the believer to speak the Word with boldness. He also helps us and makes intercession for us. He strengthens and equips us. The spirit of counsel will teach you to know the truth. He would instruct you and help you make good decisions. He will remind you of the teachings of Christ and reveal unto you the deep things of God and what the Lord has prepared for those who fear him. The things which no eye has seen, no ear has heard, and no heart can imagine. The counsel of God being revealed to us by the spirit, so we work and live by the Spirit's directions and guidance and the ways of God. In decision making, when you rely on the spirit, He is the one that would help you excel and be successful in life.

Prayer: *I pray the counsel of the Lord takes you to higher places of the earth and opens more doors for you.*

Launching Deeper: John 14:16,17, Romans 8:16, Ephesians 3:16, John 16:14.

Hebrew Word Study: "geburah"—strength, might (Strong's Hebrew: 1369).

August 13

RUACH KOL KAVOD KOL HASHEM

רוח עד קָבוד עד השם

The Spirit of Glory and of God

"If you are reproached for the name of Christ, blessed are you, for the Spirit of glory and of God rests upon you. On their part He is blasphemed, but on your part He is glorified" (1 Peter 4:14, NKJV).

The same spirit that rested upon Christ rests upon you, the Spirit of glory Who gives the victorious exhibition of perfection in times of persecution and afflictions. There is a kind of divine honor and the weight of His glory that comes upon those who go through challenges in serving Him. When the Spirit settles in you, He imparts His power and glory upon you to replace any kind of reproach and shame. You are secured under His shadow as you journey through life. He abides in the hearts of those who go through any disappointments in their plans in life. When we stay in His secret place of His presence, we can hear His voice clear, and His directions are visible in every decision. He gives good counsel and brings God's glory in time of trouble, for the temporal affliction can not be compared with the eternal weight of glory that awaits the believer, for The Spirit of glory empowers you with abundant grace and truth and fulfills every desire for goodness and work of faith with power, so that the name of Jesus may be glorified.

Prayer: *I pray you find favor before the Lord and let Him show you His glory, goodness, grace, and mercy, receive the benefits of the covenant, and do marvelous things.*

Launching Deeper: Numbers 11:25,26, 2 Kings 2:15, Isaiah 11:2, 1 Thessalonians 1:10-12.

Hebrew Word Study: "toqeph"—power, strength, energy (Strong's Hebrew: 8633).

August 14

Elohim Shuv

אלוהים שוב

God of Restoration

"'For I will restore health to you And I will heal your wounds,' says the LORD, 'Because they have called you an outcast, saying: 'This is Zion; no one seeks her and no one cares for her'" (Jeremiah 30:17, AMP).

The Lord's appointed time to restore his people has come. The God of restoration will fulfill His Word to His people when they follow His commands. If they are scattered, He will gather them back to their land and restore their fortunes and have mercy upon them. The psalmist prayed to the Lord that he would restore the joy of his salvation and restore health to live in his presence. In the book of Joel, due to the disobedience of the Israelites, the Lord caused his army of locust to invade their farms; it invaded their corn, the wine, and their oil-olive tree, grains destroyed, wine dries, and oil languishes, and fades away, and farmers are put to shame. Spiritual invasion in a believer's life is an attack on the blessings that have been given to you. With fasting, repentance, and consecration, the Lord will be jealous and have pity upon his people to restore his provision by sending rain and sending the corn, the new wine, and the oil. He will restore protection by driving away the armies and restore his goodness unto you by doing great things. He will restore the continuous flow of the grain, His Word, continuous flow of the wine, His joy, continuous flow of the oil, the anointing, and His blessings in your life.

***Prayer:** I pray the Lord restores all that has been taken from you and gives you rest in all areas of your life.*

Launching Deeper: Jeremiah 30:13, 3:22, 33:6, Isaiah 56:8.

Hebrew Word Study: "shub"—to turn back, return (Strong's Hebrew: 7725).

August 15

Ruach kol Chen

רוח קול חן

Spirit of Grace

And I will pour on the house of David and on the inhabitants of Jerusalem the Spirit of grace and supplication; then they will look on Me whom they pierced. Yes, they will mourn for Him as one mourns for his only son, and grieve for Him as one grieves for a firstborn.

Zechariah 12:10 (NKJV)

The believer here totally depends on the spirit of grace throughout His Christian life. The grace of God is the unmerited favor, the favor we do not deserve that grants us the ability to do the will of God through his grace. He has called you into the eternal glory of Christ and has restored unto you his righteousness and made you strong, given you an established foundation in faith. And He has made His spirit of grace to abound upon you, so you would have all that you need and be equipped into every good work. It helps you and replaces all our weaknesses. The spirit of grace helps us to go before the throne of grace with confidence and receive his mercy in time of need. The spirit of grace helps you in time of weakness, makes you to be who you are in Christ and work through you by his grace, and sets you apart for himself. and increases the grace upon your life.

Prayer: *I pray the spirit pours upon you with grace and power and cause you to be a great witness in Him.*

Launching Deeper: Hebrew 10:29, Proverbs 1:23, Isaiah 32:15, 44:3,4.

Hebrew Word Study: "shaphak"—to pour out (Strong's Hebrew: 8210).

August 16

Ruach Hakodesh

רוח הקדושה

Spirit of Holiness

"And declared to be the Son of God with power according to the Spirit of holiness, by the resurrection from the dead" (Romans 1:4, NKJV).

The spirit of holiness rest upon us, God is spirit, and they that worship him must worship him in truth and in Spirit. The Lord commands us to be blameless and holy as he is holy, perfecting holiness in fear of God as our bodies are the temple of God. We offer our self onto him, holy and pleasing to God, which is our spiritual service of worship. The spirit of holiness dwells in us so we would know him, and with the seal of holiness without which no one will see the Lord, He is the one that establishes our hearts in blamelessness and holiness by causing us to increase in love. The fruit of holiness, His mercy and grace, love and kindness, righteousness prepares you to eternal life. He has chosen you as his own possessions, a holy nation so we can show forth His goodness, that is His covenant relationship with you, and He has qualified you into His Inheritance in the kingdom. For the spirit makes you holy and helps you to live a holy life.

***Prayer**: I pray the perfection of the Lord come upon you to show forth His power in Jesus' name.*

Launching Deeper: 1 Thessalonians 3:13, 1 Peter 2:9, 2 Thessalonians 2:13, 1 Corinthians 6:11.

Hebrew Word Study: "qadosh"—sacred, holy (Strong's Hebrew: 6918).

August 17

Ruach Da'at

רוח ד'ת

Spirit of Knowledge

"The Spirit of the Lord shall rest upon Him, The Spirit of wisdom and understanding, The Spirit of counsel and might, The Spirit of knowledge and of the fear of the Lord" (Isaiah 11:2, NKJV).

The Spirit of knowledge gives the truth about the Father, for the Spirit searches the deep things of God for us. Jesus knew the Father, seen the Father, was with Him in the beginning and revealed who the Father is to us. The knowledge of the Father is the truth. He knows all things and reveals Himself as the truth. The knowledge of God will fill the whole earth as waters cover the sea. All scriptures center on the idea of knowing God and conforming to His eternal will. Ignorance of Him and refusal to know the Lord are condemned many times in the scriptures. This is what will damn the soul. What are knowledge and the Spirit of knowledge, the state of obtaining information about someone or something This is a characteristic of the Spirit of God, who dwells in us and gives us the ability to obtain information about the will, intents, plans, strategies, and purposes of God for our lives. Knowledge of Him helps you to trust in Him. When you get to know that He is your provider, your defender, your deliverer, your healer, the one who gives you eternal life, the one who shows the way, and guides your and fulfills his promises concerning your lives, you keep your faith in Him alone and He rewards you.

***Prayer:** I pray the Spirit anoints you, teach and give you the knowledge of truth, and set you free to prosper.*

Launching Deeper: Jeremiah 31:34, Psalm 43:3, John 8:32, 1 John 5:13, 2 Peter 1:1-8.

Hebrew Word Study: "daath"—knowledge (Strong's Hebrew: 1847).

August 18

Ruach kol Yirat Hashem

רוח קול יראת השם

Spirit of the Fear of the LORD

'The Spirit of the Lord shall rest upon Him, The Spirit of wisdom and understanding, The Spirit of counsel and might, The Spirit of knowledge and of the fear of the Lord" (Isaiah 11:2, NKJV).

The Lord told Moses and the people of Israel to recognize how far He has brought them. He has delivered them from the Egyptians and has led them to conquer and possess the land. Which He promised his fathers, now all that the Lord requires from them is for them to fear the Lord their God, walk in His ways, love Him, serve Him with all their heart and their soul. The initial step of acquiring wisdom is an element of living right with the Lord. The reverential fear of God is honoring His awesome nature, The Spirit of the fear of God rests upon the believer, and He bows in awe and in reverence of His creation, His self-existence, His holiness, His Word, His mercies and compassion, and His judgment. The blessings of the Lord are conditioned in reference to Him. He gives us the heart to fear Him for our own good; He is pleased with those who fear Him and reference His name. When you give reverence to the Lord, you do what is right to receive rich understanding and discover knowledge, for the whole duty of man is to fear the Lord and keep His commandments. The fear of the Lord fades all other fear away and takes away the fear of men. No one can hurt or touch you as you set your heart to fear the Lord.

Prayer: *I pray as you look at life and wonder how God has made your life to be full of His Glory, you will keep on blessing and fearing His name.*

Launching Deeper: Jeremiah 32:39, Psalm 111:10, Job 28:28, Deuteronomy 4:6.

Hebrew Word Study: "nuach"—to rest (Strong's Hebrew: 5117).

August 19

Ruach kol Chayyim

רוח קול ים

Spirit of Life

"Now after the three-and-a-half days the breath of life from God entered them, and they stood on their feet, and great fear fell on those who saw them" (Revelation 11:11, NKJV).

The sustenance of life is the breath of God, the spirit of God. He is the life-giver who supports spiritual and natural life. The spirit of life that breathes into every void and lifeless conditions, it impacts upon the believer a new law that determines his rule of action and rule of behavior. He set him free from the law and power of sin by the life of Christ, which is given by the Word, and it's made manifest in the believer's life to quicken and empower. The Spirit of life is the manifestation of the life of Christ Himself. Walking and living the spirit gives new life, true life, and abundant life, which springs into eternal life to make you free from the yoke and deeds of death. The Spirit plants new purpose, new plans and strategies, new desires and new guidance that causes you to live a righteous life. The life that flows gifts of the Spirit like a fountain of water that never dries. The Lord said He would pour water on the thirsty land, and on the dry land, He would pour His Spirit upon you and His blessings upon your offspring.

Prayer: *I pray the spirit of life fills every dryness in your life and causes His freshness to spring forth in you.*

Launching Deeper: Romans 8:2,11, Ezekiel 37:5-14, Isaiah 44:3, John 4:14,15.

Hebrew Word Study:"mezimmah"—purpose, discretion, device (Strong's Hebrew: 4209).

August 20

Ruach Hakodesh Elohim Chayyim

רוח הקדושה אלוים חיים

Spirit of the Living God

"Clearly you are an epistle of Christ, ministered by us, written not with ink but by the Spirit of the living God, not on tablets of stone but on tablets of flesh, that is, of the heart" (2 Corinthians 3:3, NKJV).

The heart became the spiritual tablet that carries the testimony of a transformed life and a life written by the finger of God in the believer. Paul is testifying about the greatness of the Living God and of what He has done, transforming the lives of the believers in Corinth. They have been conformed into the likeness of Christ by the spirit of the living God; they decide to do His will and commit themselves to be faithful to Him. The spirit helps you in the understanding of the Word of God and to assist you to live His life, that is, the life of Christ. When we practice his goodness and His mercy, His love, and forgiveness, when we practice sharing His love and humility and service, we are being seen as an epistle that is read by the outer world, and we emanate the mind of Christ. When we walk in our own ways, the kind of life letter we show does not inspire our world when we are willful and self-centered. We will put the pen in our own hands to write our own letters, which is in line with the divine letter to bring glory to the Spirit of the Living God.

Prayer: *I pray your life be an epistle that displays the power and grace of God to your world.*

Launching Deeper: Romans 8:5, 1 Corinthians 8:5-10, 2 Corinthians 6:16, Joshua 3:10, 1 John 2:6.

Hebrew Word Study:"shalach"—to send (Strong's Hebrew: 7971).

August 21

Ruach HaEmet

רוח האמט

Spirit of Truth

"The Spirit of truth, whom the world cannot receive, because it neither sees Him nor knows Him; but you know Him, for He dwells with you and will be in you" (John 14:17, NKJV).

No darkness can withstand the power that comes with the illumination of the Word, which is the truth. The spirit of truth leads the way towards the knowledge of truth and the fullness of the truth of God. He reveals treasures hidden in the Word and a revelation of Himself. The world cannot perceive the truthfulness of the spirit because it's under the influence of deceitful spirits who lead to falsehood and darkness. Spirit of truth reveals the verity of the Word of God and all truths that relate to Christ and the Father and of the kingdom, for there is deliverance in His truth. The truth declared is what sets you free from captivity. The believer with the spirit of truth can perceive and receive what the Father gives. He also reminds you what Jesus thought and His intentions into the future and the understanding to know more about His ways, for He searches the deep things of God and makes it known to you to make your ways successful in all you do.

Prayer: *I pray the Spirit of truth guide you and lead you into a deeper revelation of Him.*

Launching Deeper: John 15:26, 16:13, 1 John 2:27, Romans 8:9.

Hebrew Word Study: "gelah"—to reveal (Strong's Hebrew: 1541).

August 22

RUACH CHOKHMAH BINAH

רוח צ׳וקהמה בינה

The Spirit of Wisdom and Understanding

"The Spirit of the LORD shall rest upon Him, The Spirit of wisdom and understanding, The Spirit of counsel and might, The Spirit of knowledge and of the fear of the LORD" (Isaiah 11:2, NKJV).

Give thanks to the Lord, who, by His wisdom, created the universe. The Messiah, with the spirit of wisdom and of understanding, could discern and perceive the right and wrong of human actions, The spirit of wisdom that rests upon Him was seen in His ministry, His teachings and preaching, and the actions He took and His dealings with men. He acted wisely in the affairs of men. His wisdom was extraordinary even when He was a child, His understanding of the Word and the answers He gave the priests in the temple when they asked Him questions about the law astounded them. In His ministry, the people wondered where His wisdom was from because His wisdom was with authority, He was obedient to the Father, and that's what pleases the Father. Received guidance by the spirit in Christ and the knowledge of Him that is, the treasures of wisdom, knowledge and His understanding which is beyond human comprehension.

***Prayer**: I pray let His spirit rest upon you this day and give you His understanding without measure.*

Launching Deeper: Ephesians 1:17, Colossians 2:3, 1 Corinthians 1:30.

Hebrew Word Study: "chakam"—to be wise (Strong's Hebrew: 2449).

August 23

OZ YESHUATI

עוז ישותי

Strength of My Salvation

"O God the Lord, the strength of my salvation, You have covered my head in the day of battle" (Psalm 140:7, NKJV).

In Paul's description of the spiritual Armor, the helmet that covers the head is salvation. It protects the head against any attack. Salvation gives the believer the assurance of his deliverance. The believer's security depends on the Lord. And we have obtained the salvation of the Lord Jesus by his grace, giving us the power to reject ungodliness and worldly passions and to leave righteousness in Him, as we hold on to it for His appearance. As our deliverer, He gives us freedom from distress and the ability to pursue His way, the ability, and the strength through the Holy Spirit to walk in His purpose and do His will. In the Strength of our Salvation, you have forgiveness of sin by grace; you have abundant life by grace, you also have eternal life by grace, and you can do the will of God by His grace.

Prayer: *I pray the strength of salvation preserves you in all seasons and takes you to a higher dimension in Him.*

Launching Deeper: Psalms 18:1,2,35; 27:1, 28:7,8, 118:14.

Hebrew Word Study: "sakak"—to overshadow, to cover (Strong's Hebrew: 5526).

August 24

Cherev kol Gaavah

צ׳רב עד גבה

Sword of His Majesty

Happy are you, O Israel! Who is like you, a people saved by the Lord, The shield of your help And the sword of your majesty! Your enemies shall submit to you, And you shall tread down their high places.

Deuteronomy 33:29 (NKJV)

His love for us will cause him to leave his everlasting glory to come and give himself as a ransom for your life. He loves you as a sinner and loves you as a believer, and cares for you. When we are overwhelmed and in distress, our God commands us to transfer every form of heaviness to the broader and infinite shoulder of His. "Casting all your care upon Him, for He cares for you" (1 Peter 5:7, NKJV). For there is none as great and powerful as our Sword of Excellence, none as stable, immovable and dependable, awesome in praiseworthy, glorious in holiness, perfection in His handiworks. See the Lord move with His Sword in His hands in that situation on your behalf and make these declarations for the day; The Lord will go for you like a mighty warrior, He will lift His Sword in majesty like the king who prevail against your enemies in Jesus' name, for He is the Most High.

Prayer: *I pray every enemy be threshed before you, as the Sword of excellence fights on your behalf.*

Launching Deeper: Judges 7:20, Psalms 7:12, 45:3, 84:11.

Hebrew Word Study: "ezer"—a help, helper (Strong's Hebrew: 5828).

August 25

HAPPORETZ

ה"הפורץ"

The Breaker

The breaker comes up before them: they have broken up, and have passed through the gate, and are gone out by it: and their king shall pass before them, and the Lord on the head of them.

Micah 2:13 (KJV)

When an army is attacking a city in the olden days, mostly there were walls and gates around the city, iron gates that need to be broken through. The army has to break through the walls and the gates in order to reach the city. This happened in Jericho with Joshua and the people of Israel in Judges 6. The Lord gives them instructions as they followed, the walls and the gates were broken down, the Lord broke through the walls and gates for them to conquer the city. The Messiah will go before you, the presence of the army commander, the mighty man of war and mighty in battle, will take the lead and break through every obstacle. He will break in pieces, gates of bronze, and cut through bars of iron and level every mountain. The Breaker will open before you the two live gates and break through the doors open that no one will shut. He breaks through every obstruction and sets the captives free, bringing out the prisoners from prison and matching on triumphantly with songs of deliverance. If the enemy put hindrances and blocks to hinder any flow of blessing, the breaker will breakthrough every gate for you in Jesus' name.

***Prayer**: I pray the Mighty warrior goes ahead of you to make the way straight for you and opens great doors for your life.*

Launching Deeper: Exodus 32:20, 33:14, Isaiah 42:7,13-16, 45:1,2, 49:9,24,25, 63:9, 52:12.

Hebrew Word Study: "parats"—to break through (Strong's Hebrew: 6555).

August 26

HaGadol V'HaNorah

הגאודול והנורה

The Great and Dreadful

And I prayed to the Lord my God and made confession and said, O Lord, the great and dreadful God, Who keeps covenant, mercy, and loving-kindness with those who love Him and keep His commandments.

Daniel 9:4 (AMPC)

Daniel consistently seeks the Lord in prayer and petition with fasting. When he realized Jeremiah's prophecy for Israel's seventy-year captivity had passed, he went before the Lord, who is faithful to His promises and made confessions and petitioned the Lord who is great and dreadful, and greatly to be praised. His name greater than any other gods and does wonderful acts and deeds for His people, exceedingly abundant and above all that we can think or imagine. Daniel pleads for His love, His mercy, His grace, and His faithfulness in all His nature and His perfection, which display His greatness. He is dreadful in His judgments, His wrath, and His vengeance. We stand in awe of Him; He is to be feared and to be trusted. You will not be terrified by anything, for the Lord is with you. He is the God who is great in keeping His covenant and devoted to His love and mercy.

Prayer: *I pray the Lord remembers His covenant of blessing and peace with you and your children's children.*

Launching Deeper: Jeremiah 10:6, Psalm 96:4, Matthew 5:35, Exodus 3:20, Malachi 1:4, Nehemiah 1:5.

Hebrew Word Study: "aheb"—to love (Strong's Hebrew: 157).

August 27

KOREM

כורם שם

The Husbandman

"I am the true vine, and my Father is the husbandman" (John 15:1, KJV).

The Father is the great Possessor of the vineyard; He is the one who connects all his children to the Vine, who is Christ Jesus. As the Lord of the spirit world, He himself cultivates the plant, makes it deeply rooted in the field of His kingdom, and trains it to grow fruitfully. The husbandman makes us well established in His kingdom and causes us to enjoy every blessing of the vine as branches. The branch of the Lord is gloriously beautiful, and the fruit is excellent and attractive. When He plants, He puts a wall of protection around it, digs a winepress in it, plants that do not bear fruit He takes away, and the one that is fruitful He prunes to make it more fruitful. The Husbandman, who is the Father, prunes by discipline and tests that the believer goes through. His pruning yields and maintains a closer relationship with Him and sustains faithfulness. Any plant that He did not plant is pulled out. He is the one that grafts others into the branch to share the nourishment of the Vine. As you stay connected to Him, you will lack nothing and be established in all His blessings.

***Prayer**: I pray you continues to yield fruitfulness as a branch of Him and His anointing flow through you as you stay connected.*

Launching Deeper: Isaiah 5:1, Psalm 80:8, Ezekiel 19:10, Matthew 15:13, 1 Corinthians 3:9.

Hebrew Word Study: "matta"—place or act of planting, a plantation (Strong's Hebrew: 4302).

August 28

El HaNistar

הנסטר

The Invisible God

"Now unto the King eternal, immortal, invisible, the only wise God, be honour and glory for ever and ever. Amen" (1 Timothy 1:17, KJV).

Not even the most perfect man upon the face of the earth can see God and live. Through His mercies and grace and the blessedness of Him, some have seen His back and have beheld a certain part of him. Well, He is invisible. We can see these invisible attributes in creation, and it displays His awesomeness in every creature. The imperfectness of human nature cannot stand the perfection of the Holy God and to behold His beauty. His holiness and perfection require purity of the heart to behold His glory because He is a spirit, as Jesus said, we should worship him in spirit. Jesus is the reflection and the image of the Father. If you see the Son, you have seen the Father, for He has made the invisible Father known to all in holiness and purity, in Christ you can have a view of Him. He is invisible and would be revealed in the future, and the saints shall see Him and see His face, and His name will be on their forehead, you will behold His beauty, and His presence will never leave you.

Prayer: *I pray let all the earth adore and bless the invisible God whose beauty is seen in His creation.*

Launching Deeper: 1 Timothy 6:16, Exodus 33:20, John 1:18, Colossians 1:15, Hebrews 11:27, Revelation 22:4.

Hebrew Word Study: "yophi"—beauty (Strong's Hebrew: 3308).

August 29

HASHEM GIBBOR MILCHAMAH

השם גיבור מילצ'מה

The Lord Mighty in Battle

"Who is this King of glory? The LORD strong and mighty, The LORD mighty in battle" (Psalms 24:8, NKJV).

The Lord gave the Israelites a command that whenever they go to war, and they draw near to the battle and see the chariots and the army bigger than themselves, they should not be afraid, For the Lord who is mighty in battle will go ahead of them and fight the battle and give them the victory. He is the king of glory, the mighty warrior who conquers the enemies at every battle. You should know that the powers of the enemy are under your feet. You are more than a conqueror, and if God is for you, who can be against you? The Lord has given you authority and power to overcome the force of evil in the name of Jesus. The Lord Mighty in battle is strong to destroy every stronghold. He is strong and mighty to destroy every altar in high places lifted to fight against your life. Any form of continuing conflicts, the Lord will destroy in the name of Jesus. He overcomes every principality, every dominion, and satanic rulership. He is mighty in battle to contend with any force that contends with you and gives you the victory.

Prayer: *I pray let the Mighty Man in battle do the things that Him alone can do for you and cause you to triumph in Jesus' name.*

Launching Deeper: Psalms 45:3-6, 50:1, 93:1, Exodus 15:3,6.

Hebrew Word Study: "nakah"—to smite (Strong's Hebrew: 5221).

August 30

HaBoneh

הבונה

The Builder

"For he waited for the city which has foundations, whose builder and maker is God" (Hebrews 11:10, NKJV)

The faith of Abraham marvels at all of us. He believed God, and the Lord credited Him as righteous. When He was called and given the covenant of blessing and to have a promised land to him and his descendant, even though His children possessed their physical inheritance as promised, He still looked and expected the spiritual promised land and a city in the heavens, the one whom only the Father Himself will build, for the Most High is the Great designer, architect, and builder of all things. He builds creation upon His Word, and creation still stands till today. Paul said, if our earthly house of this temple is dissolved, the Lord is building a house that is not made of natural hands but built-in eternity in the heavens for His people. Jesus declared He will build His church, and the gates of hell cannot prevail against it. When He builds, it's everlasting, and its foundation can never be destroyed. Let the Builder build your life, build your family, build your children and build your spiritual life on the solid foundation, the rock that can never be moved at any time.

Prayer: *I pray the Builder build your spiritual life and construct you into the totality of Him*

Launching Deeper: Hebrew 3:4, 13:14, 21:2, 11:16, Revelation 21:14, Isaiah 14:32, 2 Corinthians 5:1.

Hebrew Word Study: "yasad"—to establish, found, fix (Strong's Hebrew: 3245).

August 31

HaRuach kol Chayyim

הרא"ה קול ים

The Breath of Life - Revelation 11:11

"Now after the three-and-a-half days the breath of life from God entered them, and they stood on their feet, and great fear fell on those who saw them" (Revelation 11:11, NKJV).

In the Valley of the Dry Bones, the Lord called Ezekial in the spirit to observe the multitude of dry bones. He asked him if these bones could live again. Ezekiel did not hesitate but referred it back to the Lord and said, "O Lord you know all things." Then the Lord commanded Him to prophecy to the bones to hear the Word of the Lord, that He will cause the Breath of life to enter them and they shall live, when Ezekiel prophesied, the multitude of bones were covered with flesh, the Lord commanded him to prophecy the four winds to bring breathe, breathe came upon them, and behold they heard the voice of the Lord and were raised up as a mighty army of the Lord. When everything looks dead, prophecy the breath of God to bring life and fulfillment, the spirit quickens dead situation to bring hope. His breath of life upon us quickens and helps us to live His life, as the spirit came upon the Lord Jesus in the time of baptism and empowered Him. by His breath, He created the heaven and the earth and caused man to live as a living soul. The breath of Him indwells in you to rise as a mighty person of valor.

***Prayer**: I pray His breath of life come over you and let things be in the manifestation of His power.*

Launching Deeper: Ezekiel 37, Job 33:4, Psalm 33:6, Genesis 2:7.

Hebrew Word Study: "naba"—to prophecy (Strong's Hebrew: 5012).

September

And I have declared to them Your name, and will declare it, that the love with which You loved Me may be in them, and I in them."'

John 17:26 NKJV

September 1

Elohei HaEmes

אלוהי האמי

The Only True God

"And this is eternal life, that they may know You, the only true God, and Jesus Christ whom You have sent" (Johm 17:3, NKJV).

He is the only true God; there is none like Him. Fictitious deities give big names to themselves, but they are not who they say they are by nature. John said He is the true God and eternal, for Christ gives us the understanding to know the true God. His ways are true and just, many have presented themselves as gods to be worshiped, and men have trusted in false gods, but among the thousands on the earth, different gods of various nationalities, none is true. In all His deeds and glorious power and living and loving as the True God of heaven, He will bring all of them to judgment, and the nations cannot stand His wrath; dominion belongs to Him. In fact, the earthquakes and trembles at His presence, the rocks shatter before Him. The Only True God is to be feared and to be praised. His grace and mercies are true, and truth goes out of His mouth and cannot be changed. All knees will bow to Him, and every tongue will proclaim His allegiance.

Prayer: *I pray you receive more illumination in His truth to direct your path.*

Launching Deeper: Jeremiah 10:10, Deuteronomy 4:39, 2 Chronicles 15:3, Isaiah 43:10,11, 45:5,6,10,11.

Hebrew Word Study: "batach"—to trust (Strong's Hebrew: 982).

September 2

HaMelech HaOlamim

המלך האולימים

The King Eternal

"Now to the King eternal, immortal, invisible, to God who alone is wise, be honor and glory forever and ever. Amen" (1 Timothy 1:17, NKJV).

He is the King of the never-ending kingdom, and His authority and dominion go throughout every generation and all ages. The Eternal King reigns and rules forever. He is above all creation. He is the eternal king who gives eternal life. He was before all time, the self-existing One. He is the originator of time and determines the start of ages and the end of ages. Kingdoms of the world and governments do not last through the ages and have limited time. Their dominion and authority always end at a point, and their memories are no more, but the God of all ages exists through every generation and rules in the affairs of men in every generation. He lifts kingdoms and brings down kingdoms to fulfill His purpose and plans through the times that men may know that he is the great God, and the knowledge of Him will cover the earth as waters on the earth. The King Eternal sustains and provides, equips, and empowers you with grace and favor, and will not relent in keeping you safe in His peace.

Prayer: *I pray the King Eternal be glorified in your life in Jesus' name.*

Launching Deeper: Psalm 145:13, James 5:44, Romans 2:7,10, Colossians 1:15, 1 Timothy 6:16.

Hebrew Word Study: "dor"—period, generation (Strong's Hebrew: 1755).

September 3

Hashem kol Ahavah

השם קול אהדות

God of Love

"He who does not love does not know God, for God is love" (1 John 4:8, NKJV).

For His great love, His children are not consumed. For His great love, He protects and provides for them, His greatest and deepest expression of His character, and His great commitment in the relationship to His children. For He is love, and when we abide in Him, His love is perfected in us. It shows we are born of Him, and we know Him. He demonstrates His gracious love to us by sending forth His only son to come and die for our sins, with eternal love, He has loved us to draw us unto Himself and from everlasting to everlasting; He extends this love unto all who fear His name from generation to generation, remembering His covenant with us. This love of God is unfailing and rich unto us and has caused us to be called children of God. In His love, He defends and protects His people like a father will carry the son, and continues to set His love on you and He has chosen you. He has kept his oath of promise and has redeemed you from the captivity of slavery, from the hands of the enemy, and His love extends even to the unlovely.

Prayer: *I pray His love will engulf you as you share with the unlovable.*

Launching Deeper: Psalm 69:27, 89:2, 105:8, 128:6, 1 John 4:9-10, John 15:13, 3:16.

Hebrew Word Study: "aheb"—to love (Strong's Hebrew: 157).

September 4

HaTekhiyyah HaChayyim

תחיית המתים והחיים

The Resurrection and the Life

"Jesus said to her, "I am the resurrection and the life. He who believes in Me, though he may die, he shall live" (John 11:25, NKJV).

He is the personality called life, and where He is, there is the fulness of life Wherever He is, light springs up, the life gives illumination to men and causes men not to be condemned but to be redeemed and have abundant life, which is given to all who believe in Him. They will be raised from the dead and quickened in the last day into eternal life. None will be lost in Him, for He is the personality of resurrection, resurrected by the power of the Holy Spirit, and lives forever. The keys of death and Hades are in His possession, and He gives life to whomsoever that He wills and gives them abundant grace and gift of righteousness, the ones that do not believe in Him forfeits the life given and inherits the wrath of God, for He is the true life, the way of life that leads to the father, resurrected for all so that all will follow suit. Let His resurrection power quicken and revive you to do more in Him.

Prayer: *I pray His resurrection be your portion in every aspect of your life, and His decrees be the theme of your songs wherever you go.*

Launching Deeper: John 5:21, 6:39, 40, 44, Romans 5:17, John 5:26, 6:35, 3:36, Job 19:25-27.

Hebrew Word Study: "zaqaph"—to raise up (Strong's Hebrew: 2210).

September 5

HaAlmavet HaShem

הקב"ה

The Immortal God

"Who alone has immortality, dwelling in unapproachable light, whom no man has seen or can see, to whom be honor and everlasting power. Amen" (1 Timothy 6:16, NKJV).

He is the incorruptible mighty One. There is no mortality in Him. He is the God and who never dies. We ascribe all honor, power, dominion, and glory unto Him. He gives us the heart to seek and know Him as our immortal and ever-living God, who is there forever for you in times of challenges. Through the knowledge of Him, we have access to all things pertaining to life and godliness and His exceedingly and great promises. We have become partakers of the divine nature of eternal life. He will strengthen and empower you in all your ways. He has been active throughout the ages and has never disappointed or fail anyone He calls. The Immortal God has given unto us an immortal inheritance that fades not, reserved in heaven for all His children. The seed of your spiritual birth is incorruptible by the immortal Word of God, you will triumph over your enemies, and know you are justified and vindicated in Him.

Prayer: *I pray any form of hopelessness be transformed into His eternal hope and His glory come upon your life in Jesus' name.*

Launching Deeper: 1 Timothy 1:17, Romans 11:36, Psalm 145:13, John 5:14.

Hebrew Word Study: "nachalah"—possession, inheritance (Strong's Hebrew: 5159).

September 6

Dvar HaChayyim

דבר הים

The Word of Life

"That which was from the beginning, which we have heard, which we have seen with our eyes, which we have looked upon, and our hands have handled, concerning the Word of life" (1 John 1:1, NKJV).

The Lord gives His Word now and then. In every season, there is a Word He gives concerning activities and situations. You really need to pay attention to His voice to hear what He says in that moment. There is the Word He gives in line with the present. Jesus says he who has ears let him hear what the Spirit is saying. He reveals Himself to His people through the Word. He makes us understand the Word, and the evil one will not take it from our hearts. The Word takes root in us for us to have a deeper understanding of the things of the spirit, worries, and cares of life will not choke it. The Word of Life will bear fruit in your life. You will understand what goes on in the spirit with your heart. His Word brings fire in every chapter of evil, and it is hammer destroying every form of wickedness, healing the sick, and building up the believers, for He is the ultimate Author of His own Word, which reaches out to you in any situation and blesses your life to be fruitful.

Prayer: *I pray, as you meditate, and dig deep in His Word of Life, let all you do be successful and prosperous like Joshua.*

Launching Deeper: 1 Samuel 3:21, Mark 4:23, Matthew 13:1, Ephesians 6:16, Joshua 1:8.

Hebrew Word Study: "sakal"—to be prudent (Strong's Hebrew: 7919a).

September 7

DVAR HASHEM

דבר השם

The Word of God

"He was clothed with a robe dipped in blood, and His name is called The Word of God" (Revelation 19:13, NKJV).

The Word of God is the Word of truth and Grace. The spoken Word brings results. It is the power that manifests things into existence. There are no flaws in it, it's trustworthy and perfect in its works. From Genesis to Revelation, not even a Word fails. None of the Words promise failed. He is the Word of God that became flesh and dwelt with men. The Word who is God eternal and lifted above all things. The Word of God is sweet and full of His delight. His Word is irrevocable, active, and living. It is the sword of the spirit and regarded as food for the spirit that makes the spirit to be nourished and continue to flourish. The Lord commanded the prophets to eat the Word and eat the scroll from which they could declare His Word in power to the people. As Peter told the believers to crave the pure spiritual milk of the word, I pray you crave and stay in His word so you may grow in salvation, for its active and results in great deeds. Through Christ, the Word, all things were made, he rules and sustains the order of creation. The Word established creation, let it establish great things in your life.

Prayer: *I declare be blessed by the Word, and let things be turned for your favor as you proclaim the goodness of the Word*

Launching Deeper: John 1:1, James 1:21, Psalm 17:4, 33:6, Psalm 147:18, Hebrews 12:4, Isaiah 55:11.

Hebrew Word Study: "reshith" beginning, chief (Strong's Hebrew: 7225).

September 8

HaKeren Yeshuati

קרן ישותי

The Horn of Salvation

"The LORD is my rock and my fortress and my deliverer; My God, my strength, in whom I will trust; My shield and the horn of my salvation, my stronghold" (Psalms 18:2, NKJV).

The horn is a symbol of royal dignity and power, for strength and honor. Animals with horns use their horns for defense and for attack. Horns are also used for trumpets and to hold oil for anointing, horns of the altar are a place of refuge and are to be smeared with the blood of the sacrifice. The psalmist saw the protection of the Lord as a deliverance from his adversaries. The Horn of Salvation is his source of strength and safety. The Lord declared He will exalt the horn of His servant David and raised a horn of salvation in the family. That horn will drive away the enemies and defend them. The Lord causes your horn to grow and make it as strong as iron, and the horns of the wicked are cut off. The horns in Zechariah's vision were the strength and power of the nations that had scattered the people of Israel. They have lifted themselves against God's people, and He commanded they be cut off. Like Hannah, the Lord will exalt your horn and bring you to great honor and dignity, a place of His strength and power.

Prayer: *In favor of the Lord, the door will be open to you, doors of power and excellence. His favor will make you mighty upon the land.*

Launching Deeper: 1 Samuel 2:1, Zechariah 1:18-21, Luke 1:69.

Hebrew Word Study: "magen"—a shield (Strong's Hebrew: 4043).

September 9

Adir Hashem

אדיר השם

The Glorious Lord

"But there the glorious Lord will be unto us a place of broad rivers and streams; wherein shall go no galley with oars, neither shall gallant ship pass thereby" (Isaiah 33:21, KJV).

When there is no river in Jerusalem, the Lord Himself will be a source of streams for the land, The glorious Lord will Stream down to provide water for the people, and every nourishment will be provided and be the benefit for them. He will be onto His people, streams of light and grace and mercy. Every dry land had become a land flowing with springs of water to His children. He will cause us to have peace like a river and our righteousness like waves of the sea, and He will be our God, and we will be His people, and we will be present in His glorious presence and A glorious union. We will have with Him and give His glorious power to His children. The glorious Lord reveal His glory in the works of His hands and in His name, for His glory shines over the earth and shines over you.

***Prayer**: I pray the Lord's presence fills your life like broad rivers to bring fruitfulness and increase into your life.*

Launching Deeper: Psalm 29:3, Acts 7:2, 2 Corinthians 4:4-6.

Hebrew Word Study "nahar"—a stream, river (Strong's Hebrew: 5104).

September 10

HaEl Hagadol HaGibbor

הלל הגדור הגיבור

The Great and Powerful God

You show unfailing love to thousands, but you also bring the consequences of one generation's sin upon the next. You are the great and powerful God, the Lord of Heaven's Armies.

Jeremiah 32:18 (NLT)

The power of God is unlimited. He is all-powerful and can do everything that he wills. With Him, all things are possible. His throne is established for ages and forever. He rules in power and has clothed himself with strength, and established the world that can never be moved. Whatever He purposed, He establishes it. No one can fathom the deep secrets of His power; they are higher than the heavens and deeper than the deepest. His name displays His might and power, and there is no one like Him. We see power and might in the work of redemption; He is mighty in saving His children; great in loving His children, and is powerful in having mercy upon them to redeem and to call his children to His kingdom. Through the proclamation and declaration of the gospel, the Great and Mighty God showed forth His wonders in His son Jesus Christ; He is powerful in keeping His promise and fulfilling His plans and purpose in your life, His greatness is seen in the weakness of His children. Through His power, you can defeat every work of darkness. Let His might and power be praised.

***Prayer:** I pray let His powerful intentions and splendid plans for your life never be thwarted, and let all be fulfilled in Jesus' name.*

Launching Deeper: Psalm 68:35, 2 Corinthians 4:7, Ephesians 6:10, Philippians 3:10.

Hebrew Word Study: "chesen" royal, power (Strong's Hebrew: 2632).

September 11

HaHeikhal

ההיכל

The Temple

"But I saw no temple in it, for the Lord God Almighty and the Lamb are its temple" (Revelation 21:22, NKJV).

The Lord promised the Israelite He will make His dwelling place among His people and be their God. In the revelation of John the Apostle, towards the end part of his encounter, where the Lord showed him the new Jerusalem, the scripture tells us that there was a loud voice that declared the dwelling place of God is now with men; He is going to be among them and make His habitation with His people. The Lord God will be our God, and we His people, the owner of our lives, and allow nothing to harm us. There will be no need of a new temple like the one Solomon built for worship in Israel. This temple is going to be replaced with a glorious and honorable presence of the Lord, for the Lord Himself will be our temple, in the closeness of Him, where we would have direct and immediate and uninterrupted communion with Him and the Lamb forever; therefore, we would not think of going to the temple to pray but have Him as our Temple and worship Him eternally.

Prayer: *I pray His presence abides with you all the days of your life as you keep communing with Him.*

Launching Deeper: Revelation 1:8, 11:17, 1 Kings 8:27, 2 Chronicles 2:6.

Hebrew Word Study: "miqdash"—a sacred place, sanctuary (Strong's Hebrew: 4720).

September 12

HaZabad kol Othim

חב"ד עד עתים

The Giver of Signs

"Ask a sign for yourself from the LORD your God; ask it either in the depth or in the height above" (Isaiah 7:11, NKJV).

When the angel of the Lord came to Gideon, he told him he was going to rescue the people from the Midianites, and Gideon kept on asking the Lord for a sign if the Lord was going to use him for that assignment. First thing he asked the Giver of Signs to give Him was a fleece wet with dew and its surroundings dry, and the Lord gave him that sign. The next sign Gideon asked was the opposite to happen, the fleece dry and the surroundings wet, and the Lord did that without delay. The Giver of Signs being so gracious and patient, answered Gideon's prayers and showed His power. By these signs, the Lord gave an assurance of His presence to Gideon and to encourage him. Signs given to Gideon subdued every fear; the Psalmist prayed that the Lord will show him a sign of His goodness and his enemies be ashamed. As the Lord gave Hezekiah a sign to let Him know He will do what He promised as He did for Moses when he was asked to go to Egypt, Let the Lord show you His wonders and give you a sign of His favor and let His supernatural encounter be your portion in the days ahead.

Prayer: *I pray the Lord gives you a sign this day of His goodness and His power and the great things to be done in your life.*

Launching Deeper: Psalm 86:17, Isaiah 38:7, 8, Judges 6, 1 Kings 13:3, Isaiah 7:14.

Hebrew Word Study: "oth"—a sign (Strong's Hebrew: 226).

September 13

HaShem kol Ahavah Shalom

השם קול אחדות שלום

The God of Love and Peace

"Finally, brethren, farewell. Become complete. Be of good comfort, be of one mind, live in peace; and the God of love and peace will be with you" (2 Corinthians 13:11, NKJV).

To be at peace with someone means you are in a relationship of love and loyalty. The God of Love and peace inaugurates His covenant of peace. He delights in the welfare of His children. His peace is not only the absence of hostility but maintenance of calmness. He causes His children to take pleasure in the abundance of peace, peace with long life, peace in the work of their hands, peace, and security in your place of dwelling. When He blesses you with peace, He rejuvenates your prosperity to flow like rivers that never runs dry and appoint His love as the overseer of your life "Instead of bronze I will bring gold, instead of iron I will bring silver, instead of wood, bronze, And instead of stones, iron. I will also make your officers peace, and your magistrates' righteousness" (Isaiah 60:17, NKJV). He does not take His love away from you at where He establishes His peace. He makes the latter glory be greater than the former, let this be established in your life.

***Prayer**: I pray the Lord equips you with His strength and peace and make you full of His love with faith.*

Launching Deeper: Genesis 37:4, 45:24, Mark 9:50.

Hebrew Word Study: "shalom"—completeness, soundness, welfare, peace (Strong's Hebrew: 7965).

September 14

HaMvorach HaRibbon HaYachid

המבורך והיחיד

The Blessed and Only Potentate

"Which He will manifest in His own time, He who is the blessed and only Potentate, the King of kings and Lord of lords" (1 Timothy 6:15, NKJV).

Like clay upon the potter's wheels, the potter turns the clay how He wants, molds and shapes, and brings to beautiful design. The clay cannot question the potter why He shapes, turns it, and presses it in any way that he wants, so the Blessed God is sovereign in all He does. He does what He pleases, and all He wishes in heaven and upon the earth and created and made them. All exists because of Him. No one questions or stands against what He does, and no one can undo what He does. His love and devotion are so great. With Him all is possible, He rules as king upon His throne high above in heaven, and His throne endures forever. His sovereignty is forever in the heavens and the earth, and there's no one like Him. He is sovereign over men and has the power to exalt and power to cast down. As the Blessed and Only Potentate Lord, His mercies upon you are sovereign, His favor, His grace, and salvation for you are sovereign, it is the same way His blessings for you are supreme, and no force of darkness can take it away from you, .

***Prayer:** I declare His light shines in your darkness for gracious and compassionate are the deeds of the Lord.*

Launching Deeper: Psalm 93:1, Isaiah 40:22, Daniel 7:9, Jeremiah 49:38, Matthew 5:34.

Hebrew Word Study: "nazir"—one consecrated, devoted (Strong's Hebrew: 5139).

September 15

ELOHEI KOL CHEN V'CHESED

אלוהי קול חן נגד חסד

The God of All Grace

"But may the God of all grace, who called us to His eternal glory by Christ Jesus, after you have suffered a while, perfect, establish, strengthen, and settle you" (1 Peter 5:10, NKJV).

By the grace of Adonai, we are saved. By His grace, we have the gift of God. By His grace, our prayers are answered, by grace, we have the favor of God, and by grace, Abel, Noah, Moses, and Mary found favor in the sight of the Lord. This grace abides with us all. God is the source of all unmerited favor and mercies unto His children. He supplies every kind of grace that the believer will need to requite every weakness and helps the believer to do the impossible and overcome every weakness to serve the Lord in righteousness and to minister in all callings and gifts. Whether to preach, to prophesy, and to serve in various ministries all to bring His purposes to completion. His calling you into His kingdom makes you a steward of His manifold grace, adopted, justified, and built up to receive an inheritance to keep on growing in this grace and knowledge of the Lord Jesus who anoints you with His glory.

***Prayer**: I declare praise to the Lord, all people, old men and children, and let them all praise the name of the God of all Grace.*

Launching Deeper: Acts 20:32, 13:43, Colossians 1:3-6, Hebrews 13:9.

Hebrew Word Study: "chen"—favor, grace (Strong's Hebrew: 2580).

September 16

HaShem Eloheinu

השם אלוהינו

Ruler of All, The Omnipotent

"And I heard, as it were, the voice of a great multitude, as the sound of many waters and as the sound of mighty thunderings, saying, 'Alleluia! For the Lord God Omnipotent reigns!'" (Revelation 19:6, NKJV)

The Ruler of All shows forth His power and spreads His fame over the earth. The Omnipotent God chooses His people as His possessions and makes everything to work according to His plan and intentions. He also raises kings to proclaim His name on the earth. All kingships and rulership are His. The Ruler of All can pluck and bring down nations and plants them in places He intends, and by His will and purpose. If they do not, He brings them down. Deities are subjects to His rulership and sovereignty. He is the great God above all gods; who makes kingdoms, rulers, powers, and authorities and disarm their evil forces and triumph over them. All things were made for Him to show forth His dominion and rulership over them all. He will rescue you from those that oppress you; for this reason, the Son of God was made manifest in you to display God's omnipotence and also destroy the works of the devil.

Prayer: *I pray the Omnipotent Father will increase you to have dominion and subdue your territory and have the good of it.*

Launching Deeper: 1 John 3:8, Psalm 95:3, Exodus 18:11, Deuteronomy 10:17, Daniel 2:47, Colossians 1:16, Revelation 12:7-10.

Hebrew Word "malak"—to be king or queen, to reign (Strong's Hebrew: 4427).

September 17

ELOHEI RUCHOT HANEVI'IM

אלוהי רוצ'ו הנביאים

The God of the Holy Prophets - Rev 22:6

"Then he said to me, 'These words are faithful and true.' And the Lord God of the holy prophets sent His angel to show His servants the things which must shortly take place" (Revelation 22:6, NKJV).

John is receiving this revelation as authentication and confirmation of what the Lord had shown the Holy prophets in the old times. The Holy Prophets were His agents to do his biddings and to give divine information to His people, not their own words but His divine oracles to the people of God. They were faithful and humble servants but had divine power and influence. The Holy Prophets, both great and minor, receive from the Holy God through various means, through trances, visions, and dreams. He spoke through them and transferred His ideas and intentions to them. The prophecy about you can be the past, what is presently happening and what must shortly take place. He can reveal supernatural visions of the future. The carnal mind cannot discern what's happening in the spirit. Leaders and governors of nations do not know Him and are incapable of understanding His directions. Jesus reminded the apostles that all the prophets wrote about Him will be accomplished, right from Moses to the last prophet; none will fail. His Word and promises for you will not come void but will surely be fulfilled in Jesus' Name.

***Prayer**: I pray the Lord give you the grace and the anointing He gave His prophets and do more great works in Him.*

Launching Deeper: Revelation 22:7, Genesis 41:32, 1 Corinthians 7:29, Luke 18:31.

Hebrew Word Study: "chalom"—a dream (Strong's Hebrew: 2472).

September 18

CHAYYEICHA V'HAORECH YAMEICHA

’חיאישה נגד ’אורך ימיחה

The Life and Length of Our Days

That you may love the LORD your God, that you may obey His voice, and that you may cling to Him, for He is your life and the length of your days; and that you may dwell in the land which the LORD swore to your fathers, to Abraham, Isaac, and Jacob, to give them.

Deuteronomy 30:20 (NKJV)

Towards the latter part of Moses' life, he gave the command to the people of Israel to remember what the Lord has done for them. How the Lord has kept His promises to bring them to the promised land, the land of blessings and fulfillment, so He gave the command and said, He set before them life and prosperity, blessings and curses; therefore, they should choose life and live and have long life. They are to love the Lord and be obedient to His commands and His judgment by holding closely to Him and never to neglect His Word, for He is their life, the source, and giver of life. The one who sustains, maintains, and preserves life. He is the same God who prolongs your life and causes you to enjoy the life He has given you to its fullest, when you keep abiding in Christ Jesus by faith in Him and by keeping our steps with the Holy Spirit, the fountain of abundant life, He lets you fulfill the number of your days upon the earth with dominion and blessings.

Prayer: *I pray the Lord be the strength of your life and see Him in His light.*

Launching Deeper: Exodus 23:25-27, Deuteronomy 4:40, Psalm 37:3, Deuteronomy 30:6,16.

Hebrew Word Study: "yom"—day (Strong's Hebrew: 3117).

September 19

HaNavi

הנביא

The Prophet

"The Lord your God will raise up for you a Prophet like me from your midst, from your brethren. Him you shall hear" (Deuteronomy 18:1,5 NKJV).

Now at the Beautiful Gate, a miracle happened: the mighty name of Jesus Christ, called upon by Peter, healed a lame beggar. Many people wondered about the miracle and how it happened, and it gave Peter the opportunity to talk about the authority behind the name Jesus and the miracle. Jesus of whom the Jews did not accept and was crucified, whom God the Father raised from the dead, which he Peter had been a witness, is that name the lame man believed in and is healed. Peter confirmed that there is the fulfillment of a prophecy declared by Moses and all the prophets, that a Prophet will be raised among His people, and they will hear Him and be saved. Among the people, He is recognized as One whom they expected, the Carrier of the saving Word from God speaking with authority about God's plans, purposes, and blessings. Jesus as the Prophet pronounced the blessings of God and also announced judgment to those who rejected Him. The Spirit of God anointed Him, and every testimony about His mighty works and outstanding miracles is the Spirit of Prophecy, the originator and significance of all prophecies.

Prayer: *I as you pray to Him, let Him reveal more unto you, and fulfill the word of prophecy upon your life.*

Launching Deeper: Acts 3:11-26, Luke 2:25, 7:16, 24:19, John 1:21-25, John 4:19.

Hebrew Word Study: "nabi"—a speaker, prophet (Strong's Hebrew: 5030).

September 20

Ma'oz kol Chayyim

מעוז קול ים

Stronghold of My Life

"The LORD is my light and my salvation; Whom shall I fear? The LORD is the strength of my life; Of whom shall I be afraid?" (Psalms 27:1, NKJV)

Adonai is the strength and power of His people; He increases the strength of the weak and gives salvation to His children, for their deliverance and their honor rest upon Him. He's always with us and subdues every fear, our strength every morning, and the one who rescues us from every time of trouble. When we are with Him, we will not be afraid. The Stronghold of our Life is the one who empowers and helps us. He upholds us by His right hand and delivers us. He makes our feet like hinds' feet and causes us to walk in high places. The stronghold of my life, my trust, and confidence are in Him alone. He is your sustainer and anchor. You are strong in him and in the power of His might. We stand firm in faith in His grace and in His Word. For He always renews the strength of those who wait on Him, and in every aspect of their lives, He has become our stronghold.

***Prayer**: I pray the Lord will be your strongman and stronghold of your life and let Him overthrow any strong man against you in Jesus' name.*

Launching Deeper: Psalms 18:1,2, 46, 19:14, 28:7,8, Isaiah 41:10, 33:2.

Hebrew Word Study "saad"—to support, sustain (Strong's Hebrew: 5582).

September 21

EVEN NEGEF

אפילו נגף

Stone of Stumbling

"And he shall be for a sanctuary; but for a stone of stumbling and for a rock of offence to both the houses of Israel, for a gin and for a snare to the inhabitants of Jerusalem" (Isaiah 8:14, KJV).

Unbelief caused a sanctuary, an inviolable asylum, and a rock of refuge to become a fatal stumbling block. The Jews could not see Jesus as they expected, they looked forward to see a king to deliver them from the Romans, but He came as a poor servant telling the truth, fulfilling prophecy, healing the sick on the sabbath, claiming sonship, and claiming to be God, so with jealousy and hatred they crucified their Savior, causing a great stumbling block to them. Walking in love is staying in the light that illuminates our understanding and positions our hearts in the love of Christ. In contrast, hatred is a trap to oneself and closes on its prey. It brings darkness to the path and blocks the vision of Him who walks in it and causes Him to stumble, therefore being a stumbling block to himself and to his outside world. Let His love fill our hearts, and His light shine in our path, for we are all living stones being shaped and prepared for God's spiritual building project of royal priesthood and having the privilege and responsibility of offering acceptable spiritual sacrifices to the Father through Christ our Lord.

Prayer: *Let all stumbling block of hatred be removed from the heart, let His light of love shine in the heart in Jesus' name.*

Launching Deeper: Luke 2:33, Luke 20:17,18.

Hebrew Word Study: "Eben (Even) Ezer"—The Stone of Help (Strong's Hebrew: 68, 5828).

September 22

Geza kol Yishai

גזה קול ישי

Rod Out of Jesse

"The Reign of Jesse's Offspring There shall come forth a Rod from the stem of Jesse, and a Branch shall grow out of his roots" (Isaiah 11:1, NKJV).

Isaiah's prophecy about the Savior, a descendant of Jesse of the Tribe of Judah, the roots of Jesse, and out of the lineage of kings and greatness now comes the greater king who comes forth, the Messiah, coming from the common and the lowly. Jesse was a commoner in the city of Bethlehem where the prophet Samuel went to anoint the second king of Israel, the shepherd who was of the desert taking care of sheep and did not have the qualification of a king and did not look like one, but the Lord of Lords who looks into the hearts of men and knows the spirit of men saw the offspring of Jesse as the one that will fulfill what's in His heart, so He chose and anointed Him, from this lineage is the humble servant, a shoot from Jesse, an everlasting plant, born into a poor family in Bethlehem of Judea. Christ was God but took upon Himself an image of a bondservant and obeyed the Father to the cross, and so God exalted Him to His glory. The Lord will shoot you forth to greatness and power, do not despise smaller beginnings, when it looks like all hope is gone and there is no hope, remember He has started working it out to bring it to a wonderful expected end.

Prayer: *I pray that you branch out to the manifestation of His glory and power.*

Launching Deeper: Isaiah 6:13, 11:10, 53:2, Micah 5:2, Ruth 4:17, 1 Samuel 17:58.

Hebrew Word Study "geza"—a shoot from the stump (Strong's Hebrew: 1503).

September 23

HaTzenach

הצמ"ח

The Branch

"Hear, O Joshua, the chief priest, You and your companions who sit before you, For they are a wondrous sign; For behold, I am bringing forth My Servant the BRANCH" (Zechariah 3:8, NKJV).

If the accuser brings Joshua and his companions before judgment to be prosecuted as sinners, wearing filthy clothes, the Lord will send forth His servant, the Branch, as a sign of righteousness to intercede on their behalf. The One who would grow out of this place and build a temple is beautiful and glorious, and those that are ingrafted in Him produce fruit of excellence, for the people of Israel, the one who grew out of the stem of Jesse. One who rules wisely as king upon the throne of David and executes justice and righteousness upon the land, that through Him all who believe would be made righteous. The Branch springs forth and grows; He is such as an example of life to which all men would look up to. He is full of the richness of the heavenly fruits, being Himself the fruitfulness of grace, salvation, and the blessings of the Father. A branch of hope that will spring forth to bring fulfillment of God's intentions for your life.

Prayer: *I pray let the Servant, the Branch intercede on your behalf and be a canopy of righteousness unto you.*

Launching Deeper: Isaiah 4:2, 11:1, Jeremiah 23:5, 33:15, Zechariah 6:12.

Hebrew Word Study: "Zemorah"—branch, twig, shoot (Strong's Hebrew: 2156).

September 24

HaNes kol Haamim

נס קול הים

The Ensign of the People

"And in that day there shall be a root of Jesse, which shall stand for an ensign of the people; to it shall the Gentiles seek: and his rest shall be glorious" (Isaiah 11:10, KJV).

He is a sign of hope for the people, the sign of the banner of salvation that flies across the nation, and as a symbol of light given revelations to the Gentiles who did not know the Lord God. He is the Son of man who is lifted on the cross and draws all men unto himself to have eternal life. Even the Gentiles are granted repentance from the Father as they put their hope in the Son of man. The ensign is Adonai lifted to gather the scattered sons and daughters across the nations and give them rest. By His work of righteousness, He would bring them to a peaceful dwelling of everlasting peace. Those that have not seen His glory and heard about His name and fame would see the established sign from afar on the mountain of Zion and would be called into His presence proclaiming the glory of God among the nations. When Christ the ensign to the people is lifted, as we continue to preach the good news, the Gentiles will come to the light of the knowledge of God, and their lives will be transformed to have everlasting hope, they have peace and eternal life, and the salvation of the Lord rest upon them to lead their lives in the knowledge of Christ.

***Prayer:** I pray His ensign of light arises upon you to radiate His presence to the Lost world.*

Launching Deeper: Luke 2:32, John 3:14, 12:32, Acts 11:18, Isaiah 11:12, 28:12, 49:22.

Hebrew Word Study: "haphak"—to turn, overturn (Strong's Hebrew: 201).

September 25

HaEved kol HaShem

העבודה קול השם

The Servant of God

"Behold my servant, whom I have chosen; my beloved, in whom my soul is well pleased: I will put my spirit upon him, and he shall shew judgment to the Gentiles" (Matthew 12:18, KJV).

Christ is the delighted and chosen Servant of the Lord filled with the Holy Spirit to serve God and to bring justice to the nations. He is the fulfillment of what the prophets spoke. He was anointed to preach and teach the good news to the poor and to declare deliverance, salvation, and eternal life to those that are bound, in captivity, and have been blinded by the prince of this world. The Servant of the Lord proclaimed the true Word of God and released the oppressed from any form of yoke. He was obedient to the Father to come and live among men, took the form of a man, and ministered to the people and to his disciples to fulfill what was written about Him. The Servant served the Father's will and shew forth the way, the lights and the door, and give himself as the bread of life and a sacrifice on the cross for those that would believe in him. He was the humble Servant who walked in humility, and when He completed his task, He was exalted and given the name that was above every name, and by the mentioning of the name Jesus, every knee bows to set as an example for all believers. As we take up a servanthood heart and serve the Lord in humility, He will be our lifter, and He will exalt us and fill our lives with His glory.

Prayer: *I pray the Lord subdue your enemies, and in your outgoings, the Lord be with you and defend you.*

Launching Deeper: Matthew 3:17, Isaiah 42:1, Matthew 12:17, 17:5, Luke 4:18, John 3:34.

Hebrew Word Study: "yighah"—obedience (Strong's Hebrew: 3349).

September 26

MALACH HAELOHIM

מלאך האלוהים

The Angel of His Presence

"In all their affliction He was afflicted, And the Angel of His Presence saved them; In His love and in His pity He redeemed them; And He bore them and carried them, All the days of old" (Isaiah 63:9, NKJV)

The Lord appeared to Moses as an angel and spoke to him about the deliverance of his people in Egypt. He told Moses He heard their cry, and has seen the oppression, and has come to deliver them. The Angel of the presence of the Lord has the form and symbol of the Lord's presence, the image of the glory of God who is the Messiah. Moses declared that if His presence does not go with the people, then they will not take the journey. He should not lead them. He led them through the wilderness and carried them all the way as a man carries his son and as an eagle carries the eaglets on his wings; The Angel of His presence took them through to the promised land by His great power, set His affection on them and redeemed them with His mighty hand from the house of slavery. The Mighty One surrounded them and guarded His people as the Apple of His eye and also commanded that they put away foreign gods and serve the Lord their God. Angel of the presence of the Lord is with you to protect you, to keep you, and to guide you to the fulfillment of His Word concerning your life.

Prayer: *I pray He walks with you every step of the way and never leaves you till all His plans for you are accomplished.*

Launching Deeper: Acts 7:30, Exodus 3:7, 23:20, 33:14,15, Deuteronomy 1:31, 4:37, 7:7, Isaiah 43:1-4, 46:3.

Hebrew Word Study: "nasah"—to lift, carry, to take (Strong's Hebrew: 5375).

September 27

HaMesarep HaUmetaher

המסארף האומטהר

The Refiner and Purifier

He will sit as a refiner and a purifier of silver; He will purify the sons of Levi, And purge them as gold and silver. That they may offer to the Lord An offering in righteousness. Malachi 3:3 (NKJV)

Gold in its raw state does not look attractive, but it's taken through the refinery to be washed and passes through the fire, meltdown, and shaped to the desired design and comes out as a beautiful ornament. The Lord God, by the prophecy of the prophet Malachi, declared Christ as a purifier and a refiner of silver to the house of Levi and the house of the priests. Christ, by preaching the gospel, will purge and refine the church. He will purify and bring the reformation through the working of the Holy Spirit. With patience and love, He would cleanse them and, by the washing of water by the Word, to bring out their best. The refining of the fire cleanses everything that is not of the Lord and brings out the perfection of Christ in us. It fills us with love for the service of God and causes us to do good works in His praise. The work of Christ Jesus as the Purifier and Refiner turns you to be a vessel of honor suitable for the Master's use, filled with His power and anointing working miracles to His glory.

Prayer: *I pray you will be unto Him a sacrifice of praise in righteousness; His spoken Word in you, burn and destroy the works of darkness.*

Launching Deeper: Psalms 4:5, 51:19, 66:10, Proverbs 17:3, 25:4, Isaiah 1:25, Jeremiah 9:7, Ezekiel 20:38.

Hebrew Word Study: "taher"—to be clean or pure (Strong's Hebrew: 2891).

September 28

Cheleq kol Yacov

כלק קול יעקב

Portion of Jacob

"The Portion of Jacob is not like them, For He is the Maker of all things; And Israel is the tribe of His inheritance. The LORD of hosts is His name" (Jeremiah 51:19, NKJV).

People inherit various possessions with different values, wealth and riches are very common inheritances that individuals can acquire, some in enormous value, but none can be compared to the Great "I AM" as the inheritance or the Portion allocated to a person. Yahweh is Jacob's inheritance, and Jacob is Yahweh's inheritance (Deuteronomy 32:9, Jeremiah 10:16). The Lord of hosts is His name. He is the portion established for Israel; He is the one that can make all things possible. His great providence is your portion. His power and love endure for you. He empowers and gives strength to the weary. Jacob's inheritance is not like the other gods. Idols of the pagan nations are worthless, all are handmade, and those who rely on them become just like them. His people should never be afraid of these idols, for they cannot do any harm or do any good. Portion for Jacob, the God of Israel is the true living God, you are His chosen and treasured possession, and He is faithful to His covenant relationship with you and will not fail He will complete His part of the covenant for your life.

Prayer: *I pray the Portion of Jacob showers you with His grace and mercy and let every challenge in your life tremble at His wrath.*

Launching Deeper: Deuteronomy 32:9, Psalms 73:26, 16:5, Jeremiah 10:16.

Hebrew Word Study: "nachalah"—possession, property, and inheritance (Strong's Hebrew: 5159).

September 29

HaRofeh

הרופא

The Physician

"When Jesus heard that, He said to them, "Those who are well have no need of a physician, but those who are sick" (Matthew 9:12, NKJV).

The Lord is the Physician of the spirit, soul, and body. He heals the pain and sickness of the body, be it emotional sickness, heart-brokenness, sorrows, anxieties, fears, and every emotional turmoil, oppressions of the mind, and guilt of the sins of the hearts that injures the conscience and brings defilement to the soul. Christ, the Physician heals the brokenhearted and binds up their wounds; He heals the disease of sin and brings recovery of forgiveness. He takes away our sins as far as the east from the west and remembers them no more. The Physician cures from the bondage of iniquities and transgressions by the remedy of His precious Blood shared for all who believes in Him. He is the author of healing and heals His children from all diseases, and gives the image of His salvation. The Great Physician brings good health, restoration and reveals His abundant peace extended to you like a river. He, being the Sun of Righteousness, will arise upon you and overshadow you with virtues of peace, soundness, strength, and healings from all afflictions.

Prayer: *I pray let no disease come near your dwelling, receive His divine immunity from any pandemic in Jesus' name.*

Launching Deeper: Jeremiah 30:17, 3:22, Isaiah 58:8, Galatians 5:22.

Hebrew Word Study: "marpe"—healing, cure, health (Strong's Hebrew: 4832).

September 30

ELOHIM SALACH

אלוהים סלאך

The God Who Forgives

"You answered them, O LORD our God; You were to them God-Who-Forgives, Though You took vengeance on their deeds" (Psalms 99:8, NKJV).

The only God who pardons and blot out all the sins of His penitent and never remembers them. He is slow to anger, full of loving kindness and mercies. The Forgiving God who not only forgives sins but also our transgressions and iniquities. He has promised to hear us from His throne room and forgive and restore us back to Himself anytime we humble ourselves, seek His face and turn from every evil way. We cannot claim to be without sin. Sin is a nature of man, we were conceived and brought forth in a state of wickedness, and by His mercies, He grants us the ability to come before Him, confess our sins and repent in our hearts. He forgives and purifies us from all unrighteousness by the blood of Jesus, the Lamb of God who takes away the sins of the entire world, cleanses us, and makes us as white as snow according to the riches of God's Grace. The Forgiving God delights in mercy and loves you, no one like Him who pardons, He is always faithful to forgive when we confess.

***Prayer:** I pray His love overshadows and restore you to His goodness and mercies forevermore.*

Launching Deeper: Exodus 34:5-7, Isaiah 43:25, Nehemiah 9:17, Micah 7:18,19, 1 John 1:8,9.

Hebrew Word Study: "anah"—to answer, respond (Strong's Hebrew: 6030).

October

Help us, O God of our salvation, For the glory of Your name;
And deliver us, and provide atonement for our sins,
For Your name's sake!' (Psalms 79:9 NKJV)

October 1

HaRe'a kol Choteim

ידיד החוטאים

The Friend of Sinners

"The Son of Man came eating and drinking, and they say, 'Look, a glutton and a winebibber, a friend of tax collectors and sinners!' But wisdom is justified by her children" (Matthew 11:19, NKJV).

The tax collectors were not very popular in the time of Jesus. It was said that they demanded from the people more than what was expected of them and were corrupted, but those are the ones that Jesus will welcome into His company to dine with, by this attitude He won their heart and transformed their lives. They looked upon Him for hope and found it, an act that many did not understand, as the Son of a Holy God to associate with sinners and walked with them. The Pharisees criticized Him for such an association with sinners. He defended Himself to the Pharisees that, if people are not well, they are the ones who need the doctor, not those who are well, they humble themselves before the Lord; Jesus, the Friend of Sinners, shows His love for them by His death on the cross and invites all to be part of His kingdom of friendship, as He said He stands at the door and knocks whoever hears His voice and opens He will come in as a friend and dine with them.

Prayer: *I pray the Almighty will be your closest friend, and His company will be your delight.*

Launching Deeper: Revelation 3:20, James 4:8, Luke 7:34, 7:39. 19:7, Joshua 1:5.

Hebrew Word Study: "merea"—friend, companion (Strong's Hebrew: 4828).

October 2

HaShachar

השחר

The Dayspring

"Through the tender mercy of our God, With which the Dayspring from on high has visited us" (Luke 1:78, NKJV).

The birth of John brought Joy to the house of Zachariah. He blessed the Lord and praised His name for his promises that have been fulfilled and for bringing the Dayspring to deliver them from their enemies. He praises the Lord, who has shown them mercy and has kept his covenant made to Abraham. The tender mercies of the Lord have been revealed to them and have visited. The Dayspring, which is the light of the dawn, has visited the people of Israel. He is the Messiah that has brought light to the people in darkness and visited them to bring His favor and blessings. It has also brought them the lights of the world, showing a new door is opened onto them. It is the beginning of a new day, a day of hope and vindication, the acceptable year of the Lord to bring deliverance and to bring His power. To guide you to the peace of God. The Dayspring would remove every obstacle out of your way and straighten your path, He will arise and shine upon you, see the Dayspring showing forth his goodness towards your life by the multitude of His loving-kindness and mercy, and He will bring you to your promise land.

***Prayer:** I pray the Dayspring enlighten your path for you to know more of Him, and shine upon all that belongs to you*

Launching Deeper: Psalm 25:6, Isaiah 63:7,15, Numbers 24:17, Isaiah 11:1, Zechariah 3:8.

Hebrew Word Study: "yasad"—to establish, found, fix (Strong's Hebrew: 3245).

October 3

Kol Berakah Avi

קול ברקה אבי

All Generous Father

"Every good gift and every perfect gift is from above, and comes down from the Father of lights,with whom there is no variation or shadow of turning" (James 1:17, NKJV).

He is the one who provides what is good to his children, He remains the same, and his love and kindness never end. Parents know how to provide for their children. Children may need clothing,they may need food and education, others may need motivations, if we know how to provide all these things, how much more Our Father in heaven who loves us more than we can think of, and who has a covenant with us and has promised to never leave us or forsake us. The All Generous Father has endowed us with gracious and wonderful gifts and every spiritual blessing from the heavens; He has filled the earth with His unfailing love; He blesses and makes prosperous and provides for the poor, and onto the sinner, He shows His love and mercy. His generosity is displayed through the death of Christ to give us redemption and eternal life. His generosity has given us sanctification and fields us with the Holy Spirit. You have his wisdom, his comfort, strength, and his encouragement, so you never lack.

***Prayer**: I pray the All-generous God continues to provide for you all that blessings that pertain to life.*

Launching Deeper: Joel 2:28-29, Philippians 4:19, Jude 1:2, John 3:16, Psalm 130:7.

Hebrew Word Study: "nadib"—inclined, generous, noble (Strong's Hebrew: 5081).

October 4

MATANAH HASHEM

מתנא השם

Gift of God

Jesus answered and said to her, "If you knew the gift of God, and who it is who says to you, 'Give Me a drink,' you would have asked Him, and He would have given you living water"

John 4:10 (NKJV)

When the Samaritan woman came to the well and saw Jesus, she was amazed and became more amazed when Jesus asked her for some water. And wondered how Jesus would ask her, a Samaritan, for some water to drink. Jesus responded that if she knew who He is and what the Gift of God is, she would rather ask Him of the living water. Jesus implied that there is a gift from God that gives water that is living, a garden spring that flows streams of living water and springs of salvation, the Gift of God is the water of life that quenches every thirst springing into eternal life, this water will also flow from our lives to quench the thirst of others, the Lord Jesus, the Gift of God giving unto humanity, all will come to Him and drink freely. As the Samaritan woman asked Jesus to give her this Gift so she will have rest of coming to the well continually, so the Lord gives you rest from all troubles and challenges by His Gift of living waters.

Prayer: *I pray His gift of living water satisfy and quench every thirst of your spirit and nourish you continually.*

Launching Deeper: John 4:14, 7:37,38, Ephesians 2:8, Revelation 7:17, 21:6, 22:1, 22:17.

Hebrew Word Study: "zebed"—endowment, gift (Strong's Hebrew: 2065).

October 5

HaShem kol Otot v'Mofetim

שריר הכרוב השם נ' מופתים

The God of Signs and Wonders

"I thought it good to declare the signs and wonders that the Most High God has worked for me" (Daniel 4:2, NKJV).

The evidence of the presence and power of God is displayed in our world, His uncountable signs and wonders through his authority and sovereignty. Supernatural deeds are manifested in the scripture. This shows he is the all-powerful and all-knowing God. He multiplied His signs and wonders in the land of Egypt when He delivered His people from Pharoah's oppression by his mighty hand. By His signs and plaques, He brought them out, and brought them into the promised land, and made a name for Himself, a glorious name to this day. His signs and wonders encourage our faith and give us directions, as Elijah prayed on the mount of Carmel that the Lord will answer by His sign of fire to burn the sacrifice, that the people may know that the Lord God is the exceptional God. Elisha also picks the mantle that Elijah left and stood by the Jordan and called upon the name of the God of Elijah, and it parted into two. Great miracles performed by the Lord Jesus also showed His power and authority over nature, and mighty miracles He will do in your life as the God of signs and wonders.

Prayer: *I pray the Lord performs His signs for you and cause you to enter His gates with thanksgiving and go into His courts with praise*

Launching Deeper: 2 Corinthians 12:12, Psalm 135:9, Deuteronomy 6:22, John 4:48, Jeremiah 32:21, Daniel 6:27.

Hebrew Word Study: "mopheth"—wonder, sign, portent (Strong's Hebrew: 4159).

October 6

MA'OZ KOL HAEVYON

מעוז קול האוון

Stronghold for the Helpless

For You have been a strength to the poor, A strength to the needy in his distress, A refuge from the storm, A shade from the heat, For the blast of the terrible ones is as a storm against the wall.

Isaiah 25:4 (NKJV)

The love of God is shared with all people, the needy and the helpless, those in affliction and in persecution. This gives us a picture of the time of Jesus' crucifixion where He also called upon the Father and said, "My soul is exceeding sorrowful even unto death......" (Mark 14:34 NKJV) He was helpless and in distress of the soul, and the heart had pounded, his physical strength was failing, he was being discouraged, clear display of human nature and the necessity of the divine strength. When all hope is gone, know the Lord's presence and power are there to deliver and keep you as your stronghold. When you feel helpless, He declares the enemy destroyed, and every plan of the wicked cannot stand His presence. Know You are secured in his power when all hope is gone. Know there is something within your spirit and in your heart that would be quickened by the spirit of the Lord. He never fails and will always empower you by His grace, which is sufficient for you.

Prayer: *I pray the Lord sends you help from Zion and be stirred by His Spirit to do great in His kingdom.*

Launching Deeper: Isaiah 11:4, 14:32, 29:19.

Hebrew Word Study: "maoz"—a place of safety, protection (Strong's Hebrew: 4581).

October 7

HaRum v'Nasa Echad

הא רום נגד נאס"א אחד

The High and Exalted One

For thus says the High and Lofty One Who inhabits eternity, whose name is Holy: "I dwell in the high and holy place, With him who has a contrite and humble spirit, To revive the spirit of the humble, And to revive the heart of the contrite ones.

Isaiah 57:15 NKJV

Isaiah's vision of the Lord in chapter 6 speaks of the Majesty and exaltation of the throne and habitation of the Most High. His dwelling is High and Holy, and yet He dwells with the lowly and contrite in heart. Even though He lives in heaven in bodily form, He communes with the humble in spirit to bring revival, healing, and restoration. He is High above and does not change in time. His nature is holy in words, in His ways and works, He is infinitely exalted, the impure cannot engage in His presence and his dwellings. The High and Exalted also dwell in the temple of men. His Shekinah glory fills the temple in time of worship, and priests could not stand in the fullness of His glory, Highly exalted in His great light to shine upon the universe. The High and Exalted One promises His blessings on all who fear His name. He is merciful and long-suffering, loving and faithful, who lives in your heart and in your Spirit to uplift and empower you and to make all things beautiful in His own time for your life.

Prayer: *I pray the Lord will be lifted in every aspect of your life and be your stronghold who thrust the enemy before you.*

Launching Deeper: Isaiah 6:1, Psalms 83:18, 97:9.

Hebrew Word Study: "rum"—to be high or exalted, rise (Strong's Hebrew: 7311).

October 8

HaBikkurim Moshiach

הביקורים מושיץ'

Christ, the First Fruit

"But each one in his own order: Christ the firstfruits, afterward those who are Christ's at His coming" (1 Corinthians 15:23, NKJV).

Paul explaining the resurrection to the church of Corinth, that if Christ had risen from the dead, they also would rise from the dead; if not, the basis of our faith is meaningless. There is no hope for every believer, all the preaching of the gospel is of no value, believers who testify about Christ will be false witnesses. Resurrection is the glorious hope of the believer. Christ's resurrection with an immortal body is the first fruit of those who have fallen asleep. As proof, he appeared unto the brethren who had gathered to worship on different occasions, and they all saw Him physically as He foretold them. First fruit is the best of the harvested crops given as an offering to the Lord, recognizing the goodness and blessings of God. He is the first fruits from the dead, raised by the power of the Almighty God to proclaim the glorious light to the lost. He will raise all believers by the sound of the trumpet, and all will be changed into His glorious radiance, and that is our hope, our joy, and our boast in the Lord.

Prayer: *I pray the glory of the Firstfruit be your portion, be strong and be of good courage to do great upon the land*

Launching Deeper: Matthew 16:27,28, Acts 26:23, 1 Corinthians 3:23, 6:14, 15:20-23, Revelation 1:5.

Hebrew Word Study: "parah"—to bear fruit, be fruitful (Strong's Hebrew: 6509).

October 9

Rosh Marashah v'Koachim

ראש השנה נגד קוכים

Head of Principality and Powers

"And you are complete in Him, who is the head of all principality and power" (Colossians 2:10, NKJV).

When we are filled with Him who is the fullness, we receive His fullness, His divine auction run through in us. All authority and powers in heaven, upon the earth, and under the earth is given unto Him by the Father and are made His footstool, and He rules amid them. He disarmed all principalities and powers and exposed their deeds and has displayed that their powers are weakened by overcoming them on the cross. Through the atonement of His blood, He has purchased men and delivered them from the grip of spiritual wickedness in high places. Though we wrestle with principalities, in the name and the power of the Lord Jesus Christ, they are defeated and are put under your feet. He is raised above all rule and authority, and dominion and every other name, for by Him and for Him all were created. You are seated with Him in the heavenly place and make manifest the manifold wisdom of God to the rulers and authorities in the heavenly places.

***Prayer**: I pray the Lord trains your hands to war and causes you to run through troops and bring every wicked principality down in Jesus' name.*

Launching Deeper: 1 Corinthians 15:25-26, Acts 2:32-35, Psalm 110:1, Ephesians 4:8.

Hebrew Word Study: "sar"—chief, ruler, head, captain, prince (Strong's Hebrew: 8269).

October 10

KOL KOFER

מזוודת קול

Ransom for All

"Who gave Himself a ransom for all, to be testified in due time" (1 Timothy 2:6, NKJV).

Ransom is a price to set something or someone free from captivity. In the Old Testament, there are laws concerning the procedure of ransom in so many forms. Ransom can be paid for something or someone who has been devoted to the Lord. They were to be redeemed. Widows could be ransomed from poverty or of any misfortune, and also if a person is guilty of something, the person could be ransomed instead of receiving a punishment, and that is what Our Lord Jesus did for us. His death on the cross was a ransom for all. His soul was made an offering for our sins and reconciliation for our iniquities that produced everlasting righteousness. We have been purchased with the precious blood of Christ, a costly price paid for the salvation of all. The Father's desire is that all will be saved, that none will be lost. This gives us a reason to pray for all to be saved. He gave the nations their ransom. He will give anything for your ransom and drive every enemy out of your sight. For nothing can take you out His hands.

Prayer: *I declare as you acquaint yourself with Him, and be at peace and let good come your way and let His favor never leave you.*

Launching Deeper: Job 33:24, Isaiah 53:6, Matthew 20:28.

Hebrew Word Study: "kopher"—the price of a life, ransom (Strong's Hebrew: 3724a).

October 11

HaOseh Gadol Peleh

האוזה גדל פלה

The Performer of Great Wonders

"Who is like You, O Lord, among the gods? Who is like You, glorious in holiness, Fearful in praises, doing wonders?" (Exodus 15:11, NKJV)

This title depicts the uniqueness of the God we serve. There is no God like our God who performs wonders. The performer of Great Wonders is incomparable. David speaks of the greatness of the acts and deeds of the Lord in his life in Psalm 71, how the Lord had been exceedingly faithful in His covenant with Him right from his youthful days till the time he was old. The Performer did marvelous things in his life; He gave him victory in battle. He saved, sustained, taught, and comforted him in troubles. His creation cannot be fathomed. His blessings are exceedingly great upon every fiber of creation with outstanding activities, His miracles are unspeakable and exceed every boundary, His salvation unto men is everlasting, His peace passes all understanding, and His faithfulness and blessings is immeasurable. The Doer of Great wonders will command victory for you this day. He has sustained you from birth and preserved you, all that seek to hurt you are disappointed and ashamed. He is doing great wonders for you, and you will praise Him continually.

Prayer: *I pray the Lord who performs great wonders will work marvelous breakthroughs for you and bless you with covenant blessings.*

Launching Deeper: Psalm 71, Psalm 136:4, Joshua 3:5, Psalm 72:18, 86:10.

Hebrew Word Study: "pala"—wondrous works (Strong's Hebrew: 5381).

October 12

Saad Kol

סעד קול

Upholder of all Things

Who being the brightness of His glory and the express image of His person, and upholding all things by the Word of His power, when He had by Himself purged our sins, sat down at the right hand of the Majesty on high.

Hebrews 1:3 (NKJV)

He is the sustaining providence power of all things, the one who steers and pilots all things. The bearer of the pillars of the universe, in persons, big and small, great and the feeble, good and bad, comprehensive in all activities and events and not only The Creator. Preserving the work of His hands, sustaining and feeding them, providing for everything necessary for life, ruling, exalting and throwing down, punishing and empowering, healing and making things in all His operations, all according to the workings of His plan and purposes. No matter how the events of the world go in times and in the ages, He is actively involved in the universe; He is Lord over all and reigns over all, nothing has ever stopped the movement of creation as He created until The Upholder of all things declares so. By Him, everything consists and exists. His decrees and precepts are to be observed, and they stand forever, and He upholds all things by the power of His Word. He will uphold you with His righteous right hand and keep you constantly. He will uphold you to accomplish His promises for your life and will not stop until all is done.

Prayer: *I pray the upholder of all things sustains you and your generation in His blessing for eternity in Jesus' name.*

Launching Deeper: Psalm 75:3, John 1:4, Colossians 1:17, Revelation 4:11.

Hebrew Word Study: "takan"—to regulate (Strong's Hebrew: 8505).

October 13

FOROISGEIER

פורויסג'ייר

The Forerunner

"Where the forerunner has entered for us, even Jesus, having become High Priest forever according to the order of Melchizedek" (Hebrews 6:20, NKJV).

The king of Salam appeared to Abraham as a sign of His presence and of peace in a time of warfare, for He alone does wonderful things and brings peace in times of chaos, He is giving you the peace that passes all understanding and does not withhold His love and faithfulness from us. Christ, the Forerunner, came to bless and stand in as a representation of The Father, Who has become our High Priest to appear in the heavenly temple and to present offerings of Himself on our behalf. His priesthood is forever and continues to make intercession for us and goes ahead of us to prepare a place and keeps on preparing us to take part in His everlasting glory, introducing us into the heavenly presence of the Father. With such hope, we stay assured in our faith in God, that no matter the challenges and storms of life, our advocate and Forerunner has secured our glorious hope, putting things together whiles equipping us by the Spirit to bring the will of the Father to fulfillment, and to come and transport all believers to take possession of what He has prepared for them.

Prayer: *I pray the Forerunner will go ahead of you and make way for you. He will make the crook place straight and remove blockades out of your way.*

Launching Deeper: John 14:2, Psalm 110:4, Hebrews 2:17, 3:1, 4:14, 5:6, 1 Peter 3:22.

Hebrew Word Study: "mahar"—to hasten, prepare (Strong's Hebrew: 4116).

October 14

Yeshu'ot Panay

ישות פאנאי

Help of My Countenance

Why are you in despair, O my soul? And why are you restless and disturbed within me? Hope in God and wait expectantly for Him, for I shall again praise Him, The help of my countenance and my God.

Psalm 43:5 (AMP)

David encouraged himself after his trials and the wrath of God against him. He spoke to his soul, the center of his emotion, to hope and trust in the Lord. By the Lord's mercies, he can forget his sorrows. He is the Only One who will make his countenance cheerful and graceful; He will bring healing to his emotional unrest and make His heart glad, for no matter how long weeping will last in the night, there is a joy that will rise in the morning as the sunrise upon God's people. He will make sure no challenge overwhelms you as you keep honoring His Name. Despite the depth of the bitterness, just a Word from Him will cause the tempest to be peaceful. Jesus, the Health of your countenance, has the power over any distress to bring healing and joy to your emotions and restore you to a countenance of good health and reveal His abundance of peace unto you. You will find joy and praise His name in His presence.

Prayer: *I pray the Lord commands His deliverance and gladness into your spirit and continue to be strengthened by the joy of the Spirit.*

Launching Deeper: Jeremiah 30:17, 33:6, Matthew 9:12, Psalm 42:11.

Hebrew Word Study: "yachal"—to wait, to be patient (Strong's Hebrew: 3176).

October 15

NOTEN LEHEM KOL BASAR

גילין מוסיקה לחם קול בזאר

Giver of Food to All Flesh

"Who gives food to all flesh, For His lovingkindness endures forever" (Psalm 136:25, AMP).

One of God's activities that are not very visible is His providence for all creatures. Every life depends on His sustenance. He has ordered that the needs of His creation be met. Their eyes are upon Him for food, and His hands are open to satisfy the needs of all creatures in all seasons. From the beginning, He commanded that every seed-bearing fruit is given as meat for man. He makes the grass to grow for livestock. The same way He commanded Noah to take food for all the animals He took to the ark, just imagine such a great task to find a particular meal for every kind of animal that he took into the ark, but the Lord provided for Him to find and sustained hundreds of animals for forty days, from the smallest to the biggest of them all, the plant-eating to the flesh-eating animals. The Giver of food to all flesh made it possible for all to be fed for that long. He is good to all with compassion and gives food to the hungry; He is your provider; the sparrow does not plant seeds but has food; He is mindful of you to provide your needs and will not forsake you, cast your cares upon Him and see Him give you rest and providence.

Prayer: *I pray the Giver of food to all flesh will continue to provide for you in every aspect of your life. You will not lack any good thing from Him.*

Launching Deeper: Psalms 104:21, 27, 145:9, 145:7.

Hebrew Word Study: "lechem"—bread, food (Strong's Hebrew: 3899).

October 16

Chayyei Olam

חי עולם

Eternal Life

And we know that the Son of God is come, and hath given us an understanding, that we may know him that is true, and we are in him that is true, even in his Son Jesus Christ. This is the true God and eternal life.

1 John 5:20 (KJV)

John testifies about the life that has been revealed and proclaimed, that's the Lord Jesus is the eternal life and whoever would confess the Son has also confessed the Father, for God has given us life in His Son so that believing in the Son grants you eternal life. He is the origin of the term eternal life, and He gives it as a gift to all who would receive by faith, and being committed to the things of God and His grace and favor; He is the life from the Father and the life which is shown forth as a light onto all men. He who believes in Him would have this eternal life. Even when the person dies by the resurrection power of the Lord Jesus, He would have life. He is the one who gives long life that continues in everlasting life, which is knowing God and enjoying His blessings. This eternal life is the glory of God and believer's portion of inheritance.

Prayer: *I pray the eternal life from the Lord be your inheritance, and may He lead you into greatness.*

Launching Deeper: Luke 24:45, John 1:18, 8:42, 14:6,9, 17:3.

Hebrew Word Study: "olam"—long duration, antiquity, futurity (Strong's Hebrew: 5769).

October 17

ELYON L'MALKHEI A'RETZ

אליון המלכי א'רץ

Prince of the Kings of the Earth

"And from Jesus Christ, the faithful witness, the firstborn from the dead, and the ruler over the kings of the earth. To Him who loved us and washed us from our sins in His own blood" (Revelation 1:5, NKJV).

He rules and reigns over the kingdom of this world, and He is from the lineage of King David. He is proclaimed as the King of Kings and Lord of Lords. His kingship is everlasting. He ruled in the affairs of men and took power from the ruler of this world by dying on the cross and became the ruler of its kings. Even though they conspired against Him, He broke them into pieces and brought them under His feet; He is the one who lives, who rules in righteousness and in justice and in peace as the Prince of Peace, giving peace to His people on earth. The ruler who gives life to the people of the earth, the ruler who blesses you and gives you His grace. His kingdom is exalted above all, all kings, all governments, all monarchs, all tribe, all people, all nations and all rulers, bow down to Him and will confess He is Lord, all will bring their glory on to him for they all are accountable unto Him.

Prayer: *I pray anything that will make war against you be conquered in His name and let His peace saturate your life.*

Launching Deeper: Psalm 51:2, Isaiah 1:6, Revelation 11:15, 17:14.

Hebrew Word Study: "kisseh"—seat of honor, throne (Strong's Hebrew: 3678).

October 18

Alpha and Omega

אלפא ואומגה

"I am the Alpha and the Omega, the Beginning and the End," says the Lord, "who is and who was and who is to come, the Almighty" (Revelation 1:8, NKJV).

He is in the beginning, performing all things and carries out his promises, and carries out his purpose and his plans. Christ is the first and the last. He called for the generations from the beginning. There is no God like Him. He is the one who was and who is and who is to come. When John had the revelation, He saw the beginning of creation and what the Lord had done, things that were going to happen even after eternity. John saw the beginning of the end, and He was commanded to write all that He saw. He is the Alpha and the Omega, so He is the beginning of all things. All that we see in creation. The self-existent God, everything began from Him and for Him, the existing God and continues to exist through eternity. When creatures stop existing, the sum and substance of all that are in the scriptures. He is in the first verse of the scriptures, in Genesis as the God who began creation and in the last verse of the scriptures, in Revelations as the one who sustained everything with His grace, the Amen, the one who has caused everything to be, and has been faithful through all, know He is faithful to keep and sustain you in His power.

Prayer: *I pray the Alpha and the Omega smile on you when there is no confidence. Let Him bring you that confidence more than anything.*

Launching Deeper: Exodus 3:14, Isaiah 41:4, 44:6. Revelation 1:4, 4:8, 11:17, 15:3. 16:7.

Hebrew Word Study: "techillah"—a beginning (Strong's Hebrew: 8462).

October 19

Ruach Hakodesh Edut

הרוח, העד שלנו

The Spirit, Our Witness

"But the Holy Spirit also witnesses to us; for after He had said before" (Hebrews 10:15, NKJV).

The Spirit is reliable and consistent in His words and works; He is the Faithful counselor; he bears testimonies about the work of Jesus. When Jesus was baptized, He descended on Him to authenticate and empower Him to fulfill His assignment. The Spirit upon the believer assured Him that Jesus is with us, and in us, we remain in Him. The Spirit, our Witness, teaches and reminds us of all that Jesus spoke and helps us to know that Jesus is of the Father. This is the Source of confidence in the believer's faith and as a Child of God. He is trustworthy, and His truth is unchangeable; He speaks the truth about Jesus and His goodness and the love of the Father to us. When Jesus came upon the earth by His love and by His mercies, He healed the sick and set the captives free. The Spirit testifies about His wonders and miracles, His Word to the poor, and forgiveness of all our sins, and His death on the cross to redeem us. The Spirit, our witness, shows the faithfulness and truthfulness of Jesus and His promises concerning our lives and authenticates that He will perform every Word for your life in Jesus' name.

***Prayer**: I pray people from afar, from the north, south, east, and west will confess Jesus comes in the flesh and He is Lord, and is of the Father.*

Launching Deeper: 1 John 4:2,3, Acts 5:32, 1 Corinthians 12:3, Romans 8:15,16, Revelation 1:5, 3:14.

Hebrew Word Study: "ed"—a witness (Strong's Hebrew: 5707).

October 20

Ruach HaTovah

התובא

His Good Spirit

"You also gave Your good Spirit to instruct them, And did not withhold Your manna from their mouth, And gave them water for their thirst" (Nehemiah 9:20, NKJV).

The Good Spirit of the Lord leads us on level grounds and speaks to us. As Jesus said, whoever hears, let him hear what the Spirit says to the church. The Good Spirit is always speaking, giving counsel and directions at all times. He is involved in our daily lives and in every challenge, praying and interceding for us, with groaning and words that cannot be uttered in situations we do not know how to pray. Nehemiah recognized the help of the Spirit to the Israelites. Through their journey in the wilderness, the Lord provided for them and protected them all the way. He calls and commissions his servants unto services and callings and ministries in diverse operations. He is the fulness that indwelled in Jesus and assisted Him in His ministry. After His forty days fasting, He came back in the power of the Good Spirit in healing and deliverance; The same Spirit dwells in you to bear the fruits of the spirit, His love, faithfulness, kindness, peace, patience, gentleness, and self-control are springing up in you continually.

Prayer: *I pray the Good Spirit overshadows you with His goodness and protection and shines His light upon you.*

Launching Deeper: Psalm 143:10, Romans 15:30, Galatians 5:22,23.

Hebrew Word Study: "sakal"—to be prudent (Strong's Hebrew: 7919a).

October 21

Ruach Patir

רוח סובלת

His Free Spirit

החופשית

"Restore to me the joy of Your salvation, And uphold me by Your generous Spirit" (Psalm 51:12, NKJV).

David prayed unto the Lord to hear Him and restore the joy of the spirit to Him. When all hope is lost, He relied and trusted on the free and generous Spirit to uphold Him. He was sustained by the mighty hand of the Lord and equipped, as we have been sustained and maintained by the grace and in His power, equipping us to do what has been entrusted in every believer. Disobedience in His Word can vex and grieve the good Spirit, and He can be quenched by not following His instructions. He has also given unto us unique gifts for the various ministries and in ministering to others; Whenever we are in need, and we call upon Him, He hears and answers. The Free Spirit reveals the truth to His Word, He is the God who keeps His Word, and they that keep His commandments are protectant and preserved from His wrath. You possess the oracles of God by revelational knowledge by the Holy Spirit; The Spirit downloads His blessings from heaven's throne room and helps you in every situation and sustains your soul so you can rejoice in His strength.

***Prayer:** I pray you will abide in His presence, and His Spirit remains with you and cause your life to bear glorious fruits.*

Launching Deeper: Romans 8:15, 2 Corinthians 3:17, Galatians 4:6,7, Psalm 54:4.

Hebrew Word Study: "chadash"—to renew, repair (Strong's Hebrew: 2318).

October 22

Ruach Mishpat

רוח משפט

The Spirit of Judgement

"When the Lord has washed away the filth of the daughters of Zion, and purged the blood of Jerusalem from her midst, by the spirit of judgment and by the spirit of burning" (Isaiah 4:4, NKJV).

The Spirit is the agent of washing and purging, convicting the mind, to wash away any form of defilement, to put away sins and transgressions, and has an appointed time for judgment, and that's why He brings to light what is hidden in darkness and exposes motives of the heart of men, The judgments of the Lord is righteous and faithful to vindicate the righteous. The Spirit of Judgement does not show favoritism to neither the rich nor the poor. In His judgment, He demonstrates His glory in justice, He defends the course of the weak and the needy and puts an end to the evil of the wicked. The spirit of judgment brings salvation to the people and brings compassion to redeem His people from the bonds of suppression and punishes the wicked of their sins. He charges the nations, and His righteous judge reveals His holiness; His judgment reveals His power and might, and it reveals His mercy. With his mighty right hand, He delivers His people, and with His outstretched arm, He sends forth His judgment.

Prayer: *I pray in your land may you possess a double portion and may he judge the wicked on your behalf.*

Launching Deeper: Revelation 18:18, Nehemiah 9:31, Psalm 78:38, Romans 2:9-11.

Hebrew Word Study:"shaphat"—to judge, govern (Strong's Hebrew: 8199).

October 23

Ruach Ba'er

רוח באר

The Spirit of Burning

"When the Lord has washed away the filth of the daughters of Zion, and purged the blood of Jerusalem from her midst, by the spirit of judgment and by the spirit of burning" (Isaiah 4:4, NKJV).

The Spirit of burning quickies you to be zealous for the things of God. It brings a great desire upon your life to do great services for God. The passion of worship propels into His presence. The zeal that burns out every form of ungodliness out of the believer's life. Spirit of burning also emanates fervency in prayer, enthusiasm, and energy. Remember, it is not good to have zeal without knowledge, nor to be hasty and miss the way. But we would like the zeal for righteousness to consume us. Elijah was very zealous for the Lord. When they forsake the covenants and break down the altars and kill the prophets, he stood for the Lord. When challenges arise, do not let the burning subside keep the fervency of the Spirit and continue with zeal. Do not let your love for His service wax cold. Let His love fill your heart to do great things for the Lord.

Prayer: *I pray your willingness for Him will increase, and He will lift you from one level to another level of His glory.*

Launching Deeper: Isaiah 37:32, Psalm 69:9, John 2:17, Proverbs 19:2, James 5:16, Isaiah 48:9-11.

Hebrew Word Study: "baar"—to burn, consume (Strong's Hebrew: 1197).

October 24

Ruach Elohim HaKadosh

רוח אלוים הקדוש

Spirit of the Holy God

Belteshazzar, chief of the magicians, because I know that the Spirit of the Holy God is in you, and no secret troubles you, explain to me the visions of my dream that I have seen, and its interpretation.

Daniel 4:9 (NKJV)

It's like one of the days that you'd have a dream that fascinates you and wonder what the dream is all about. This kind of dream made the king of Babylon afraid and terrified. He became troubled and called for the wise men on the land of Babylon, who could not give a sensible meaning to the dream, but for Daniel, through the Spirit of God, received the revelation of the dream. The people of God have an advantage over the world. Everything that pertains to life, and workings of the spirit world, the Lord in His mercy releases revelation knowledge. You possess the oracles of God by revelational knowledge of the Holy Spirit. It's download from heaven's throne room for you. You have advantages of the Divine Timings and seasons of God like the sons of Issachar, understanding by the counsel of the Spirit of the Holy God to know what to do and be successful. Follow His directions and live in it. The Spirit endows you with his gifts and skills in your calling and gives you revelational knowledge for the timing you are in.

Prayer: *I pray the Spirit gives you understanding of the times and seasons in your time to be ahead.*

Launching Deeper: Psalm 147:19,20, Romans 3:1.

Hebrew Word Study: "Nabi"—"Prophecy" in Hebrew, to speak under divine inspiration or influence (Strong's Hebrew: 5030).

October 25

YAHWEH MIVTACHI

יהוה מבטחצ׳׳י

God of My Confidence

"For You are my hope; O Lord GOD, You are my trust and the source of my confidence from my youth" (Psalm 71:5, AMP).

When the Amalekites raided Ziklag, after David and his men had gone to fight the Philistines, they took their wives and children as captives for slaves. When David and his men returned and saw Ziklag burnt, they cried until they found no strength to cry, David became distressed because they decided to stone him, but David found confidence and strength in the Lord. His confidence was that God did not bring him this far to leave him. He inquired from the Lord and was given the permission to pursue the enemies, for victory was granted to him, the Lord fulfilled His Word and gave him victory. He hoped in the Lord and trusted in. The Lord was his source of confidence; David was stable and was not moved. Let the God of your Confidence remove every fear and place your confidence in Him. He would rescue you, let your soul find rest in Him, and do not be shaken. Trust in the name of the Lord, have confidence in His purpose and plans for your life. He has not brought you this far to leave you; all will be fulfilled in Jesus' name. Confidence in His presence and providence is what you need.

Prayer: *I pray Lord be your confidence, find rest and be safe and secured in His Mighty Arms.*

Launching Deeper: Proverbs 14:26, 1 Samuel 30, Isaiah 32:17, Jeremiah 17:7.

Hebrew Word Study: "mibtach"—confidence (Strong's Hebrew: 4009).

October 26

Hakodesh Hashem

הקדוש השם

The Holy One of God

"Let us alone! What have we to do with You, Jesus of Nazareth? Did You come to destroy us? I know who You are—the Holy One of God" (Mark 1:24, NKJV).

The Holy one born of the virgin Mary without blemish, Him whom men despised and the nations abhor. The angel Gabriel was sent to the virgin Mary to deliver a message. She was found favored by the Most High. The angel brought her the message of hope and joy and blessings. When she was wondering what kind of message it was, the angel assured her that there was no fear, for she was chosen to carry the Holy One of God in her womb. King of Israel, the Christ the one whom many will believe in and have eternal life, the Holy One of God born is the one who is unique and distinguished beyond the world, and by heavenly authority, His life and nature were set apart to do the intention and purpose of God. He performed His works in holiness and lived a life of purity, separated from sin and appointed to judge sinners. Demons recognized He was the Holy One of God and pleaded with Him not to destroy them before their time. He separated Himself as a servant to discipline God's people and to live a holy life by the grace and the empowerment of the Spirit. The grace is upon you this day to do the intentions and purpose of God for your life.

***Prayer**: I pray the Holy One anoints you with His power and glory to cast out evil.*

Launching Deeper: Matthew 1:18, 4:3, Luke 1:32, Mark 1:24, 34.

Hebrew Word Study: "chasid"—godly man, kind (Strong's Hebrew: 2623).

October 27

Gevurah Elyon

גבורה אליון

The Power of the Highest

And the angel answered and said unto her, The Holy Ghost shall come upon thee, and the power of the Highest shall overshadow thee: therefore also that holy thing which shall be born of thee shall be called the Son of God.

Luke 1:35 (NKJV)

When Mary did not know how the prophecy and the word of the angel were going to be fulfilled, the angel revealed to her that the power of the Spirit would overshadow her to cause everything said to come to pass. The Power of the Highest quickens a person to live a life that will cause God's intentions and plans to be fulfilled. The Power of the Highest shows forth the manifold wisdom to the world in a believer and displays His power upon the earth, with an outpouring to bring transformation. Even the desert changes to be a forest, and there is justice and righteousness, the Power of the Highest will rest upon you this day to give you wisdom in decision making, understanding in matters, counsel for directions, strength to replace every form of weakness and give you knowledge in the revelation of His Word with the fear of God in serving Him.

***Prayer**: I pray let the Power of the Highest overshadow you and bring the blossom and abundance of blessings and transformation in your life.*

Launching Deeper: Isaiah 11:1, 2, 29:17, 28:6, 29:17, 35:2, 44:3, 59:21.

Hebrew Word Study: "menuchah"—resting place, rest (Strong's Hebrew 4496).

October 28

HaMenachem

המנחם

The Comforter

"And I will pray the Father, and he shall give you another Comforter, that he may abide with you forever" (John 14:16, KJV).

Jesus assured the believers that it was the Father who had sent Him to come and fulfill an assignment, and He has come that they will have an abundant life as they believe in Him. As they believe in Him, they will do greater works by His ascension to the Father. The believers should not hesitate to ask whatever they want and need, the Father will do for them, and they will glorify His name. Even though it's important that He returns to the Father, His ascension to the heavens will cause a release of the Comforter. When He leaves, He will not leave them alone He is going to ask the Comforter, the Spirit of God, to be with them. He is the one that will help you and comfort you, you will not be left comfortless, He is with you, the Comforter will give witness of Him and testify about Christ and all that He's came to do, He is the one that will give you directions into all truth and comfort your spirit.

***Prayer:** I pray He Comforts you in times of challenges and strengthens and anoints you to do great things.*

Launching Deeper: John 14:18, 26, 15:26, 16:7-15.

Hebrew Word Study: "anah"—testify (Strong's Hebrew: 6030).

October 29

Ruach HaBanim

רוח הבנים

Spirit of Adoption

"For ye have not received the spirit of bondage again to fear; but ye have received the Spirit of adoption, whereby we cry, Abba, Father" (Romans 8:15, NKJV).

The Father has given us all the privileges of being children of the kingdom family. He has adopted us through Jesus and by the indwelling of the Holy Spirit. The Spirit in our hearts makes us cry Abba Father and shows our close relationship with Him. We are no longer slaves but sons adopted and given an everlasting name by the leading of the Spirit. When we follow the Spirit, He calls us the sons of God, by the Spirit of adoption, the Father executives. His providence and care with love upon us. The Spirit also makes intercession for us as He knows the deep things and the will of God for your life. Before you ask, the father knows, for you have the privileges and the blessings as a child of God, and He has eternally secured you with an inheritance by the Spirit as you produce His likeness by His grace.

Prayer: *I pray every yoke of slavery be broken out and stand firm in the liberty received through Jesus.*

Launching Deeper: Galatians 4:6,7, Isaiah 56:1-8, Jeremiah 3:19.

Hebrew Word Study: "ben"—son (Strong's Hebrew: 1121).

October 30

Ruach Hakodesh Havtachah

רוח הקדוש חב"ד

The Holy Spirit of Promise

"In Him, you also trusted, after you heard the word of truth, the gospel of your salvation; in whom also, having believed, you were sealed with the Holy Spirit of promise" (Ephesians 1:13, NKJV).

Every promise of God always comes to fulfillment with prayers, Jesus assured the apostles of the promise of the Father. He asked them to wait for the Spirit of Promise, who will give them abilities and grace to operate. The promise of the Father is for both the Jews and Gentiles and for their descendants; this was fulfilled on Pentecost day. You see that location, availability, and obedience are important to the fulfillment of the promise, preparing you to receive the promise, even though Jesus gave the promise, He asked them to wait, wait upon the Father in prayer and in being connected to him to receive. When you are baptized in the Holy Spirit, you are immersed in Him. His help and strength are available, and you are sealed with Him to be identified as His child and authenticated in His power. You are distinct among all, and He takes ownership of you. When you are born of the Spirit, you are of the Spirit with power to fulfill every promise for you.

Prayer: *I pray every shame and reproach be removed and receive double honor and all promises of Him be fulfilled in your life.*

Launching Deeper: Ephesians 4:30, John 6:27, Romans 4:11, Mark 16:15,16.

Hebrew Word Study: "omer"—promise, thing, word (Strong's Hebrew: 562).

October 31

Elohim shel Shadrach, Meshach, Abednego

אלוהים של שדרך, מש"ך, עבדנגו

God of Shadrach, Meshach, and Abednego

Nebuchadnezzar responded and said, "Blessed be the God of Shadrach, Meshach, and Abed-nego, who has sent His angel and rescued His servants who believed in, trusted in, and relied on Him! They violated the king's command and surrendered their bodies rather than serve or worship any god except their own God.

Daniel 3:28 (AMP)

During trials, the presence of the Lord is always with his people. It is the strong faith in you that will quench every fiery dart. The king of Babylon, by his power, ordered an image to be set for all the people to worship, he spoke, that those that would not worship his image would be cast into a fiery furnace, when Shadrach, Meshach, and Abednego took a decision to defy the king's command, far be it from them to serve other gods, they were cast into the fire, but an angel of the Lord came to deliver them; the king realized and acknowledged that the king of the Jews is the all-powerful God; He is the Almighty, that He truly exists before ages, and there is no God like Him, and none can be compared to him. He is worthy of praise and blessings, worthy of honor and great and greatly to be praised. Among other gods, there are none. The faith of Shadrach Meshack Abednego stood still, and they were delivered. The king made a decree to alter a previous decree that the Jew might not serve any other God but their own God because they trusted in the name of the Lord and did not conform to the idol worship in the land. Keep trusting in Him and see His deliverance.

Prayer: *I pray the God of Shadrach increases your faith and lets His deliverance come to you.*

Launching Deeper: 1 Chronicles 16:25, Daniel 3:29, Psalm 22:4,5, Isaiah 12:2.

Hebrew Word Study: "pelach"—to pay reverence, to serve (Strong's Hebrew: 6399).

November

An altar of earth you shall make for Me, and you shall sacrifice on it your burnt offerings and your peace offerings, your sheep and your oxen. In every place where I record My name I will come to you, and I will bless you. (Exodus 20:24 NKJV)

November 1

ELOHIM KOL DANIEL

אלוהים קול דניאל

God of Daniel

I issue a decree that in all the dominion of my kingdom men are to [reverently] fear and tremble before the God of Daniel, For He is the living God, enduring and steadfast forever, And His kingdom is one which will not be destroyed, And His dominion will be forever.

Daniel 6:26 (AMP)

The decree not to pray to any other god was against Daniel's prayer life, and to the God he serves. When the decree was made, he went to his room and opened his windows, and continued with his practice of prayer, defying every order not to do so. The decree was that anyone who disobeys would be cast into the lion's den, at this point, Daniel feared God than to fear lions who will devour him. He knew his God whom he prayed to every day, and will not conform to pressure to deny his God; it was his way of life to be in the presence of God every day, and The Lord proved Himself on Daniel's behalf and sent an angel to rescue him from the lions' den. As you walk in fear of God, His protection is assured, and his peace is in abundance, negative decrees against you will be turned around to bring you favor, people around you will fear and tremble before the God that you serve. They will know that He lives forever, The God of Daniel is the all-powerful, and His kingdom is unshakable and dependable, unchangeable, His purposes are valid, his promises are fulfilled, and providence are certain for your life as you keep your confidence in Him alone.

Prayer: *I pray as you trusted in the protection and preservation of God of Daniel, the living God let Him shut the mouths of the lions on your behalf.*

Launching Deeper: Daniel 4:34, Deuteronomy 5:26, Psalms 2:11, 99:1-3, 119:120.

Hebrew Word Study: "sholtan"—dominion (Strong's Hebrew: 7985).

November 2

Olam Ruach

עולם רוח

The Eternal Spirit

"How much more shall the blood of Christ, who through the eternal Spirit offered Himself without spot to God, cleanse your conscience from dead works to serve the living God?" (Hebrews 9:14, NKJV)

By the everlasting power, Jesus received the full measure of the Spirit and was led to the wilderness, tempted and tested. He waited upon the Lord to receive the anointing to preach good tidings, bind up the broken-hearted, declare freedom to the oppressed and declare spiritual prison gates opened, performing miracles and cast out devils by the power of the Eternal Spirit. He went through sufferings to redeem us, His own people rejected Him, by betrayals but carried the sins of the world upon Him, He submitted willingly to suffer and was crucified, a unique sacrifice without blemish and spotless to God, an atonement to establish an everlasting covenant of eternal redemption, where you are forgiven of your sins, and sanctified by the blood once and for all, through the Eternal Spirit you have the eternal love of the Father bestowed upon you, and He has freely given you all things, for you are predestined, called, justified and glorified.

Prayer: *I pray the Eternal Spirit will revive you, be your refuge and thrust your enemies and destroy them.*

Launching Deeper: Deuteronomy 33:27, Isaiah 57:15, Jeremiah 10:10, Romans 8:29.

Hebrew Word Study: "qedem"—front, east, formerly (Strong's Hebrew: 6924a).

November 3

Ruach HaNevu'ah

רוח הנביעה

The Spirit of Prophecy

And I fell at his feet to worship him. But he said to me, "See that you do not do that! I am your fellow servant, and of your brethren who have the testimony of Jesus. Worship God! For the testimony of Jesus is the spirit of prophecy.

Revelation 19:10 (NKJV)

Is the Spirit of the Father who speaks through His servants to give the Word of prophecy and caused them to testify and witness about Him with power, He is the One Who teaches all things, reminds and directs what he hears to the believer, the words of Jesus. This is testifying about Jesus. The ultimate revelation of all prophecies is the power of the Lord Jesus. It reveals who He is, whether predicting the future or admonition believers; He is the perfect sacrifice, slain from the foundations of the earth to save the world. The Spirit of Prophecy, who is Jesus, who comforts us and grants us peace. He lovingly cares for His own. And perfects us to live the life manifesting Him unto His praise and Glory. As we depend on Him, He is there to carry your burdens and grant you rest. His stripe and wounds heal every sickness and disease. He will quench your thirst as the living water and gives you life as you take His bread of life.

Prayer: *I pray an angel will be released to bring you good tidings and establish you in His goodness.*

Launching Deeper: Revelation 1:9, 12:11, 17, 22:9.

Hebrew Word Study: "“naba”—to prophecy (Strong's Hebrew: 5012).

November 4

Elohei Eliyahu

אלוהי אליהו

The God of Elijah

He took the mantle of Elijah that fell from him and struck the waters and said, "Where is the LORD, the God of Elijah?" And when he too had struck the waters, they divided this way and that, and Elisha crossed over.

2 Kings 2:14 (AMP)

Elisha continued from where Elijah stopped. He trusted God and called upon the name of the God of Elijah to silence idol worshippers on the land. As a servant of the prophet Elijah, he had witnessed most miracles that were done by the power of God in his manservant. Elijah's prophecies were fulfilled, his prayers were answered, he was a prophet of action. He prophesied droughts and prophesied rain, and it was fulfilled; the Lord used him on Mount Carmel where he challenged prophets of Baal and called down fire to consume the sacrifice. On the day he was taken to heaven, Elisha followed him all day as he knew it was His Master's time to go. The God of Elijah gave the double portion of the anointing to Elisha, and he also received mighty miracles in the name of the Lord. He called upon the God of Elijah to part the waters, and the Lord answered. The God of Elijah will grant unto you the double portion anointing to break every yoke out of your life. He would use you. He will fulfill His Word in you and would answer your prayers and take you to the next level in Jesus' name.

Prayer: *I pray when you call upon the name of the Lord, let the Lord bring answers as He heard Elijah.*

Launching Deeper: Judges 6:13, 1 Kings 18:36-39, Psalm 42:2,10.

Hebrew Word Study: "addereth"—glory, a cloak (Strong's Hebrew: 155).

November 5

ECHAD GIBBOR HA'ALILIYAH

אחד גיבור הגליליה

The One Mighty in Works

"You are great in counsel and mighty in work, for Your eyes are open to all the ways of the sons of men, to give everyone according to his ways and according to the fruit of his doings" (Jeremiah 32:19, NKJV).

The God of the Earth commands His people to recite His acts and deeds upon the earth and praise His name continually, for there is no greater power and might that can execute His acts. He made the heavens and the earth amid the lightning and the rain in the mountains and called forth the wind. He is the all-powerful who sets His signs and wonders on the earth according to His will, and all stand till today, and no one can stop Him. By His mighty works, He has made a name for Himself throughout generations. He is mighty in works by delivering His people with His righteous right hand. Through His mighty deeds, His name is declared in all nations, and the earth blessed and praised His name from the rising of the sun until the setting. He is the One to be feared; He is the king of the nations. The nations cannot stand His anger. He is One Mighty in Works. Is there any work too hard for Him to do in your life? Your health, your family, your marriage, and spiritual life is His concern, He will work all things together for your good.

Prayer: *I pray the Lord will perform mighty works for you in an instant and bring to fulfillment His wonders for you.*

Launching Deeper: Exodus 15:11, Daniel 4:35, Psalms 66:5, 77:14, 89:5,7.

Hebrew Word Study: "adar"—wide, great (Strong's Hebrew: 142).

November 6

TZUR MICHSHOL

צור מישויל

Rock of Offense

"He will be as a sanctuary, But a stone of stumbling and a rock of offense. To both the houses of Israel, As a trap and a snare to the inhabitants of Jerusalem" (Isaiah 8:14, NKJV).

Our Rock of Defence and their Rock of Offence

Those who would not believe in the Savior and rebel against Him will fall to their hurt. No one can run against a fixed rough rock and come uninjured. The Jews rejected the Messiah and were offended by His birth, His poor parents, His upbringing and education, His ministry, and crucifixion. In their reasoning, God would not cause the Messiah to be crucified, anyone who is hanged on a tree is cursed (Deuteronomy 21:23). It was shameful and degrading to die in this manner. To them, the Savior, who is the Anointed of God, cannot be accursed, making this concept offensive to the Jewish religion. His teachings and doctrines of truth and liberation are offensive to the world because it exposes the weakness of human works to gain righteousness before the Holy Father. He chooses the foolish things of the world to confound the wise. The Rock that defends those who believe in Him and the Rock that rejects those who don't believe and are offended by Him. As a believer, He is a precious stone and a Rock of defense. He defends you and keeps you safe and stable in His salvation.

Prayer: *I pray the Lord be your Rock of defense and a refuge in your time of challenges and uncertainty.*

Launching Deeper: Isaiah 28:16, Luke 2:34, Romans 9:32,33.

Hebrew Word Study: "mikshol"—a stumbling block (Strong's Hebrew: 383).

November 7

Chesed

אהבה ואהבה

My Lovingkindness

"My lovingkindness and my fortress, My high tower and my deliverer, My shield and the One in whom I take refuge, Who subdues my people under me" (Psalm 144:2, NKJV).

The Originator of love is the Lord God Almighty, and He loves with an everlasting love. His greatness and His power are displayed in His lovingkindness for all people to see and bless His name, and this distinguishes Him from any other god. His love and divine providence are there for all. When the enemy surrounds us, He lifts a standard to preserve and protects us, for His love, He will plead your cause and repay those who do evil against you. He will not forget you but would rescue you from violence and cut the wicked off, for He is God, your goodness, and even if the mountains are removed, and the hills are shaken, the Lord will not remove His lovingkindness from you and His covenant will not be broken. He blots out our sins by His love and blesses those who come to Him for help. According to His great compassion and love, the Lord will do to you many good things and delight in you to favor and bless you.

Prayer: *I pray, for His great love you will not be consumed, for His compassion will never fail, and they are new every day.*

Launching Deeper: Jeremiah 31:3, Exodus 15:13, 34:6, 2 Chronicle 6:42, Psalms 6:4, 32:10.

Hebrew Word Study: "chesed"—goodness, kindness (Strong's Hebrew: 2617).

November 8

ISH MAKHOVOHT

איש הצער

Man of Sorrows

"He is despised and rejected by men, A Man of sorrows and acquainted with grief. And we hid, as it were, our faces from Him; He was despised, and we did not esteem Him" (Isaiah 53:3, NKJV).

The love and humility of Christ were demonstrated in His sufferings through to the cross, the path the Father laid to bring salvation to the world. The prophets foretold His sufferings and His death. God's declaration in Genesis concerning the woman and the serpent also showed what was going to happen to the seed of the woman, that the serpent will strike His heel and He will crush the head of the serpent, depicting the suffering He will go through. The sins and guilt of the entire world were put on Him. He was judged as a sinner. Isaiah described Him as the Man of Sorrows. He foretold the disciples what will happen to Him, how He will be delivered to the gentiles to be condemned and to be put to death. Christ, the Man of Sorrows, was mocked, and spat upon, and flogged. His appearance was disfigured and betrayed by a disciple; He was crushed and suffered and rejected by His own people, scorned and despised. He went through sorrows just for your sins, bore all the pains to redeem you and grant you His salvation and eternal life.

Prayer: *I pray for the faithfulness of the Lord for you, let kings see you and rise for what the Lord will do for your life.*

Launching Deeper: Mark 10:33, 34, Luke 18:31, John 1:10,11, Psalm 22:6,7, Isaiah 49:7, 52:14, 53:10.

Hebrew Word Study: "bazah"—to despise (Strong's Hebrew: 959).

November 9

Mashgiach Nefashot

משגיח נפשוט

Bishop of our Souls

"For you were like sheep going astray, but have now returned to the Shepherd and Overseer of your souls" (1 Peter 2:25, NKJV).

He is the overseer, the superintendence, who is appointed by the Father to watch and supervise the body of Christ. He is the universal Bishop of the souls of the church and fully committed to take care of them. Those that go astray, he brings them back. Those that are lost, He seeks after them and delivers them from the prey. He takes care of the weak and heals the sick. By the blood of the eternal covenant, He protects the souls of every believer, not excluding the body and spirit. By their relationship with God, He leads them to springs of water and clears their way. When they scatter, He gathers them and deals patiently with those that are ignorant. In our weakness, He grants us His strength. He Himself bore the weakness of our bodies and took up our pains upon Him. He is the chief Shepherd who would grant unto his church the crown of glory. Jesus is the Bishop of your soul. He leads and directs your path and increases His grace upon your life while leading you from glory to glory.

Prayer: *I pray the Lord will contend with Him who contends with you. And turn to confusion those that are against you in Jesus's name.*

Launching Deeper: Hebrew 3:1, Acts 20:28, 1 Peter 5:4.

Hebrew Word Study: "sarak"—chief, overseer (Strong's Hebrew: 5632).

November 10

NAGGAR

הנגר

The Carpenter

"'Is this not the carpenter, the Son of Mary, and brother of James, Joses, Judas, and Simon? And are not His sisters here with us?' So they were offended at Him" (Mark 6:3, NKJV).

In His hometown Nazareth where He grew up, Jesus had been with His people, and He is now teaching in the synagogue. They had become familiar with Him and despised Him as they knew Him to be a carpenter and knew His siblings; they questioned the level of His wisdom and knowledge and asked where did He learn all these things, but it did not matter, as whether they grew up with Him, the grace and the spirit of God was upon Him to do the works of the kingdom of the Father. Even though the people who knew Him looked down and despised Him which did not stop His operations. He could not do much because of their unbelief. Being the carpenter does not stop the anointing, it shows His humility. Jesus was also a skilled man apart from His ministry. He had learned a handicraft in a village and was from very humble with much knowledge of the law. He was thought to learn a trade and set an example of being diligent in all He does. Be skillful and diligent in all your endeavors and let the anointing cause you to do great works for Him.

***Prayer:** I pray you will not be ashamed or humiliated, for the Lord GOD helps you in all you do.*

Launching Deeper: Isaiah 49:7, 53:2,3, 1 Peter 2:4.

Hebrew Word Study: "yoneq"—a young plant (Strong's Hebrew: 3126).

November 11

Yahweh Mekaddesham

יהוה מקדשם

The Lord Our Sanctifier

"Moreover I also gave them My Sabbaths, to be a sign between them and Me, that they might know that I am the Lord who sanctifies them" (Ezekiel 20:12, NKJV).

It was required in the law for them to observe the sabbath and keep it holy, as a sign of the covenant that should be kept in all generations, as a sign that He is the one who sanctifies them and keeps them holy before His presence. By their obedience to God's statute and laws, they are being set apart as His own possession, and He qualifies them as His chosen nation. The presence of the Lord in their midst shows His faithfulness to be with them, and that requires their unique preparation to receive Him as the Most Holy God who promotes His Holiness in their midst to maintain His presence with them. He commands purifying His people and distinguishes them as a treasure unto Himself, for every nation to know that we are His people; it is keeping His commandment and being obedient to Him by His Spirit that helps us to stay in Him to receive His strength and grace. The blood of Jesus sanctifies our spirit, soul, and body and makes us acceptable in the Father's presence.

***Prayer**: I pray the blood of Jesus speaks better on your behalf. Let it speak his goodness and favor for you.*

Launching Deeper: Ezekiel 37:28, Exodus 19:5,6, Leviticus 20:8.

Hebrew Word Study: "qadash"—to be set apart or consecrated (Strong's Hebrew: 6942).

November 12

Mashbiach Sheovn Yammim

משבך שבן ימים

One Who Still the Roaring Seas

"You who still the noise of the seas, The noise of their waves,
And the tumult of the peoples" (Psalms 65:7, NKJV).

At the rebuke of the Supreme Sovereign, the raging sea flees, manifestation of His power over nature depicts Christ's divinity when He declared peace be still, the storms calm down, for He is the maker of them all and set boundaries to the waters that they would not cross to cover the earth. Any form of chaos represented by the waves is subdued by His authority and power. He has set a guard against it and rules them. If the floodwaters rise when the rivers raise their voices, and the sea lifts its storming waves. He hushes and mutes their voices, every terror and tumult raging in the mind to be restless and the soul in distress, He declares by His Word silence, and taking you to a state of tranquility, a state of the totality of His goodness and prosperity where you can increase without obstructions and hindrances and advance in fruitfulness, let every tempest and billows that tosses in your life be vanquished by the command of the One Who still the roaring seas and bring you His perfect and undisturbed peace.

***Prayer**: I pray let the voice of the waters pounding confusion, and chaos be silent and hushed at the power of His thundering voice.*

Launching Deeper: Matthew 8:26, 89:9, 107:28,30.

Hebrew Word Study: "eti"—still, (Strong's Hebrew: 2089).

November 13

Zera kol La'ishah

אפס קול לשיה

Seed of The Woman

And I will put enmity between you and the woman, And between your seed and her Seed; He shall bruise your head, And you shall bruise His heel" (Genesis 3:15, NKJV).

Paul gave a word that the God of peace would crush the enemy under our feet in the garden of Eden when the serpent deceived the woman, and she took the food that she was not supposed to take, an order given by the Father they disobeyed when the Lord came since they had disobeyed His command, He pronounced curses upon all of them, upon the serpent, upon the man, and upon the woman, and He said the seed of the woman would crush the head of the serpent. This was a prophecy concerning the Lord Jesus, and it was a sign about the virgin that would conceive and bear a Son, who would be seated upon the throne of David to reign forever, and his name called, the Lord with us, Emmanuel. He said He would spoil principalities and powers and make a public show of them, for the assignment of the seed of the woman was to crush the head of the serpent, for the promise of the seed is made to the church, and for the Eminence of the seed brings judgment against the prince of the world, the enemy is crushed under your feet by the blood of the Seed and you are more than a conqueror.

***Prayer**: I pray the Lord will show forth His signs and cause you to triumph over your enemies in Jesus' name.*

Launching Deeper: Psalm 132:11, Isaiah 7:14, Romans 16:20.

Hebrew Word Study: "zera"—sowing, seed, offspring (Strong's Hebrew: 2233).

November 14

YOTZER NE'EMANIM

יוצר נאמן

Faithful Creator

"Therefore let those who suffer according to the will of God commit their souls to Him in doing good, as to a faithful Creator" (1 Peter 4:19, NKJV).

Peter was encouraging the believers to have faith in the Lord even in their suffering, for the Lord is faithful He will not fail them, their suffering well equipped them to be more effective and be closer in their relationship to the Lord Jesus Christ. They should be confident and have hope in Him, for it is the cost of godliness, and it also stabilizes their service in the things of God. It develops our trust and reliance on the Lord and our character and fellowship. He is the Faithful Creator who keeps His covenant to his creation. He provides and takes care of His children as He made them. The Faithful Creator is faithful to His covenants and devoted onto you to be with you, and to deliver you from any type of challenge and in sufferings even though you walk through the fire, even though you walk through the storms, He is always with you and never leaves you or forsake you. He never changes, and He is true to His Word and will always fulfill His promises to creation.

Prayer: *I pray as you commit your ways to the Lord, let Him bring to pass every heart desire.*

Launching Deeper: 2 Peter 3:9, Hebrews 6:13-18, 12:7,11, 1 Peter 1:6,7.

Hebrew Word Study: "emun"—faithfulness (Strong's Hebrew: 529).

November 15

HaShamar

השמר

The Protector

"The Lord will preserve him and keep him alive, And he will be blessed on the earth; You will not deliver him to the will of his enemies" (Psalm 41:2, NKJV).

The Mighty One is the supreme safety of his people. He is your defender and the ultimate protector from any attack, oppression, and yokes, and bondages. The Lord lifts a standard of defense for the cause of the needy, crushes their oppressor, and brings safety to them when they're being exploited. He forfends not only in the physical but also preserves His people spiritually from the dangers of spiritual wickedness. The Protector also provides escape in temptation for His children to stand, for greater is He that is in you than He that is of the world. Give thanks, for, in all things, you are more than a conqueror. He secures you by his presence with you, never forsakes you, gives protective angels a charge to defend you. His Promises are yeah and amen that He will deliver the needy who cry to Him and have no help. The Protector will guard you from men of violence from pestilence and from sicknesses. No plague will come near your dwelling, for He who keeps you is Strong and Mighty.

Prayer: *I pray every yoke, pointing of the finger, and speaking of wickedness is taken away from you by the Protector in Jesus' name.*

Launching Deeper: Psalms 121:4, 57:1, Proverbs 30:14, Ezekiel 18:10-13, Amos 4:1, James 5:1-6.

Hebrew Word Study: "shamar"—to keep, watch, preserve (Strong's Hebrew: 8104).

November 16

Av Yisroel

אב ישראל

Father to Israel

They shall come with weeping, And with supplications I will lead them. I will cause them to walk by the rivers of waters, In a straight way in which they shall not stumble; For I am a Father to Israel, And Ephraim is My firstborn.

Jeremiah 31:9 (NKJV)

A Father's natural aptitude will cause Him to treat His child like a lost gem found. He is present, consistent, and shows love and commitment. The Lord declared to Pharoah that Israel is His firstborn and has appointed Him as His covenant first child and the highest of the kings of the earth, and as a Father to Israel; He leads them from captivity of Egypt through the wilderness; took care of them, provided and brought them to the promised land as he promised. He did them good and did not forsake them. When they needed water and were hungry for food, he had compassion and gave them manna and water. His paternal relationship to Israel showed in His love and His sustenance of this relationship between Him and the descendants of David to the coming of Christ to die for their sin and all people. As a Father to Israel, He disciplines and corrects them when they disobey and does not allow them to stumble, and gives them the inheritance of the nations. As a believer, you are adopted into this family and kingdom and the heir to the kingdom's blessings.

Prayer: *I pray as a child of the Father of Israel; the Lord sustain you and provide and turn every darkness away from you.*

Launching Deeper: John 1:12-13, Romans 8:14-17, 1 John 3:1, Ephesians 3:14-15, 4:22, Deut 14:1, 32:6.

Hebrew Word Study: "bekor"—firstborn (Strong's Hebrew: 1060).

November 17

HaZicher Yesod

הזיכר יסוד

The Sure Foundation

"Therefore thus says the Lord God: "Behold, I lay in Zion a stone for a foundation, A tried stone, a precious cornerstone, a sure foundation; Whoever believes will not act hastily" (Isaiah 28:16, NKJV).

There is nothing like having a close encounter with someone famous, so you can tell friends how excited you were when you met the person. Peter had walked with Jesus for a while from the time he was called to be an apostle, and at Caesarea Philippi, Jesus took the shot of asking them what was going on in the news about Him. What names are they calling Him? They gave Him some names. He turned it to them and asked, "What do you think about me, who am I" Peter broke the tension and declared, "You are the Christ the Son of the Living God." Jesus said, "On this Rock I will build my church." On the foundation of this revelation, I will build my church. When the foundation of your faith is on the sure bedrock of Christ, not soil of worldliness that can easily be washed by rivers and storms of life, but the unmovable and unshakable base support of the eternal Rock, you will always stand strong, because you are deeply rooted in Him, and building on your most holy faith which will yield His harvest of blessing, favor, goodness, mercy, grace, strength and the anointing in every area of your life.

Prayer: *I pray you build on the solid rock foundation and be never moved, your faith in His Word, and be unshakable.*

Launching Deeper: Jude 1:20, Colossians 2:7, Ephesians 2:20.

Hebrew Word Study: "musad"—foundation, foundation laying (Strong's Hebrew: 4143).

November 18

El Bethel

בית"ל

God of Bethel

"I am the God of Bethel, where you anointed the pillar and where you made a vow to Me. Now arise, get out of this land, and return to the land of your family" (Genesis 31:13, NKJV).

When Jacob was in distress and running away from his brother Esau, he found a place to rest and had a dream; the Lord revealed Himself to him and confirmed His presence with him; He assured to give him the land and keep the covenant with him and his children. The Lord promised not to leave him until He fulfills His promises and the blessing established. Waking up from his dream Jacob recognized the place was not an ordinary one. God had appeared to him, and he saw angels ascending and descending. He acknowledged the place as the house of God and called it Bethel. Like Jacob, in every challenge, be reminded of the Lord's covenant of blessing and protection He made at Bethel, the House of God. Build an altar to worship the God of Bethel continually and honor the personal experience with Him at the place where He promised to make you prosperous with His blessings. The house of God is where you may have an encounter with Him, that would stay with you for long. He would reveal Himself to you, bless you, and accomplish his promises concerning your life.

Prayer: *I pray the Lord will deal well with you and reveal Himself to you in a supernatural way.*

Launching Deeper: Genesis 28:13-20,32:9, 35:7.

Hebrew Word Study: "matstsebah"—a pillar, stump (Strong's Hebrew: 4676).

November 19

Shomeracha

שומראצ'ה

Thy Keeper

"The Lord is your keeper; The Lord is your shade at your right hand" (Psalm 121:5, NKJV).

A security guard will guard a property, place, or person to make sure nothing bad happens to what has been entrusted with. Keeping and guarding requires no slumber when it is in the night. He is to keep watch and protect from trouble. The one that provides ultimate security gives the safest place for his children to do well. The Lord, Our Keeper, drives away the enemy from His people and destroys the adversaries. When His people took the journey to the promised land, He gave them the assurance that He would drive away the nations, the Amorites, the Canaanites, the Hittites, the Hivites, and the Jebusite. He delivered them all into the hands of his people and called them to devote the nations to destruction. When He is in charge, and He is protecting, no one can touch what He protects in time of trouble. No one can touch you when He is guarding you. The Lord hides you in His secret place and sets you up on the rock as you keep your trust in Him.

Prayer: *I pray the One who leads the starry host and calls them each by name, and none missing help you in all your endeavors.*

Launching Deeper: Revelations 7:16, Genesis 28:15, Psalms 16:8, 91:1-4.

Hebrew Word Study: "natsar"—to watch, guard, keep (Strong's Hebrew: 5341).

November 20

HAVTACHAH ELOHIM HAAV

חב"ד אלוהים הואב

The Promise of the Father

"And being assembled together with them, He commanded them not to depart from Jerusalem, but to wait for the Promise of the Father, 'which,' He said, 'you have heard from Me'" (Acts 1:4, NKJV).

When Jesus had been with the disciples after the resurrection, Acts chapter 1 tells us he commanded them not to leave Jerusalem until the Promise of the Father had come, which He declared will come to empower and equip them to be in operation in spreading the good news to the nations. The promise of the Father, whom He will send in His name to be poured upon us believers and teach in all things and all truth, and also remind us of every word that He had taught and testify about Him. He is to baptize believers in the Holy Spirit and fill them with the power of the Spirit, sealed with the pledge of our inheritance to do great works and help plant churches. The Spirit of grace anoints you for His service and fulfills the purpose of the Lord with you, and to all people to give you directions and encourage you, sanctifying you with His gifts and fruits and also empowering you to live and walk in the will of God.

Prayer: *I pray the Spirit will clothe you with His power from on high and be fruitful in His gifts.*

Launching Deeper: Acts 13:2, 2:33, Matthew 10:20, Luke 11:13.

Hebrew Word Study: "omer"—promise, thing, word (Strong's Hebrew: 562).

November 21

HaOzer

האוזר

The Helper

"But the Helper, the Holy Spirit, whom the Father will send in My name, He will teach you all things, and bring to your remembrance all things that I said to you" (John 14:26, NKJV).

The Greek word "parakletos" is called to one's aid, a helper. Our friends and relatives have been of good help, but none can be compared with the divine Help of the Spirit, whom Jesus called from the Father to be of assistance to us. The ultimate Help, the believer will need in all circumstances and the advocate who interceded for us in time of weakness. He provides divine assistance with divine authority to vanquish weakness and helplessness out of the believer, and this is what was seen in Peter proclaiming the gospel when the Spirit came upon Him. He witnessed to the people and caused a transformation of lives to occur. As a sign of His love and kindness, He comes in the name of Christ to teach us in all things, reminds us of what Jesus thought, establishes us in His new covenant of blessing with us, and causes us to display His fruits. Also As a Helper, He gives you wisdom and insight into the things of God. You are sealed and protected in Him.

Prayer: *I pray the Spirit helps you and empowers you in everything you for Him.*

Launching Deeper: John 14:16, 26, 15:16, Galatians 5:22-23, Jude 1:18,19.

Hebrew Word Study: "ezer"—help (Strong's Hebrew: 5828).

November 22

ADAM SHOMAYIM

אדם שומאים

The Man from Heaven

"The first man was of the earth, made of dust; the second Man is the Lord from heaven" (1 Corinthians 15:47, NKJV).

This is the contrast between the natural and the spiritual existence. As Adam was of the earth as the first man, Christ is the man from heaven, as Paul explained to the Corinthians. The man from the earth had a living soul, Jesus, the man from heaven, has the quickening Spirit to stir the mortal into the supernatural. He is the Creator of the heavens and the earth and descends from heaven as the Lord and as the image of the merciful and faithful Father; Jesus, the Man from heaven, comes and stands as a humble servant in serving the Father and also makes reconciliation for many to come to His kingdom. He brings justice and faithfulness and never changes, all creations, the work of His hands will perish, but He would remain the same. His years will never end. The truth and the reality of His promises, His words, and revelations of the heavenly things, are what He has seen and gives testimony about as a man from the heavens. He will lead you according to His love and grace for your life and will strengthen and keep His eye on you.

***Prayer:** I pray the Man from heaven turns things around. Instead of wood, bronze, and instead of stones, iron, and make your officers peace and magistrates righteousness.*

Launching Deeper: Isaiah 9:6, Jeremiah 23:6, Matthew 1:23.

Hebrew Word Study: "yasha"—to deliver (Strong's Hebrew: 3467).

November 23

HAAV HACHAI

האוה הי״ד

The Living Father

"As the living Father hath sent me, and I live by the Father: so he that eateth me, even he shall live by me" (John 6:57, KJV).

Earthly father-son relationship is one of the most intriguing relationships. He is supportive and loyal; He protects and shows unconditional love. These pillars exhibited by the father provide some steps for the son to thrive in life. The Living Father believes in Christ the Son, and that is something not shared by unbelievers. As believers, we call Him Our Father because we have a new standing before Him. We are living by the Living Father. By His love for us, He sent His beloved son to us, that we would live through Him. Sometimes you wonder why man puts too much confidence in their gold, diamonds, bitcoin, fame, images, worthless and lifeless idols. As a loving father will caution his child and give him instructions, so the Living Father cautions the people of Israel that the things they go after and put their trust in are worthless. When we have Christ in us, we have life and have it more abundantly on earth and live eternally. He is the dependable Living Father, and He is exalted above every other situation in your life.

Prayer: *I pray the living Father will bring life and show forth His grace and with great gift of His goodness in the world.*

Launching Deeper: John 5:26, Jeremiah 10:1-10, Psalm 18:46, 1 Thessalonians 1:9.

Hebrew Word Study: "chay"—alive, living (Strong's Hebrew: 2416).

November 24

Naveh Tsedek

נוה צדק

The Habitation of Justice

All who found them have devoured them; And their adversaries said, "We have not offended, Because they have sinned against the Lord, the habitation of justice, The Lord, the hope of their fathers."

Jeremiah 50:7 (NKJV)

Far be it from the Lord that He will not do what is right, He will not pervert justice. All His ways are just and perfect and righteous. The ways of the Lord are just. The prophet called upon Him to bring justice to His people, for He is the Habitation of justice. The God of justice is also the one who seeks justice for His children by destroying the works of darkness and restoring them to His righteousness and blessings. The law of the Lord confirms His uprightness. His will is ultimately perfect, and His actions and deeds in mighty works are displayed in His justice, it's equitable and executed fairly by punishing evil when evil is committed, and rewarding righteousness when it's done according to His Word and precepts. In Him dwells justice and faithfulness and He loves justice. He establishes justice in the reign of Christ; He requires that amid His people where His presence is, we reflect His justice and perfect ways.

***Prayer**: I pray the Lord will bring justice in your case and silence every voice of the accuser in Jesus' name.*

Launching Deeper: Jeremiah 31:23, Psalms 90:1, 91:1.

Hebrew Word Study: "naveh"—abode of shepherd or flocks, habitation (Strong's Hebrew: 5116a).

November 25

Seter

מושבים

Hiding Place

"You are my hiding place; You shall preserve me from trouble; You shall surround me with songs of deliverance" (Psalm 32:7, NKJV).

The Psalmist loved to be in the Lord's house all his days, just to behold His beauty and countenance. One thing he knew was that on the day of trouble, the Lord would conceal him in His hiding place. The Great God is the hiding place. In His glory, He will take care of you. Moses requested the presence of the Lord to be with them as they took the journey to the promised land, and the Lord said, "There is a place near me where you can hide and stand to see my glory" (Exodus 33:21). The Lord would hide you under the shadow of His wings. He would hide you in the secret place of His presence, away from the scheme and plotting of the wicked. He delivers His people from calamities and keeps His eye upon them, watching over them. He is a hiding place. In Him, you can put your trust; in Him, you can have hope and confidence, and also depend upon Him to sustain you in tough times, a preservation which never fails.

***Prayer**: I pray the Lord will make you sing His songs of deliverance, and all around you will rejoice with you.*

Launching Deeper: Psalms 17:8, 31:20, 40:2, 41:1, 50:15, 76:2, 83:3, 91:1.

Hebrew Word Study: "sether"—a covering, hiding place (Strong's Hebrew: 5643).

November 26

UMERIM ROSHI

מרים את הראש שלי

Lifter Up of Mine Head

"But You, O Lord, are a shield for me, My glory and the One who lifts up my head" (Psalm 3:3, NKJV).

In all Job's troubles, he depended on God to be the lifter of his head. One who would restore him in His place of dignity and to His place of power. David also trusted in the faithfulness of God that when challenges have surrounded him, and he is in shame and reproach, causing his head to bow down and drowned in affliction, the Lord will turn things around for him. The Lord will cause his head to be lifted above his enemies. They cannot lift up their heads against you anymore, therefore, sing praises unto the Lord, like how Pharaoh restored the butler by Joseph interpreting his dream in prison and told him on the third day the king will bring you back to serve him. He is the one that will lift you up. He would raise you and exalt you and cause you to ride on high places of the earth and be your glory. The Lifter up of your head will bless you and will not withhold any good thing from you, all to His glory, and put a crown upon your head.

Prayer: *I pray the Lord lifts you up above your enemies and His glory be seen in you and all that you do.*

Launching Deeper: Psalms 27:6, 110:7, 119:7, Luke 21:28, Judges 8:28.

Hebrew Word Study: "rum"—to be high or exalted, rise (Strong's Hebrew: 7311).

November 27

Rabah Sakar Gili

רבאח סקאר גילי

Thy Exceeding Great Reward

"After these things the word of the Lord came to Abram in a vision, saying, "Do not be afraid, Abram. I am your shield, your exceedingly great reward" (Genesis 15:1 NKJV).

The Lord appeared to Abraham to give him an assurance that he would be with him, He would protect him, he would bless him, and make his name great. The Lord said, He Himself would be the reward for Abraham as he keeps trusting Him, for the Lord would finish his work and give Himself as our greatest reward. He would be the portion of their inheritance. Everything about Adonai would be for Abraham, all about His greatness, His goodness, His mercies, His kindness, his faithfulness, his love, his provision, his protection, his grace, his righteousness, his power and dominion, all for him and his children as the Lord promised. He is your exceeding glorious reward, your service to Him, your labor for Him will not be in vain. The challenges you go through and persecution you face in serving the Lord will be rewarded greatly. As you devote yourself to do the work of God fully, you would inherit His kingdom, and His prosperity on the earth, and His eternal presence at the end.

Prayer: *I pray the Lord goes ahead of you and bring you victory in your battles and cause you to come out with great substance.*

Launching Deeper: Deuteronomy 33:26-29, Ruth 2:12, Psalm 16:5,6, Hebrews 11:6.

Hebrew Word Study: "rabah"—to be or become much, many or great (Strong's Hebrew: 7235).

November 28

MIKVEH AVOTEIHEM

מקווה אבות

Hope of Their Fathers

All who found them have devoured them; And their adversaries said, We have not offended, Because they have sinned against the Lord, the habitation of justice, The Lord, the hope of their fathers.

Jeremiah 50:7 (NKJV)

In the Great and Mighty God, the God of Israel is the one whom the fathers of Israel trusted and desired with expectations of fulfillment, and He saved and brought obtainment in their lives. They experienced His mighty hand of deliverance and how He defeated their enemies and commanded them to serve Him alone. Though they abandoned His covenant along the way, and His fury came upon them, they always turned back and remembered the Hope of their fathers and the Hope of Israel. The fathers depended on His faithfulness in the covenant He established with them, for an everlasting fulfillment and blessings, that when they call forth the name of the God of their fathers, Abraham, Isaac, and Jacob, He shows forth His mighty deed, and the nations see He is the powerful God. Base on the covenant, have hope in His grace and compassion and know He will not allow the wicked to hurt you. The Hope of the fathers will grant you wisdom above all to know more and will reveal His secrets to you. He will never fail but will fulfill and perfect His Word for your life.

Prayer: *I pray people shall see the righteousness of God in your life. And all king's glory of God upon your life as you hope in Him and praise His name.*

Launching Deeper: Psalms 22:4, 71:5, Jeremiah 2:3, 14:8, 1 Timothy 1:1.

Hebrew Word Study: "miqveh"—hope (Strong's Hebrew: 4723).

November 29

Migdal Yeshu'ot

מגדל ישות

Tower of Salvation

"He is the tower of salvation to His king, And shows mercy to His anointed, To David and his descendants forevermore" (2 Samuel 22:51, NKJV).

A fortification of rescue, where the king always relies upon and a high tower of safety from enemies is the Lord. King David depended on His salvation and knew that there was nothing he could do to save himself from any danger; it was a relationship he had with the Father that gave him the access to tap into the favor and goodness of God. The tower of salvation was full of the mercies of God, where David could find special mercy assigned to him alone called "the sure mercies of David" in which the Lord forgave him of his sins and divinely restored him fully, and also showed to David's descendants. To Solomon, when his heart was swayed by many women and he fell into sin, for His covenant with David, His Father and for his saving power, He shown him mercy. The tower of salvation is your place of refuge in time of danger, your city full of deliverance and redemption, where He brings transformation and brings peace with God to your life and with the presence of the Holy Spirit abiding with you and shows you and your descendants His compassion and His goodness and favor.

Prayer: *I pray the sure mercies of David be your portion and providence and continue to abide in His tower of Salvation.*

Launching Deeper: John 1:1, Acts 5:30-31, Psalm 32:1,2, Romans 8:17, Galatians 4:4-7.

Hebrew Word Study: "asah"—do, make (Strong's Hebrew: 6213).

November 30

HaKapporah Zevach

הקורה זאבך

The Atoning Sacrifice

"But this man, after he had offered one sacrifice for sins for ever, sat down on the right hand of God" (Hebrews 10:12, KJV).

The fulfillment of the one-time atoning sacrifice was done in Christ to reconcile humanity back to the broken relation with God. By sins and transgression, man has provoked God's anger and wrath of judgment, and the only means to bring a reconciliation once again is ("at-one-ment") an atonement of a perfect sacrifice, and since man is not in the capacity to deliver himself, the Lord provided the solution to sacrifice His own Son. His nature of mercy and his gracious love made him reluctant to bring punishment to all sinners, but He gave Himself up as a sweet-smelling sacrifice upon the heavenly altar. He made Himself a perfect one as a purification for sins once and for all and to redeem all from bondage of lawlessness by pouring His blood for us. A means to forgive all our sins, transgressions, and iniquities, and a demonstration of his covenant of love that has bought us back unto Himself and making us holy, and healing us from all sickness of the soul, spirit, and body, keeping us close and closer to Him for eternity.

***Prayer**: I pray the blood of Jesus speak better for you, it will speak well-being and restoration for you as the redeemed of the Lord.*

Launching Deeper: Titus 2:14, 1 John 1:7, Colossians 2:13,14, Acts 13:38, Ephesians 1:7,8.

Hebrew Word Study: "kippur"—atonement (Strong's Hebrew: 3725).

December

"Thus says the LORD who made the earth, the LORD who formed it and established it, the LORD is His name
Jeremiah 33:2 NKJV

December 1

MEKHONEN HASHALOM

מחונן השלום

Author of Peace

"For God is not the author of confusion, but of peace, as in all churches of the saints" (1 Corinthians 14:33, KJV).

Peter and the rest of the disciples in the boat hoped that as long as Jesus is with them, the storm raging will not overwhelm them, and Jesus did command peace. He causes order to prevail amid chaos. The spirit of the Lord moved over the waters when the earth was without form and void, and God the Father declared, let there be light, and it was light and order. He is the author of peace, the source of tranquility and calmness. He does not allow disorderliness and confusion in His presence. As the Psalmist declared that the Lord is in His holy temple, let all the earth be silent. Paul admonished the Corinthians that whenever they gather in His name as a church, all things must be done according to the will of God, everyone one performing a task amid the gathering should let peace prevail, an attribute of God who is the Prince of Peace, the originator of order and perfect rest. He is commanding peace to prevail for you. Harmony and unity bring the flow of His presence, power, and peace. Fruit of the Spirit is in you as a sign of His perfect rest. Let the Spirit take preeminence over all things for you.

***Prayer:** I pray and silence all restlessness and tumult and command tranquility to prevail for you.*

Launching Deeper: John 16:33, 14:23-27, 15:3, Acts 10:36, Isaiah 53:5, Luke 24:22-24.

Hebrew Word Study: "mishtar"—rule, authority (Strong's Hebrew: 4896).

December 2

Baal Eretze

בעל ארץ ישראל

The Landowner

Hear another parable: There was a certain landowner who planted a vineyard and set a hedge around it, dug a winepress in it and built a tower. And he leased it to vinedressers and went into a far country.

Matthew 21:33 (NKJV)

Vineyards in Palestine are planted in rows, and some planted on leveled hills with branches trailing the ground. It has fences and walls around them and winepress built close to the vineyards with guarding towers also close by. Towers are for guards to keep watch over the vineyard, to prevent thieves and wild beasts invading the garden. As workers on the vineyard are we called with various assignments in His kingdom, some cultivating the plants, some harvesting, some trodden at the winepress for juice, and some, guarding at the watchtower. He is the owner of the lands and vineyards, and we are His servants. He claims ownership of every blessing given to us; we are His stewards of everything and possessors of nothing, assigned to produce good fruits on the land by our service to him, and accountable to the gifts, talents, and ministries endowed in us by the Spirit. As He said to Adam, replenish the earth, subdue, multiply and be fruitful upon the land, use your gifts and talents to serve, replenish, multiply, be fruitful, glorify His name and receive His blessings and reward in abundance as a good steward.

***Prayer:** I pray the Lord equips you with His anointing to work His giftings and talents in you to be more effective.*

Launching Deeper: Psalms 80:8-16, Song of Solomon 8:11,12, Mark 13:24.

Hebrew Word Study: "baal"—lord (Strong's Hebrew: 1167).

December 3

ELOHEI AVI KHOL

אלוהי אבי כהול

God and Father of All

"One God and Father of all, who is above all, and through all, and in you all" (Ephesians 4:6, NKJV).

Near East in the past, when someone gives a name to something, it's now in actuality, it has an identity and subject to the authority of the person. All creation and its identity came out of the Father. He is the God and Father of them all. He has access to all that He made to be in them, a relationship to creation, and involved in what He made. The paternal relationship of what He made and His leadership is to be recognized by all on the earth. As the God and Father of all, He is in charge of all things; He is through all in every believer showing His power and love and grace by the indwelling of the Holy Spirit; therefore, we should manifest His love to the lost world as sons of God that creation waits for. He gives you authority above all things, all powers and authorities, dominions and rulers, and governments and systems and kingdoms and nations, all powers of darkness at your command, and He has conquered them all for you. In all things He executes His providence and protection and works all things in all His children.

Prayer: *I pray as everything that is born of Him overcome the world, so do you overcome all, and as you call upon His name, let Him be there to bless you.*

Launching Deeper: Matthew 12:50, Deuteronomy 4:7, 1 Corinthians 8:6, 12:6, Ephesians 2:22, 3:17, John 14:23.

Hebrew Word Study: "edah"—congregation (Strong's Hebrew: 5712).

December 4

LASABET HAMMGBIHI

לסבט האמגביהי

He Who Dwells on High

"Who is like the Lord our God, Who dwells on high" (Psalm 113:5, NKJV).

There is no one like Him, none among the heavenly beings in holiness, revered with worship and praise who does wonders. He who dwells in majesty in the highest heavens, the heaven of heavens cannot contain Him, for He is so Mighty and exalted above all, His throne established on High. Honor and dignity in Supreme with grace and mercy and rides upon the heavens, His kingdom rules over all, on high is His Sovereignty. He rules over the nations and kingdoms of the earth and sends forth His Word in power. The Lord dwells on High above the circles of the earth and above the universe with righteousness and brings the kings and princesses to nothing and meaningless. He Who dwells on High speaks in majesty on your behalf and acts in majesty in His sanctuary, giving you help, strength, and power and overthrows your enemies by His greatness and shatter them all.

***Prayer**: I pray the Lord who dwells in majesty perform great wonders for you and use you mightily to impact others.*

Launching Deeper: Psalm 118:1,16, Psalm 89:6,8, Exodus 15:11, Deuteronomy 33:26.

Hebrew Word Study: "yashab"—to sit, remain, dwell (Strong's Hebrew: 3427)

December 5

ZORE'A KOL ZERA TOV

צורה קול זרע טוב

The Sower of Good Seed

"He answered and said to them: "He who sows the good seed is the Son of Man" (Matthew 13:37, NKJV).

It was known in the past in the East that an enemy can sow poisonous seeds in the person's land they want to afflict. The parable of the wheat and tares Jesus told the disciples, was about the children of the kingdom and the children of the world. Christ is the source of the Word, and out of the Word, we have been born in the spirit as sons of the kingdom and as the good seeds planted to show forth His glory. The enemy comes to sow the tares called the sons of the wicked, who do not heed to His Word to obey and mix themselves in the wheat and are known by their fruits, but The Sower of good seeds has the patience to wait to the end, by His mercy, that all will have a changed heart and chose the narrow way to have eternal life. The Good seed produces good fruits of the Spirit, love, peace, goodness, kindness, joy, and righteousness in Christ. The Sower will plant you and establish you in Him and cause His fruits of goodness and mercies and prosperity to spring forth in you as you walk and heed to His counsel.

Prayer: *I pray any plant the Sower of Good seeds did not sow, let it be uprooted and destroyed in Jesus' name and let His good seeds bear great fruits in your life.*

Launching Deeper: Matthew 13:24-30, 4:23, 10:40, 20:1, Colossians 1:5.

Hebrew Word Study: "zera"—sowing, seed, offspring (Strong's Hebrew: 2233).

December 6

Bechir Hashem

בכר השם

The Chosen of God

"And the people stood looking on. But even the rulers with them sneered, saying, "He saved others; let Him save Himself if He is the Christ, the chosen of God" (Luke 23:35, NKJV).

The chief priest and the Pharisees accused Jesus of things He did not do and demanded that he be crucified, taking Him to Pilate and Herod, and still not finding anything to kill Him but kept on prevailing in their accusations. At Calvary, they mocked Him and said, "He saved others now let Him save himself if he is the chosen one, the Christ." Here they confirmed He was the chosen one, though rejected by men but elected and precious in the sight of God to go through this suffering to save them from their sins. He was on the cross and died so they would be redeemed. The Chosen One was the servants of the Father in whom His soul delight and upholds and filled with the fullness of the spirit. As you speak the Word, the good news to the poor, and to proclaim deliverance to those in captivity and asleep, pray for the blind to receive sight and to bring freedom. Proclaim the year, the time, and the season of the Lord's favor brings judgment to the Gentiles and justice and restorations to the nations.

***Prayer**: I pray the Lord will choose you and delight to do you good and silence the mouth of the accuser on your behalf.*

Launching Deeper: 1 Peter 2:4,6, Philippians 2:7, Luke 9:35,4:18,19, Isaiah 2:4, 11:2, 41:8.

Hebrew Word Study: "bachar"—to choose (Strong's Hebrew: 977).

December 7

Makor Mayim Chayyim

מקור מיים ים ים

Fountain of Living Waters

"For My people have committed two evils: They have forsaken Me, the fountain of living waters, And hewn themselves cisterns—broken cisterns that can hold no water" (Jeremiah 2:13, NKJV).

The Lord told Jeremiah his people have forsaken him and followed other gods; they are not obeying Him; they broke the covenant He made with them and forgot He walked with them in the wilderness and provided them with food and water. He gave them the Living water to quench their thirst. The gift of God is the living Waters which is given by Christ. Whoever drinks the living Waters would never thirst and would become a fountain of springing waters unto eternal life. With Him is the fountain of life. The rivers that flow from the throne of God full of life, in Him, all with joy will draw water from the springs of salvation, all who forsake Him thirst and do not have everlasting life flowing unto them. The fountain of living water is the sign of prosperity and hope, a symbol of God's power and His presence, a source of fruitfulness and increase, and that is where He has settled you in, a place of abundance and all provisions.

Prayer: *I pray the Lord plants you like the tree planted by the rivers of water that nourishes and cause to flourish, its leaves never wither.*

Launching Deeper: John 4:10, 11, Deuteronomy 31:16, Revelation 7:17, Isaiah 12:3, 17:13.

Hebrew Word Study: "maqor"—a spring, fountain (Strong's Hebrew: 4726).

December 8

MA'OZ L'EVYON

מעוז לביון

Strength to the Needy

For You have been a strength to the poor, A strength to the needy in his distress, A refuge from the storm, A shade from the heat; For the blast of the terrible ones is as a storm against the wall.

Isaiah 25:4 (NKJV)

When there is an invasion of the enemy against a city, mostly it's the poor and needy in distress that suffer the most. It's only the Lord Mighty, through His mercy, that provides shelter for the oppressed and delivers them from the oppressor. When the Lord who is the Strength is with the needy, he should not be in dread of the enemy. The Lord goes ahead and destroy every work of the wicked against the needy and when the enemy afflicts, He promised to draw them into confusion and totally bring them to destruction. He sustains and strengthens also in time of persecution and bodily afflictions and brings healing to the weak soul. He answers when they call and will not forsake them, as they keep trusting in Him. While others trust in chariots and horses, and in what they have in their achievements, keep your faith in Him. His name is a sanctuary for the righteous and the needy. He will establish you in Zion, in His presence, and cause your joy to increase with strength.

Prayer: *I pray the Lord will increase your joy and cause you to rejoice and inherit the land.*

Launching Deeper: Isaiah 27:5, 28:6, 29:5, 29:20, Isaiah 11:4, 14:32, 29:19, Isaiah 4:5,6, 32:2

Hebrew Word Study: "ebyon"—in want, needy, poor (Strong's Hebrew: 34).

December 9

Tzur Machseh

צור מאשה

Rock of My Refuge

"But the Lord has been my defense, And my God the rock of my refuge" (Psalm 94:22, NKJV).

Noah sought to carry out his obligations as expected. He was able to complete the ark by divine guidance. The ark became a refuge for him and his generation; it was a refuge to escape the waters of the flood. He was unique in his time; he walked with God and found favor in the eyes of the Lord; he stood out to be faithful amid the faithless, and God chose him to prepare a hiding place for the chosen creatures who would survive the flood (Genesis 7,8). Refuge is the place of shelter and protection from difficulties. A hiding place when enemies are after you. When the Lord God is your Rock of refuge, your pursuers cannot penetrate through to reach you, no arrow or spear can penetrate through the Rock when you are hiding in there. Those who chase after you will be crushed in the attempt to get close. Your refuge will not fail, you will lodge securely from any assault (Psalm 142:5). He is the ark that keeps you safe. Depend on Him continually, for there is no safe place nor rock like our God, our refuge and powerful place of deliverance.

***Prayer**: I pray as you hide in the Rock of refuge may every assault of wickedness be turned back to senders, as you depend and trust in Him may your enemies be broken in pieces and may they be crushed by the Rock in Jesus' name.*

Launching Deeper: Nahum 1:7, Psalm 27:1-3.

Hebrew Word Study: "machseh"—meaning a place of shelter (Strong's Hebrew: 4268).

December 10

HaTzel

הצל

The Shade

"The Lord is your keeper; The Lord is your shade at your right hand" (Psalm 121:5, NKJV).

The temperature of the sun's surface is about 5000 Celsius, having too much of it or prolonged exposure to the sun can cause some damages to the body even though it's over ninety-two million miles away from the earth and has some good benefit of providing vitamin D. To have a whole nation of people walking under the sun on a forty-year journey is fascinating, the heat alone could be dangerous to them, but the Lord was as a cloud pillar of shade that protected and kept them from the sun's heat during the day and a pillar of fire against the coldness of the night. He did not allow them to be smitten. In the secret place of the Almighty, He hid you from the dangers of nature and always kept you under His shadow. The presence of the Lord is onto us, a shade against any wiles of the enemy, and the Lord Our Shade will lift a standard against him when he comes in like a flood. Your help is from the Lord. When you lift up your eyes unto the hills and ask for help, He will cover you. He is your shade, and under His shadow, He would keep you from the heat of the troubles of this world and will not let the sun smite you.

Prayer: *I pray the Lord Our Shade will be with you by pillar of cloud to defend you against the sun and a refuge from the storm as a shadow of a great rock in a place of distress.*

Launching Deeper: Psalm 91:1, Isaiah 25:4, 32:2, Numbers 14:9.

Hebrew Word Study: "tsel"—a shadow (Strong's Hebrew: 6738).

December 11

ELOHEI YAANEH EISH

אלוהי יענא איש

God Who Answers by Fire

"'Then you call on the name of your gods, and I will call on the name of the Lord; and the God who answers by fire, He is God.' So all the people answered and said, It is well spoken'" (1 Kings 18:24, NKJV).

Elijah challenge Ahab to call for the prophets of Baal and Asherah, 850 of them to come to Mount Carmel, and he asked them, for how long would they allow themselves to be deceived by foreign gods if they can save them, they should build the altar and put a sacrifice on it without fire. The one who can send fire is the true God, but they did all they could to call fire and Baal, and there was no result. But when Elijah called upon The God of the heavens, the Adonai, the great "I AM" the Awesome God, Mighty one in battle. He answered by pouring out fire upon the altar, everything upon the altar was consumed by fire, the stones, the sacrifice, and the water were all consumed to let them know He is not only the Great God but also the Consuming Fire. When you call upon His name, He would answer as your act of worship, He will never fail. The God who hears your supplication will hear you that people may know and acknowledge that He alone is the great God who pays attention to the cries of His children.

***Prayer**: I pray as you call upon the name of the Lord, let your prayers ascend to the heavenly altar as an incense and let it pour down as fire to consume every form of evil deeds in Jesus' name*

Launching Deeper: Psalm 50:15, 1 Kings 18:20-39, Psalms 18:3,6, 55:16, 86:3, Leviticus 9:24, Judges 6:21.

Hebrew Word Study: "esh"—a fire (Strong's Hebrew: 784).

December 12

Mogen kol Ezer

מאי קול עזר

Shield of Help

> Happy are you, O Israel! Who is like you, a people saved by the Lord,
> *The shield of your help And the sword of your majesty! Your enemies shall submit to you, And you shall tread down their high places.*
>
> *Deuteronomy 33:29 (NKJV)*

The shield as a weapon provides a protective interruption in combat attacks by arrows, swords, sling-stones, axes, etc. And it was consistently used in the Middle Ages. The Lord, the Man of War, and the Commander of the heavenly bodies is our Shield of help in time of combat against the enemy's attacks and falsities. A defense through His Word and the help that provides everything else man will need for His survival. He gives the shield and the lights of His splendor of His glory and gives security, strength, favor, and help. His shield of salvation gives victory and upholds and sustains with His right hand. He surrounds you with blessings and favor. The shield of His faithfulness is never failing like the protection of a shield. Your faith and trust in the Lord are a shield that drives away the arrows of doubts by the enemy and his falsities through temptation. He is the refuge in which you hide and keeps you away from trouble, and delivers you from attacks, and gives you His grace and power.

Prayer: *I pray as the Lord shields you, let every enemy submit to you, and thresh every hindrance and their high places.*

Launching Deeper: Psalms 91:4, 6:12, 3:3, 32:10. 84:9-11, 33:29, 89:18.

Hebrew Word Study: "magen"—a shield (Strong's Hebrew: 4043).

December 13

BRIT AM

ברית אם

Covenant of the People

"I, the Lord, have called You in righteousness, And will hold Your hand; I will keep You and give You as a covenant to the people, As a light to the Gentiles" (Isaiah 42:6, NKJV).

In a time of His favor, He declared He would give His servant as a covenant for the people and to establish the earth to be inherited by his children. The Lord Jesus is the mediator of the covenants and the covenant Himself. He poured His blood for the new covenant and set it for many for the remission of sins and freedom from the oppression of the enemy. The covenant of the people is God's fulfilled purpose of salvation and the covenant of grace to be given. As many as would believe in Him, will receive the forgiveness of their sins, and to bring consolation in relationship to the Father by the power of the Holy Spirit. The covenant would bring a confirmation and transformation by the indwelling of the Spirit, who would help all believers to live an obedient life, where the covenant brings mercy and sets free every believer from the law of sin and death.

***Prayer:** I pray your prayers be an offering to God and your praise as sweet-smelling incense and acceptable sacrifices unto the Lord.*

Launching Deeper: Isaiah 49:8, Matthew 26:28, Luke 1:69-72.

Hebrew Word Study: "am"—people (Strong's Hebrew: 5971).

December 14

BOREH KETZOT HAARETZ

בורה קצות הארץ

Creator of the Ends of the Earth

Have you not known? Have you not heard? The everlasting God, the Lord,
The Creator of the ends of the earth, Neither faints nor is weary.
His understanding is unsearchable.

Isaiah 40:28 (NKJV)

The greatness of the Lord is unreachable. By His will and by His Word, the heavens and the earth were created. He brought forth the foundation of the earth and established justice. All the people of the ends of the earth who look up to him shall be saved. He gives strength to His children and also exalts the horns of His people. The creator of the ends of the earth has made you by his spirit and by the mighty hand for His glory that you would worship and reference his name and honor Him at all times. He is the possessor of the earth and controls and sustains it. And sets the world in order, His thunders make the waters in the heavens to roar and the clouds to rise from the ends of the earth and bring the wind from the storehouse of the heavens, He is the Lord of all the earth and all that is in it are His, and belongs to Him. His steadfast love is seen in His creation and filled with His glory and praise, and it will be filled with the knowledge of Him.

***Prayer:** I pray kings come to your light, and the brightness of His radiance upon your life attracts more favor to you.*

Launching Deeper: Psalms 96:1, 24:1, 95:4,5, 47:9, Isaiah 44:2, 45:22, 59:1, 1 Samuel 2:10, Hosea 6:3.

Hebrew Word Study: "kol"—the whole, all (Strong's Hebrew: 3605).

December 15

MALACH HABRIT

מלאכת הברית

Messenger of the Covenant

"Behold, I send My messenger, And he will prepare the way before Me. And the Lord, whom you seek, Will suddenly come to His temple, Even the Messenger of the covenant, In whom you delight. Behold, He is coming," Says the Lord of hosts.

Malachi 3:1 (NKJV)

In the world of technology, sending messages has become very easy to do. With just a touch or a click, you can send a message to thousands of people in seconds. Technological devices and gadgets have become our messengers, bearing all kinds of messages. When the prophet Malachi gave the prophecy about a messenger coming, it happened 400 years after. The Messenger Malachi prophesied about was sent by the Father, One Who will bear the message of the divine covenant. Christ Himself is the message and the covenant appointed by the Father. The message of the covenant is to proclaim His love to His children, to bring redemption, restoration to your life, and appoint you with an inheritance of His spirit to be with you. His Word of promise will abide with you and your children. By the spirit and the covenant of blessings, you can walk in His statutes, observe His ordinances, and He will establish you with His peace.

Prayer: *I pray the Lord will pour His rain on your land, bring fruitfulness for you, and His blessings on your seeds as His covenant.*

Launching Deeper: Isaiah 42:1, 49:8, 55:3, 59:21.

Hebrew Word Study: "berith"—a covenant (Strong's Hebrew: 1285).

December 16

Rea

ידידנו

Our Friend

"You are My friends if you do whatever I command you" (John 15:14, NKJV).

Friends share interests and develop deep fellowship through communication, and they know much about each other. Jesus made His disciples full partners and positioned them to unrestrained fellowship. He kept nothing from them, the things He received from the Father and absolute subject to His commands is what He required from His friends. Our Friend Jesus had made us free to be His personal representatives on earth to reproduce His works, bring forth good fruits, and show forth His glory as He represented the Father. We have received a revelation of who the Father is from His model of love, and when we obey His love commandment, we enjoy more of the intimacy of our Friend Jesus. Through His communion and your obedience to His Word, He makes known His covenant to you. In the bond of His love, there are no limitations to His perfect rest and perfect peace, no need to fear because your Friend walks by your side and commands that you cast all burdens unto Him, for He cares that much about you and is constantly mindful of you.

***Prayer:** I pray the Lord our Friend reveals secrets of the kingdom to you, as you keep His Word and love Him, let Him manifest Himself to you and remain in His love.*

Launching Deeper: Psalm 25:14, John 14:15,28, 2 Chronicles 20:7.

Hebrew Word Study: "aheb"—to love (Strong's Hebrew: 157). "rea"—friend, companion, fellow.

December 17

SHEVET YISROEL

שבט ישראל

The Scepter of Israel

"I see Him, but not now; I behold Him, but not near; A Star shall come out of Jacob; A Scepter shall rise out of Israel, And batter the brow of Moab, And destroy all the sons of tumult" Numbers 24:17 (NKJV)

It was a journey that Balaam was not supposed to take; the award given by Balak to this mission to curse Israel was something that he could not relent. But when he arrived at Peor, the Lord reminded him He is not a God who would change His mind concerning His promises and blessings for His people. The Lord caused Balaam to pronounce blessings instead of curses. He declared that out of Israel would rise a scepter, a symbol of authority and sovereignty, the scepter that will not depart from Judah until Shiloh comes, expressing the ruling power of Christ, who will reign forever and ever with justice and righteousness, and rules with power and strength. The Scepter is being extended to you this day as a sign of His favor, as king Ahazerus extended to Esther; He extended to you to empower you, to have dominion and also declared to you He would not repent of His Word concerning you. He will bring them to fulfillment, therefore arise and shine for His scepter of power, righteousness, grace, and favor is extended on you.

Prayer: *I pray the Lord who rules amid His enemies and His throne everlasting give you victory in all you do, for He is not a man, that He would repent of what He has said. Let His promises manifest in your life*

Launching Deeper: Romans 8:34, 1 Samuel 15:18,19, 1 Chronicles 28:9. 29:17, Lamentations 5:19, Psalms 110:2.

Hebrew Word Study: "shebe"—rod, staff, scepter (Strong's Hebrew: 7626).

December 18

Elohei Kol Basar

אלוהי קול בסאר

God of All Flesh

"Behold, I am the Lord, the God of all flesh. Is there anything too hard for Me?" (Jeremiah 32:27, NKJV)

He is the God of the impossible. When everything seems difficult, He comes in. Sometimes we may look up to men for solutions and find no answers, but when God is involved in the situation, it does not matter how bad it may be, He will restore the desolate place and makes all things beautiful, for the God of all flesh knows the needs of all flesh to provide for them and take care of them. He created all and unto Him shall all flesh come, and in His hands is the life of every creature and the breath of all flesh. The God of all flesh sustains the breath of every man; He will sustain you in His favor and blessings. He breathes into the flesh of man, a perishable container, His Spirit, and dwells among them, the same way He is in you and with you. There is nothing too difficult for Him to do. Every challenge of mountains and storms in your life is just a simple matter in His sight. He will perform that expectation for you, and it will be marvelous in your sight.

***Prayer**: I pray let the God of all Flesh perform His great and Mighty acts in your life and His people, and cause all men to come and bow before Him and worship and glorify His Holy name forever and ever.*

Launching Deeper: Numbers 16:22, 27:16, 2 Kings 3:18, Jeremiah 32:17.

Hebrew Word Study: "hinneh"—behold, here (Strong's Hebrew: 2009).

December 19

HaBen Hashem Beis

הבן השם ביתיס

Son Over God's House

"But Christ as a Son over His own house, whose house we are if we hold fast the confidence and the rejoicing of the hope firm to the end" (Hebrews 3:6, NKJV).

The second letter of the Hebrew alphabet is "Bet," which means "a house, household, and family." Family is established within a household, a place where one can dwell. Believers are described as God's house, the church of the living God, which is the pillar and mainstay of the truth is God's dwelling place. As the church, we dwell under the same roof and in an established home, under the same covenant. Christ is the Lord and Master of the spiritual house of God where He is. We are also the temple of the Holy Spirit, built on the solid foundation of the Chief Cornerstone and the teachings and preaching of the apostles, and we as living stones with structures of various services joined and fellowship with one another to grow His holy temple. Through Him, we can boldly come before the Father and obtain favor. Through your worship, the world will see the reality of the work of God, that you are part of the household of the redeemed and equipped and built up with the power and gifts of the Spirit to do outstanding works for the kingdom.

Prayer: *I pray the Spirit will empower you as He dwells in you and hold firmly to what He has endowed you with as you continue to profess, and His presence finds grace to help in your time of need.*

Launching Deeper: Hebrews 1:2, 4:14, Matthew 16:18, 1 Corinthians 3:16.

Hebrew Word Study: "chomah"—a wall (Strong's Hebrew: 2346).

December 20

ECHAD ACHAZ SHIVAT HAKOKHAVIM

אחד אחאז שבעת הכהנים

The One with Seven Stars

"To the angel of the church of Ephesus write, 'These things says He who holds the seven stars in His right hand, who walks in the midst of the seven golden lampstands" (Revelation 2:1, NKJV).

One who holds in His hands the seven stars, which is the messengers of the seven churches, walks in the lampstand's mist and holds the messengers in His hand, the leaders of the churches. The lampstand is for light, power, and fire, to watch and see. He is the Son of Man whose face shines like the sun in its brightest. If He holds them, none of them can be removed. Jesus is present among His church. He will not take the lampstands away, the light will shine, there will be more fire and power, and all will see the appearance of His glory, He is our God, and we are His people, there will be more miracles seen throughout the nations as the church prepares for His coming, there will be revivals springing up in cities and communities, and you are a tool in His hands to use to transform the lives of many to His kingdom, with the Seven Stars in His hand, He walks with you and talks with you, hear His voice as the Spirit speaks to you.

Prayer: *I pray the one who holds the Seven Stars and walks amid the seven golden lampstands show forth His power in the midst of His church mightily and do great miracles for them.*

Launching Deeper: Ezekiel 1:28Exodus 25:31-37, Zechariah 4:2, Ezekiel 1, 1:26, Exodus 25:31.

Hebrew Word Study: "menorah"—a lampstand (Strong's Hebrew: 4501).

December 21

MECHOKKEINU

מצ׳וקאינו

The Lawgiver

"For the Lord is our Judge, The Lord is our Lawgiver; The Lord is our King; He will save us" (Isaiah 33:22, NKJV).

Upon our hearts are written wholesome laws for us to live by them. By the empowering of the Holy Spirit, by his grace given unto us to walk and keep them, he is the only lawgiver. Through Israel, He gave His words of promises to the world. By his law, statutes, and precepts, He's able to deliver and save and redeem, and by His law, He brings judgment against his enemies, His fiery laws go out from Him, and His justice has become a light to the nations. The Law Giver calls the nations to pay attention and listen to His laws, and He will put them in their heart. They contain His instructions and His words of guidance which should not depart from our mouth, but as we keep meditating on them, our lives become more prosperous. In his laws will the nations put their hope in, for the sake of righteousness He magnifies His laws and makes it glorious, He gives his people a heart of flesh for them to walk in His statutes. His Word for you will not go void but will come to accomplish His intentions and purposes for your life.

Prayer: *I pray as you meditate on His law, be like the tree planted by the rivers of and bring forth your fruit in your season, your leaves will not wither and continue to prosper.*

Launching Deeper: James 4:12, Ezekiel 11:18-20, Isaiah 51:4-7, Deuteronomy 33:2, Psalm 147:19,20.

Hebrew Word Study: "chaqaq"—to cut in, inscribe, decree (Strong's Hebrew: 2710).

December 22

YOTZREINU

פוטר שלנו

Our Potter

"But now, O Lord, You are our Father; We are the clay, and You our potter; And all we are the work of Your hand" (Isaiah 64:8, NKJV).

The Lord instructed Jeremiah to go to the Potter's House to see how the potter was kneading clay on the wheel. He was making a vessel, and at a point, it got broken, but the potter reworked it into another vessel that seems suitable and perfect to him. The Lord told Jeremiah, this is how He makes His people and the nations of the world. They are in His hands. When the nation does not listen to His voice, He brings them to judgment, and when they heed to Him, He builds and plants them as well. He will not reject the work of his hands. He is very concerned about what He has made. He is our Potter, and He is Sovereign, and we are His own, and He has authority over us, making us according to His own purpose and will. When He is making us, we cannot question or instruct what He does. He establishes His intentions in the making and functioning of His children upon the potter's wheel. We cannot do our own thing and walk in our own ways, but follow His path and humbly be in the hands of our Maker.

Prayer: *I pray as you remain in the hand of the Potter, let Him mold you and make you what He wants you to be in His name.*

Launching Deeper: Isaiah 29:16, 45:9, Jeremiah 18:2-6, Deuteronomy 32:6.

Hebrew Word Study: "chomer"—cement, mortar, clay (Strong's Hebrew: 2563a).

December 23

Moshel Kohen

משהל טמפה

The Ruling Priest

Yes, He shall build the temple of the Lord. He shall bear the glory, And shall sit and rule on His throne; So He shall be a priest on His throne, And the counsel of peace shall be between them both.

Zechariah 6:13 (NKJV)

Our Chief High Priest rules and reigns upon His throne in the order of the kings of Salem, Melchizedek, a priest of the Most High, who also rules as a king and as a priest and has no end or beginning. He is divinely appointed and made perfect to reign as a priest forever, and also reign as a king exalted forever with the administration of justice and righteousness upon the earth from the royal lineage of David, the King of Kings who rules over the nations has called us into His kingdom as priests. He stands and makes intercession for you continually, as a sacrifice and a mediator between you and God and bears your worship, makes atonement for you, purifies you by His blood, and makes you perfect before the Father, drawing you closer to the Lord. Our Ruling Priest helps us keep the faith and the ability to call upon the Father for help in times of our needs and offer unto Him thanksgiving and praise.

Prayer: *I pray the favor of the Ruling Priest will not depart from you. His glory will dwell with you and have mercy on you.*

Launching Deeper: Psalms 21:5, 45:3,4, 72:17-19, Zechariah 6:11, Genesis 14:18, Psalm 110:4.

Hebrew Word Study: "mashal"—to rule, have dominion, reign (Strong's Hebrew: 4910).

December 24

ELOHEI HA TIKVAH

אלוהי התקווה

The God of Hope

"Now may the God of hope fill you with all joy and peace in believing that you may abound in hope by the power of the Holy Spirit" (Romans 15:13, NKJV).

Our faith in God is what pleases Him to move on our behalf and fill our spirit with His peace and joy. Paul's prayer for the Romans was that they would abound in hope in Him. We can find hope in His unfailing love and work of redemption and hold on to it. By His mighty acts and great wonders done in the past, we have the confidence in Him, for He keeps His covenants, and He is faithful and merciful to keep His Word for His people. He fulfills His promises and not a word failed, all were accomplished, and the nations saw His glory; we rejoice in the hope we have in Him. He's the God of hope, our source of hope who never disappoints, and the reliance and living a life of His Word is what empowers you as a believer. You have the fullness of the Spirit. His peace, joy, and goodness fill your life and will not put you to shame. Everyone who hopes in the Almighty keeps moving on from strength to strength and grace to grace with His perfect rest and peace.

Prayer: *I pray your trust in Him to keep His promise will not wither, for He is faithful to see you through and to protect and keep and give you the strength and blessing you need.*

Launching Deeper: Romans 15:5, Jeremiah 14:8, Joel 3:16, Romans 12:12, 1 Timothy 6:17.

Hebrew Word Study: "maoz"—a place or means of safety, protection (Strong's Hebrew: 4581).

December 25

ADON ABADIM

אדון עבאדים

Lord of the Servants

"After a long time the lord of those servants came and settled accounts with them" (Matthew 25:19, NKJV).

We know various forms of wealth multiplication in our world today. Bitcoin and others are ways people increase their money. The parable of the talents tells of the master giving out his money to His servants and comes back to reckon with them, each according to the number given base on abilities to multiply. Reckoning is always ahead of responsibilities assigned to the people of God, and we should expect His second coming and His day of judgment to call all to recount the gifts given, wealth and estates given, days of life given, and as stewards of His blessings. Preparation for the arrival of the Lord of the servants, Son of Man, is cautioned in Jesus's parables. He placed the importance of accountability in His arrival and also emphasized responsibility in what has been entrusted to every individual, both believers and nonbelievers. What are the talents He's given to you, and what have you done with it? Are you ready for His coming for His reckoning, to give account and be rewarded?

Prayer: *I pray when the Lord of the Servant comes, He will find us faithful stewards of His gifts and talents in His kingdom.*

Launching Deeper: Matthew 24:48, 18:23,24, Luke 16:1,2,19, Romans 14:7-12.

Hebrew Word Study: "chayil"—strength, efficiency, wealth, army (Strong's Hebrew: 2428).

December 26

Breshet Bri'at Hashem

ברשת ברית השם

The Origin and Author of God's creation

"And to the angel of the church of the Laodiceans write, These things says the Amen, the Faithful and True Witness, the Beginning of the creation of God" (Revelation 3:14, NKJV).

All things were made through Him, and through Him, all things exist. When the Lord said "let there be," it was the Word He declared as in John 1:1 would say "in the beginning was the Word, and the Word was with God and the Word was God." As the Lord God declared the Word and all things were created, light and darkness, the systems of the world, the sea and the creatures, the lands and animals, people, nations, governments, dominions, and authorities. He is the originator of both the visible and invisible. All are held together, the world and the body of Christ, and He has become the first in everything, and with God, from the beginning, all things came into existence because of Him. Without Him, you were not made. In Him, there is life, and there's existence. Receive and declare His glory in your life through the Word. The origin of creation is the Word who is Christ Jesus. You are called and ordained by His Word to do exploits in Him and be sustained and made perfect in Him.

Prayer: *I pray the origin of God's creation gives unto you His double portion of all His goodness and His increase.*

Launching Deeper: Colossians 1:15-18, John 1:1-5, Revelation 19:11.

Hebrew Word Study: "miphal"—a work, something made (Strong's Hebrew: 4659).

December 27

Elohei HaShalom

אלוהי השלום

God of Peace

"Now the God of peace be with you all. Amen" (Romans 15:33, NKJV).

He is the provider of perfect peace, and it is a nature of God. The Hebrew word *shalom* means peace in all areas of your life, peace in its totality. From the beginning, He spoke of peace in the obedience of His commands and the adherence to His covenants. When Gideon saw the angel and thought that for seeing the face of an angel, he was going to die; the angel pronounced peace and blessings upon His life, and there He built the altar and named it God is Peace, Jehovah Shalom, where He showed forth in His signs and wonders. The nature of His presence is peace and tranquility. When He is in a place, there is an abundance of peace. Through our Lord Jesus Christ, He grants unto us the solemnity that our Christian lives need. We have access to the Father that no matter the challenge and captivity, He grants His perfect peace, and His peace is maintained in your continuous relationship with the Holy Spirit in you. He gives the fruit of the Spirit called peace, the peace which passes all understanding, His peace which He gives unto you not as the world gives.

Prayer: *I pray His peace saturates your life in all areas and let Him be with you and cause you to be blessed in His presence.*

Launching Deeper: John 14:27, Psalm 4:8, Job 22:21, Proverbs 19:23, Isaiah 26:3, Luke 7:37-50, 1 Corinthians 14:33.

Hebrew Word Study: "amar"—to utter, to say (Strong's Hebrew559).

December 28

Ateret Tsebi

עטרת צבי

Crown of Beauty

"In that day the LORD of hosts will be For a crown of glory and a diadem of beauty To the remnant of His people" (Isaiah 28:5, NKJV).

Kings, priests, and guests were crowns as a sign of their rulership, a sign of honor and dignity, and the Lord told the prophet that He would be an ornament of royal authority himself unto His people, a crown of honor and blessings that will not fade, an everlasting crown of His glory upon them to cause them to shine and radiate His glory and beauty, a command to reflect the light of salvation and grace. His crown upon their heads also represents their consecration to the Almighty and their victory as overcomers. He is your beauty and your perfection. You will go forth and display His glory unto all nations. When the beauty of His Shekinah glory is upon you, you reflect His holiness and His righteousness, and as He shines upon you, He establishes you in His presence and blesses the work of your hands, you will behold His beauty in His presence, and His peace will rest upon you and be deeply rooted and continue to bear fruits.

Prayer*: I pray the glory of the Lord will rise on you, and His crown of you will command greatness and favor upon your life.*

Launching Deeper: Isaiah 41:16, 45:25, 60:1-3, 19.

Hebrew Word Study: "atarah"—crown, wreath (Strong's Hebrew: 5850).

December 29

ECHAD NACHAL MAFTE'ACH DOVID

אחד נחל מפטה דוד

One Who Has the Keys of David

And to the angel of the church in Philadelphia, write, 'These things says He who is holy, He who is true, "He who has the key of David, He who opens and no one shuts, and shuts and no one opens."'

Revelation 3:7 (NKJV)

The key is a symbol of authority; it gives access to an entrance or exit, upon the house of David a key is given, it tells the complete authority over the house of David, anyone who took care of this key in the time of the lineage of David must be a worthy steward, those who reign in the house of David did not put their trust and hope in Him their God, Christ the One who was of the house of David was faithful as a servant and a king and took possession of the keys of David. Here he has the key, the authority to shut, and no one opens, and when He opens, no one will shut it. The keys of the kingdom have been open to humanity that whatever those who believe bind on this earth is bound in heaven, and what we lose on this earth is loose in heaven, what a blessing and a privilege given to the children of God, that the authority to open doors through intercessions have been given to you. By the keys of David, let the heavens' door of blessings and favor be open unto you in the name of Jesus.

***Prayer**: I pray the Giver of keys will grant to you keys of breakthrough and favor, keys of the kingdom to be a blessing unto others*

Launching Deeper: Isaiah 22:22, Matthew 16:19, 1 John 5:20, Revelation 1:11,18, 3:14, 6:10.

Hebrew Word Study: "pathach"—to open (Strong's Hebrew: 6605).

December 30

SHOMER KOL HANEFESH

שומר קול חנפש

Keeper of the Soul

If you say, "Surely we did not know this," Does not He who weighs the hearts consider it? He who keeps your soul, does He not know it? And will He not render to each man according to his deeds?

Proverbs 24:12 (NKJV)

The Lord rules, abiding and ageless, in him dwells abundance of life for those who believe in Him and are chosen by Him, He keeps watch over their souls from dangers. You are made in His image, and His Spirit dwells in you, and He is obligated to preserve His image and to favor and love you. His spirit is there to guard you and direct you to the right way, which brings you to the fulfillment of life and accomplishment of His divine purpose for you. The fellowship of the Spirit is what keeps you from any snare of the enemy. The center of your emotions is your soul, and He is the one who restores your soul with His Word of comfort and strength to enlighten you and to keep you growing in His grace. He also reveals secrets to you as you walk with Him. Walking with the Lord is to be obedient to His voice of directions and adhere to His truth and be faithful to Him, for His steadfast love endures forever, in that, you will be like the tree planted by the waters whose leaves never dry up but always flourishing and that is how He keeps your soul to flourish and prosper in Him.

Prayer: *I pray the Lord keeps your soul in the bundle of life in Him, and you are preserved to the fulfillment of His purpose for your life.*

Launching Deeper: Psalm 66:9, 1 Samuel 25:29, Psalm 121:3.

Hebrew Word Study: "nephesh"—a soul, living being, life, (Strong's Hebrew: 5315)

December 31

Echad Run

אקהאד ראן

One Who Overcomes

"These things I have spoken to you, that in Me you may have peace. In the world you will have tribulation; but be of good cheer, I have overcome the world" (John 16:33, NKJV).

By the eternal life in the Son and by our faith in Him, we have overcome the world and all its rulers of darkness. For the Lord Jesus has overcome for us, He overcame the temptations of the enemy, using the things of this world could cause Him to sin, but He overcame by the Word and defeated the power of sin over man, and has set them free from bondage; He overcame and condemned the prince of this world and its powers and authorities and evil spirits there be, and finally overcame death by His death on the cross. He is resurrected and seated with the Father in the heavenly places and has given us victory and made us more than conquerors. For He has loved us to fight every battle for us and leads us in triumphal entries. He overcame by the authority of the Word of God, by His obedience to the Father's will, and by His humility as a servant to serve God and minister unto His children. Through the blood of the Lord Jesus, who is the overcomer, we have also overcome the enemy and, by His words of our testimonies, giving us the assurance and hope in Him.

Prayer: *I pray your heart will be at rest in the victory given by Christ, and you will continue to gains success in all aspects of life in Jesus' name*

Launching Deeper: Hebrews 4:15, Matthew 4:1-11, John 12:31. 6:11, Mark 1:23-27.

Hebrew Word Study "gibbir"—strong, mighty (Strong's Hebrew: 1368).

AVAILABLE NOW!

The Daily Dominion Decrees

Ignite God's Power in You and rule over your day by your Decrees.

Published by Trilogy Christian Publishing

For more information about Joyce please visit

www.joyceboohene.com

or email at info@joyceboohene.com

CPSIA information can be obtained
at www.ICGtesting.com
Printed in the USA
BVHW071506120123
656165BV00015B/399

9 781637 694664